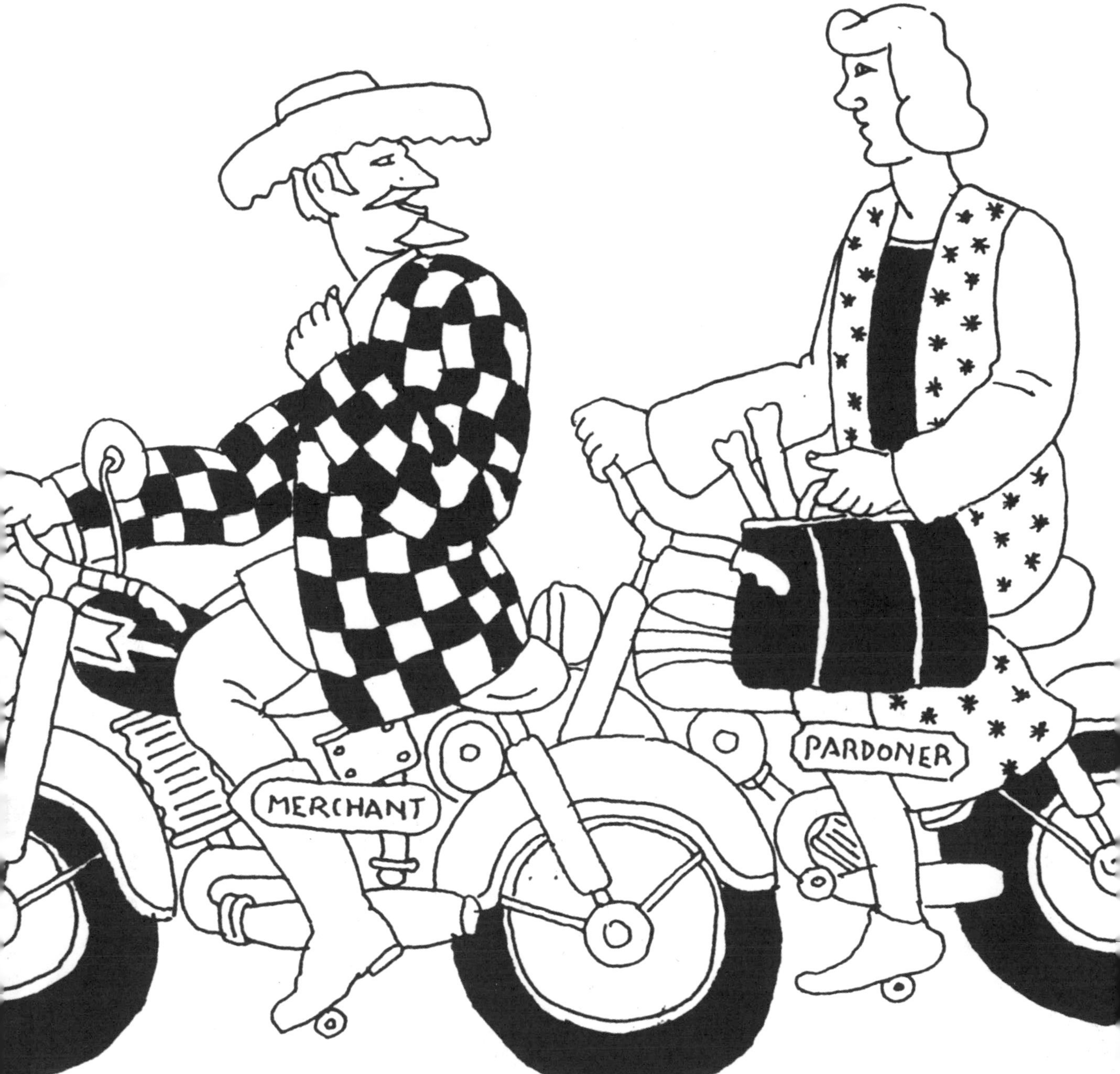
MERCHANT
PARDONER

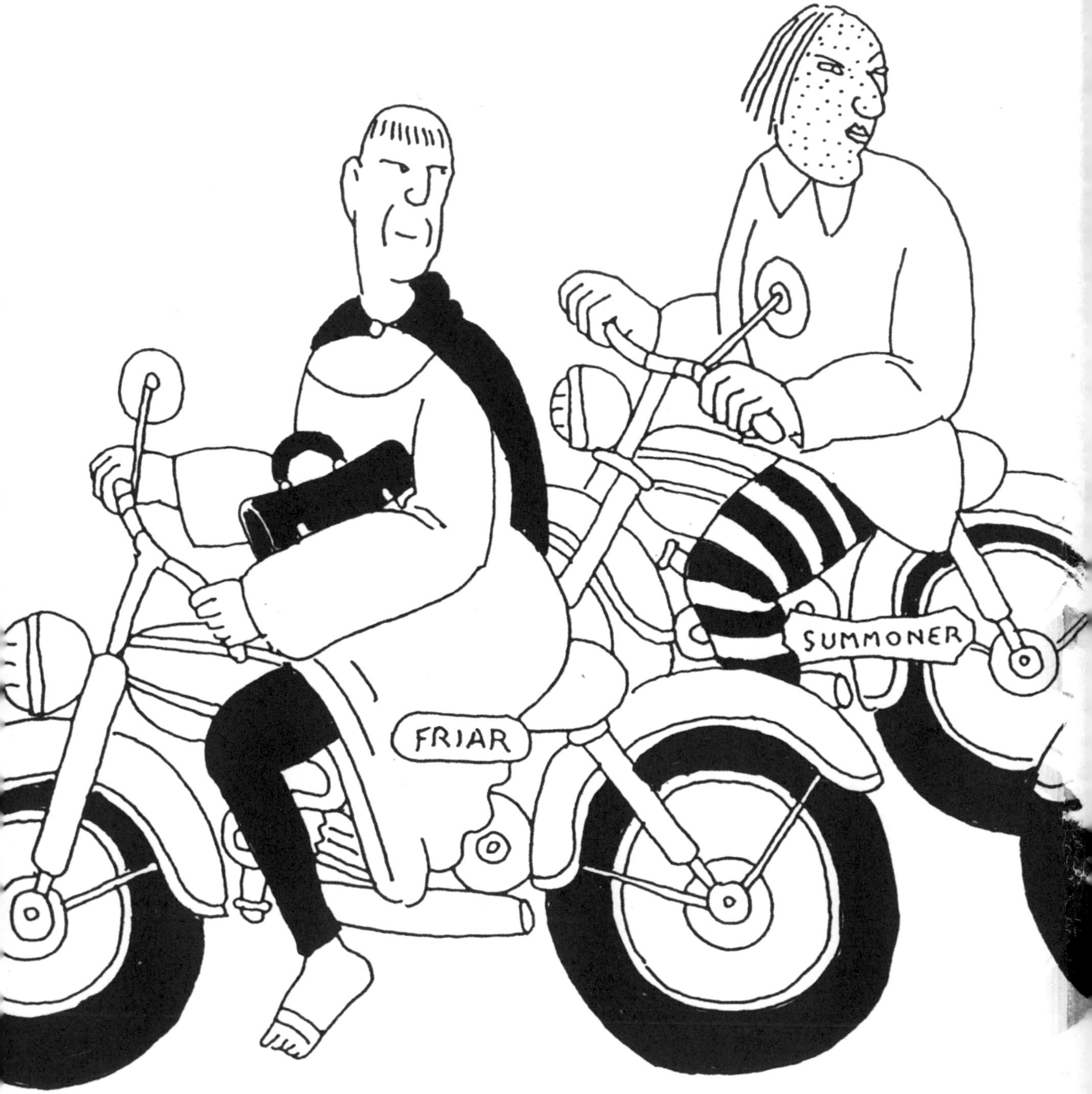
FRIAR
SUMMONER

THE CANTERBURY TALES

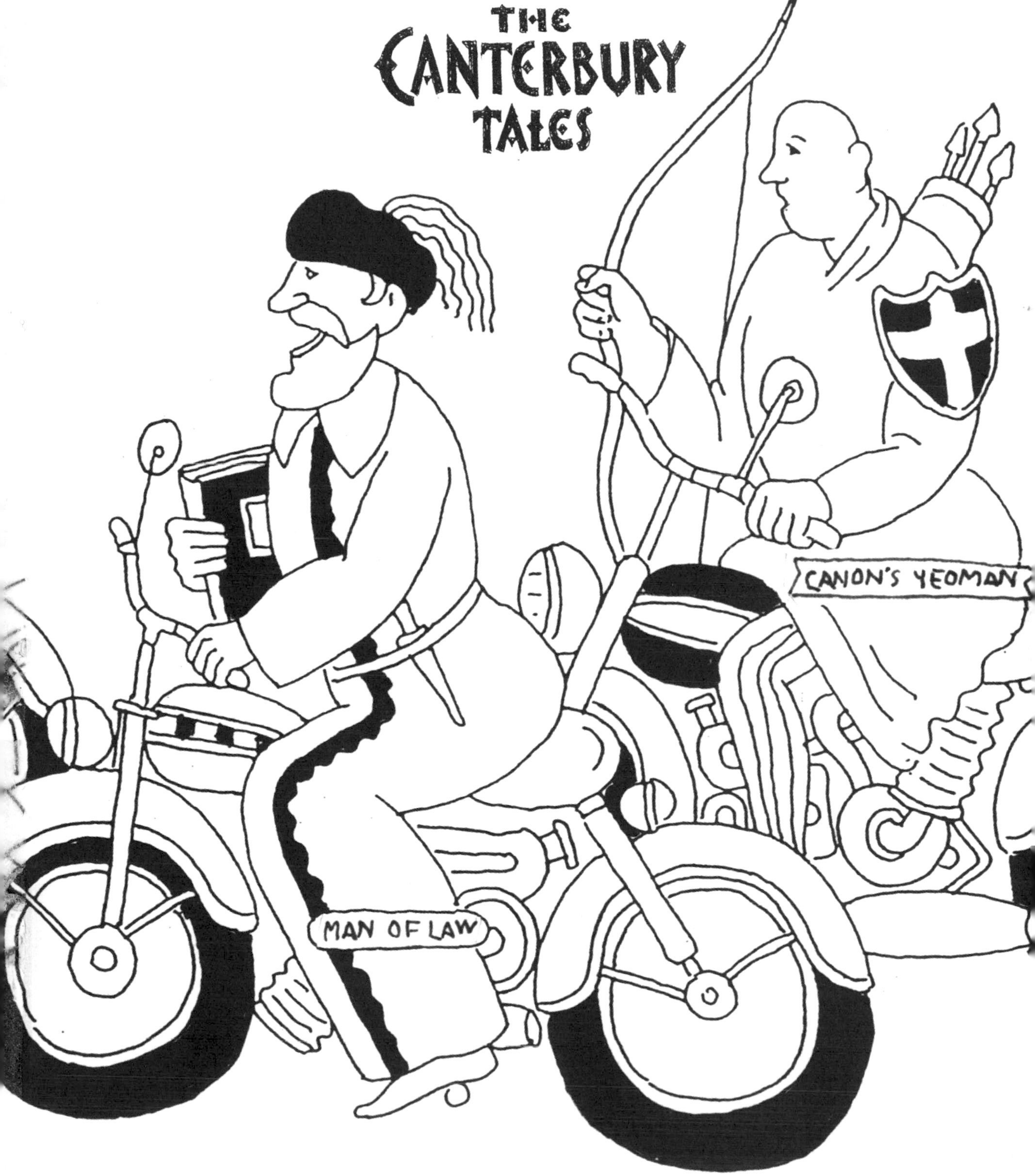
CANON'S YEOMAN
MAN OF LAW

BY THE SAME AUTHOR

DANTE'S DIVINE COMEDY

SEYMOUR: THE OBSESSIVE IMAGES OF SEYMOUR CHWAST

MOONRIDE

THE 12 CIRCUS RINGS

THE ALPHABET PARADE

THE LEFT-HANDED DESIGNER

WITH STEVEN HELLER:

ILLUSTRATION: A VISUAL HISTORY

GRAPHIC STYLE

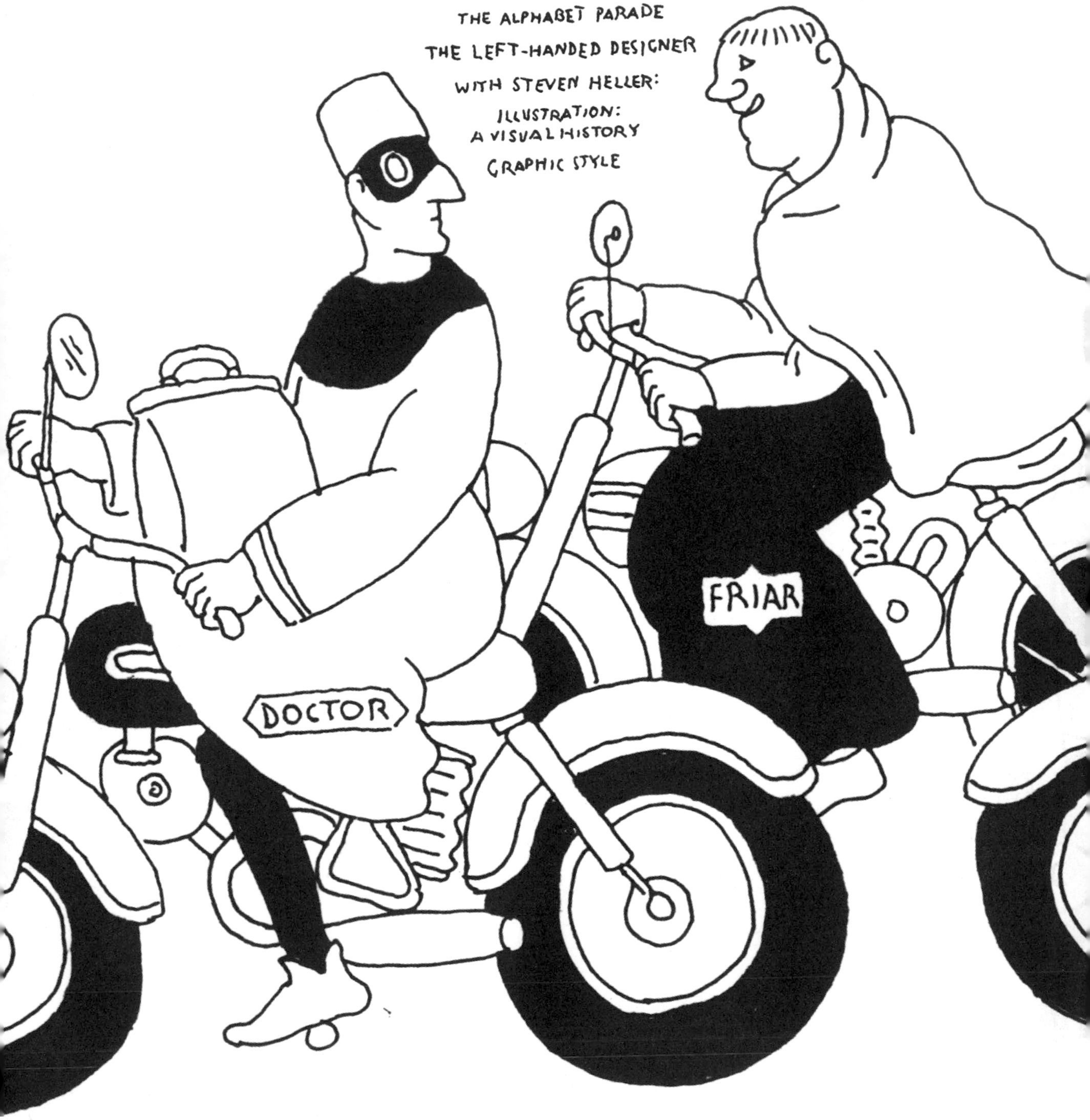
DOCTOR
FRIAR

GEOFFREY CHAUCER

THE CANTERBURY TALES

ADAPTED BY SEYMOUR CHWAST

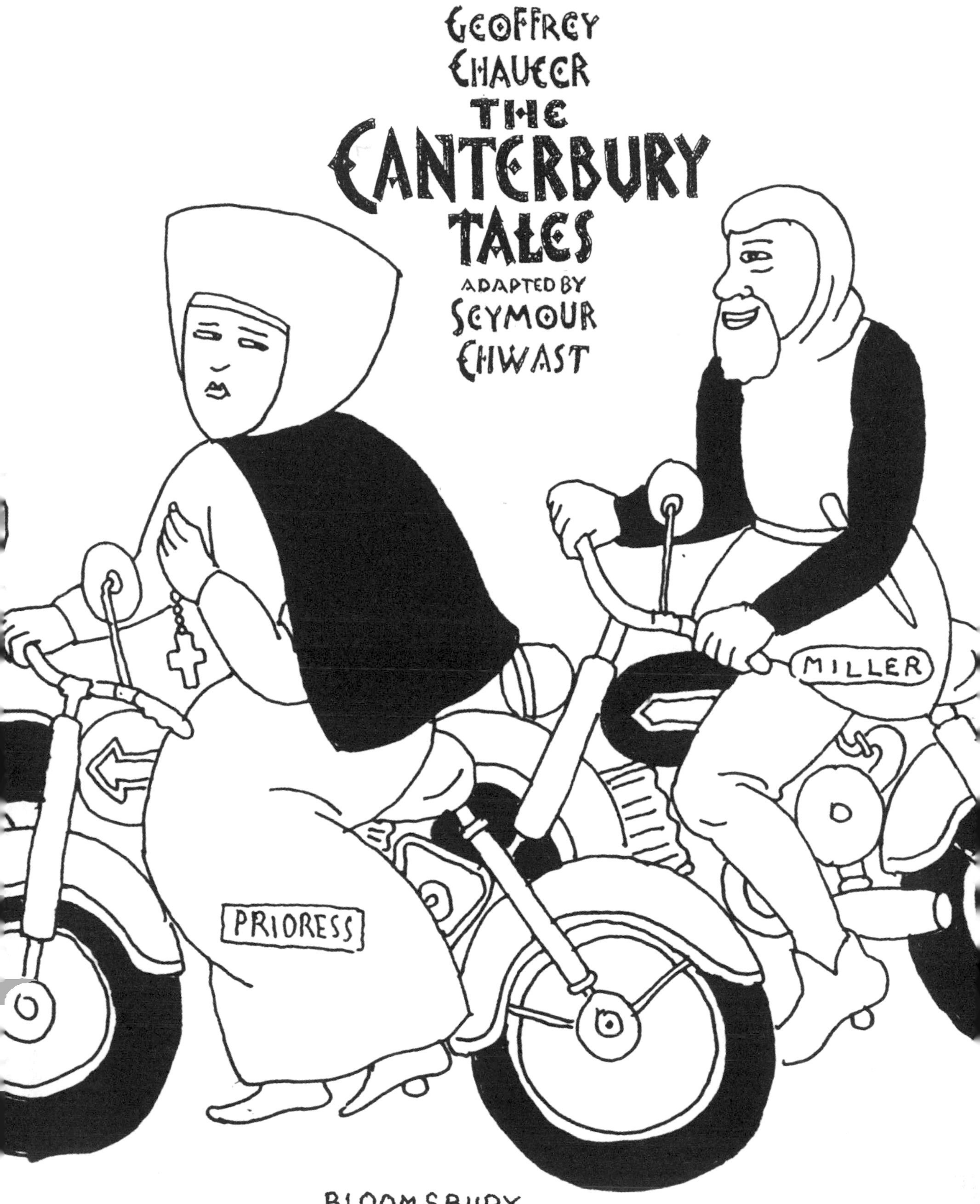
MILLER
PRIORESS

BLOOMSBURY

NEW YORK BERLIN LONDON SYDNEY

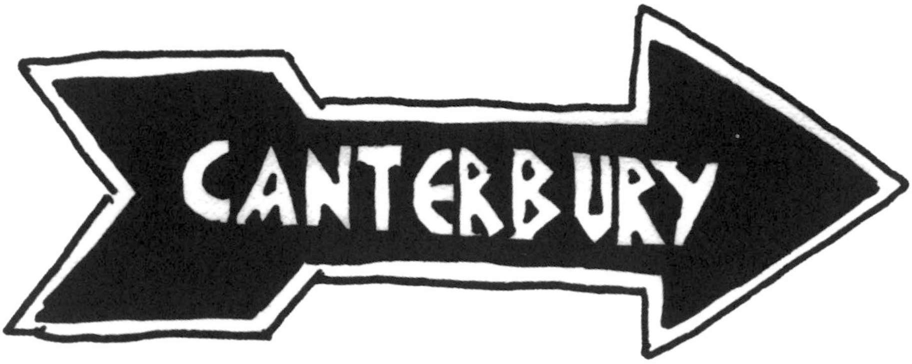
CANTERBURY

TO THE MEMORY
OF MY MOTHER,
ESTHER NEWMAN

FOR INFORMATION ADDRESS BLOOMSBURY USA, 175 FIFTH AVENUE, NEW YORK, NY 10010
PUBLISHED BY BLOOMSBURY USA, NEW YORK
ALL PAPERS USED BY BLOOMSBURY USA ARE NATURAL, RECYCLABLE PRODUCTS MADE FROM WOOD GROWN IN WELL-MANAGED FORESTS. THE MANUFACTURING PROCESSES CONFORM TO THE ENVIRONMENTAL REGULATIONS OF THE COUNTRY OF ORIGIN.
LIBRARY OF CONGRESS CATALOGING-IN-PUBLICATION DATA
CHWAST, SEYMOUR
THE CANTERBURY TALES / GEOFFREY CHAUCER; ADAPTED BY SEYMOUR CHWAST - 1st U.S. ed
p. cm.
ISBN 978-1-60819-487-2
1. GRAPHIC NOVELS. I. CHAUCER, GEOFFREY, d. 1400. CANTERBURY TALES. II. TITLE
PN6727. C499C36 2010
741.5'973 - - dc22
2010042017
FIRST U.S. EDITION 2011
1 3 5 7 9 10 8 6 4 2
ART, DESIGN AND LETTERING BY SEYMOUR CHWAST
PRINTED IN THE U.S.A. BY QUAD/GRAPHICS, TAUNTON

INTRODUCTION

GEOFFREY CHAUCER WAS BORN AROUND 1342 IN LONDON. HIS FATHER WAS A WINE MERCHANT AND HAD CONNECTIONS IN THE CHURCH. HE ATTENDED ST. PAUL'S ALMONRY AND WENT ON TO BE A PAGE AT THE HOUSEHOLD OF THE COUNTESS OF ULSTER. HIS DUTIES INVOLVED THOSE OF A SERVANT BUT HE GAINED A FINE EDUCATION, WHICH INCLUDED THE FRENCH AND ITALIAN LANGUAGES. WITH CHAUCER'S APPOINTMENT TO THE ROYAL COURT HE WAS SENT ABROAD AS A SOLDIER. HE WAS CAPTURED BUT THE KING PAID A RANSOM OF SIXTEEN POUNDS TO FREE HIM.

WITH THE DEATH OF HIS FATHER HE GAINED AN INHERITANCE AND MARRIED PHILIPPA DE ROET, WHO ATTENDED THE QUEEN.

CHAUCER'S OTHER MASTERPIECE, TROILUS AND CRISEYDE, APPEARED BETWEEN 1380 AND 1385. SHORTLY THEREAFTER HE STARTED WORKING ON THE FIRST OF THE CANTERBURY TALES, THE KNIGHT'S TALE. WHILE IT WAS HIS INTENTION THAT EACH OF THE THIRTY PILGRIMS MAKING THEIR WAY TO THE CANTERBURY CATHEDRAL TELL ONE TALE GOING AND ONE COMING BACK, WE HAVE TO BE CONTENT WITH THE TOTAL OF TWENTY-FOUR TALES TOLD ON THE WAY TO THE CATHEDRAL. CHAUCER EMBELLISHED STORIES THAT ORIGINATED FROM OTHERS OR FROM HISTORY.

THE STYLE OF THE ENTRIES RANGE FROM THE BAWDY (THE MILLER'S TALE) TO THE SPIRITUAL (THE PRIORESS'S TALE); FROM SCOUNDRELS TO SAINTS. CHAUCER'S CAREERS AND EXPERIENCES PREPARED HIM FOR THE VARIETY OF CHARACTERS AND PLOTS THAT HE EMPLOYED. EIGHTY-TWO MANUSCRIPTS SURVIVE, BUT CHAUCER DID NOT SUPPLY THE ORDER OF THE TALES. HOWEVER, LINKS FROM ONE STORY TO ANOTHER GAVE CLUES TO THE ORDER.

CHAUCER'S TOMBSTONE IN THE POET'S CORNER OF WESTMINSTER ABBEY STATES THAT HE DIED IN 1400. HE WAS POSSIBLY THE VICTIM OF THE BLACK DEATH WHICH WIPED OUT A LARGE PART OF THE ENGLISH POPULATION. HIS WORK WAS POPULAR AT HIS DEATH PARTLY DUE TO HIS WRITING IN THE ENGLISH LANGUAGE OF THE TIME. HE HAD WANTED TO DEVELOP A DIALECT UNDERSTOOD AND APPRECIATED BY ALL CLASSES. HE IS CALLED THE FATHER OF ENGLISH POETRY.

THE GENERAL PROLOGUE

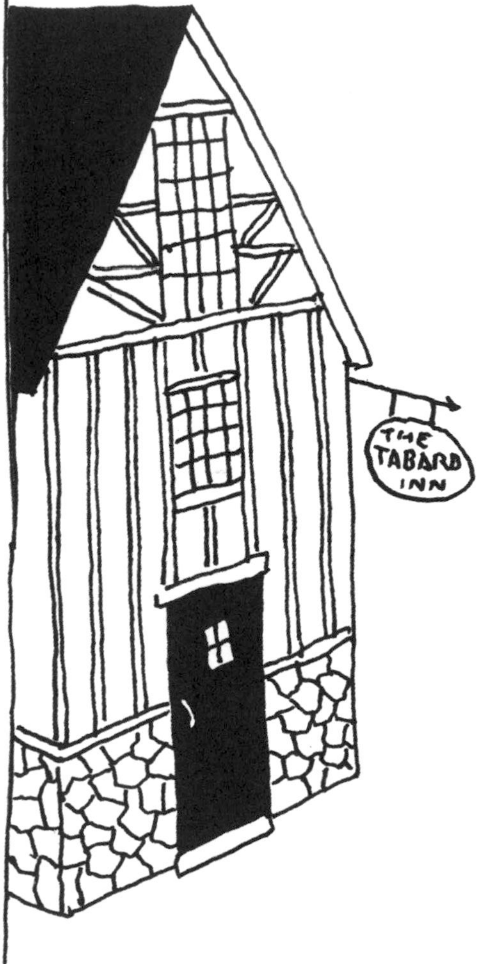
THE
TABARD
INN

IN THE TABARD INN IN SOUTHWARK, NEAR LONDON, THE OWNER, HARRY BAILEY APPROACHED TWENTY-NINE PILGRIMS. THEY WERE GOING TO CANTERBURY TO VISIT SAINT THOMAS WITH THEIR HEALTH PROBLEMS. HE SUGGESTED THAT THEY ALL TELL STORIES TO ENLIGHTEN AND ENTERTAIN THEMSELVES. I DECIDED TO JOIN THEM.

THE **KNIGHT** HAD BEEN ALL OVER THE KNOWN WORLD AND FOUGHT WITH VALOR IN MOST OF THE LANDS. HE FOUGHT FIFTEEN BATTLES IN PLACES LIKE MOROCCO, GRENADA, PRUSSIA, RUSSIA AND LITHUANIA, ALL FOR THE GLORY OF GOD.

THE KNIGHT'S SON, A **SQUIRE**, WAS WITH HIM. HE WAS A YOUTH OF ABOUT TWENTY YEARS OF AGE, ASPIRING TO KNIGHTHOOD. HIS ACCOMPLISHMENTS INCLUDED A MUSICAL VOICE, DRAWING, WRITING AND JOUSTING. HE WAS A NATURAL HORSEMAN. A WELL-MANNERED YOUNG MAN, HE WAS MADLY IN LOVE.

THE **MANCIPLE** HANDLED THE BUSINESS OF BUYING SUPPLIES FOR THE INNER TEMPLE. THIS UNEDUCATED AGENT HAD SMARTS THAT SURPASSED THE EFFORTS OF SOME OF THE BOSSES ABOVE HIM. THEIR TASK WAS TO MANAGE THE LAND OF THE ENGLISH LORDS.

THE **MERCHANT**, AN ELEGANT DRESSER, SPENT HIS TIME BUYING, SELLING, TRADING AND BARTERING. NO ONE KNEW IF HE WAS SOLVENT OR IN DEBT.

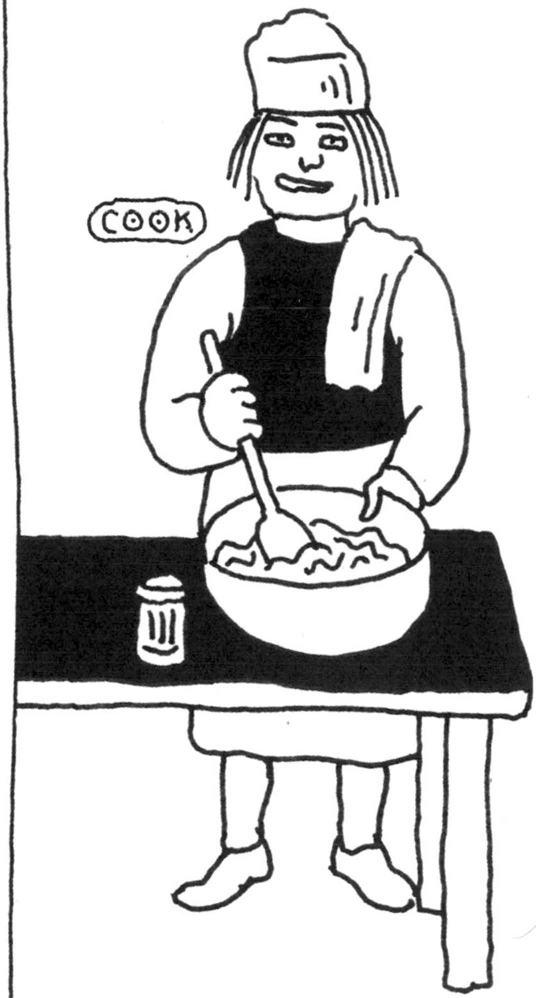
COOK

THE **FRIAR** WAS A MERRY PRIEST WHO KNEW EVERY INNKEEPER AND BARMAID IN EVERY TAVERN AROUND, FORSAKING LEPERS AND BEGGARS. HIS HOOD WAS STUFFED WITH PINS AND POCKETKNIVES TO GIVE TO PRETTY GIRLS.

THE **COOK** WAS HIRED FOR THE PILGRIMAGE. HIS CHICKEN, HARD-BOILED EGGS, MARROW BONE AND SPICES WERE DELICIOUS. HE HAD AN OPEN ULCER ON HIS LEG.

THE **CLERK**, FROM OXFORD, WAS TERRIBLY THIN. HE WOULD RATHER BE SURROUNDED BY VOLUMES OF ARISTOTLE THAN FANCY CLOTHES. HE BORROWED MONEY FROM FRIENDS TO BUY MORE BOOKS.

THE **MAN OF LAW** WAS APPOINTED BY THE KING TO SETTLE LEGAL DISPUTES AROUND THE COUNTRY. HE HAD AN INCOME ALONG WITH PRIVATE CASES AND HAD AMASSED A FORTUNE.

THE **FRANKLIN**, A LANDOWNER BUT NOT A NOBLE, LIVED AN EXISTENCE OF SENSUAL PLEASURE AND THOUGHT THAT WAS THE ONLY WORTHY GOAL IN LIFE. HE HAD BREAKFASTS OF CAKE IN RED WINE. MEAT AND FOWL ADORNED HIS TABLE ALONG WITH PIKE AND LOBSTER.

THE **PARSON** WAS AN EDUCATED MAN WHO TENDED HIS FLOCK IN A GRACIOUS AND DILIGENT WAY. HE WOULD NOT EXCOMMUNICATE ANYONE FOR FAILING TO PAY TITHES TO HIM.

THE RED-HEADED **MILLER** WAS BIG AND BRAWNY AND NOT VERY BRIGHT. HE MASTERED THE TELLING OF DIRTY STORIES AND STEALING GRAIN FROM SACKS AS WELL AS OVERCHARGING FOR HIS SERVICES. HIS NOSE HAD A BIG WART WITH GROWING HAIRS. WE SEEMED TO HAVE A MUTUAL DISTRUST OF ONE ANOTHER.

PARSON

THE **MONK** WAS A PERSONABLE FELLOW WHO LOVED HUNTING. HE HAD A STABLE OF HORSES AND GREYHOUNDS

AMONG THE PILGRIMS WAS A NUN, THE **PRIORESS**, KNOWN AS EGLANTYNE. HER MANNERS AT DINING WERE BEYOND REPROACH. SHE WOULD NEVER ALLOW A MORSEL TO FALL FROM HER LIPS TO HER BREAST. SHE SPOKE IN THE FRENCH OF STRATFORD-ATTE-BOWE, NOT THAT IN PARIS. SHE RODE WITH AN- OTHER NUN AND THREE PRIESTS.

A **SECOND NUN** AND THE **NUN'S PRIEST** ALSO TOLD TALES, ALONG WITH THE **CANON'S YEOMAN**.

THE **SHIPMAN** HAD A HABIT OF SKIMMING FROM BARRELS OF WINE ON HIS SHIP. HIS KNOWLEDGE OF THE SEA AND SHIPPING WAS UNSURPASSED. HE KNEW ALL PORTS FROM GOTTLAND TO CAPE FINISTERRE.

THE **DOCTOR** USED ASTRONOMY AND THE HOROSCOPE TO CURE HIS PATIENTS. BODILY FLUIDS, HE SAID, WERE THE CAUSE OF MEDICAL PROBLEMS. HIS CURES INCLUDED THE DUNG OF DOVES FOR SORE FEET.

THE **WIFE OF BATH** MADE CLOTH THAT WAS BETTER THAN CLOTH FROM YPRES AND GHENT. SHE WAS MARRIED FIVE TIMES BUT ALSO HAD LOVERS IN HER YOUTH. SHE ENJOYED RESPECT- ABILITY AND MADE PILGRIMAGES TO JERUSALEM THREE TIMES.

THE **REEVE** MANAGED GRANARIES, DAIRIES AND STORES VERY WELL. THE AUDITOR NEVER QUESTIONED HIM WHILE HE GREW RICH AND WAS AT PEACE WITH HIMSELF. HE HAD A LOVELY LITTLE HOUSE ON A HEATH.

THE **SUMMONER** HAD A FACE OF A CHERUB WITH CARBUNCLES. HE WAS AS HOT AND LECHEROUS AS A LONDON SPARROW. HE SUMMONED PEOPLE TO THE CHURCH COURT FOR VIOLATIONS OF CHURCH DOCTRINE.

THE **PARDONER** HAD JUST COME HOME FROM VISITING THE COURT OF ROME. HE WAS GIVEN A LICENSE FOR SELLING PARDONS AND INDULGENCES. HE CARRIED WITH HIM PIGS BONES WHICH HE SAID WERE HOLY RELCS.

SEVERAL **GENTLEMEN** WERE DRESSED IN THE LIVERY OF THEIR GUILD. THE WERE A HABERDASHER, A CARPENTER, A DYER, A WEAVER AND MAKER OF TAPESTRIES. THEIR PROSPERITY WAS SHOWN IN THEIR CHOICE OF PURE SILVER FOR THEIR KNIVES RATHER THAN BRASS.

THE **PLOUGHMAN** OFTEN HAD TO CARRY A LOAD OF DUNG. HE WAS A GOOD AND HONEST LABORER WHO DID CHRIST'S WORK FOR OTHERS EVEN IF THEY HAD NO MONEY.

OUR **HOST**, INNKEEPER AT THE TABARD, WAS ATTRACTIVE AND INTELLIGENT. HE OFFERED HIS PLAN OF ENTERTAINMENT AND AMUSEMENT FOR THE PILGRIMS. THEY AGREED AND MADE HIM THE HEAD OF THE GROUP.

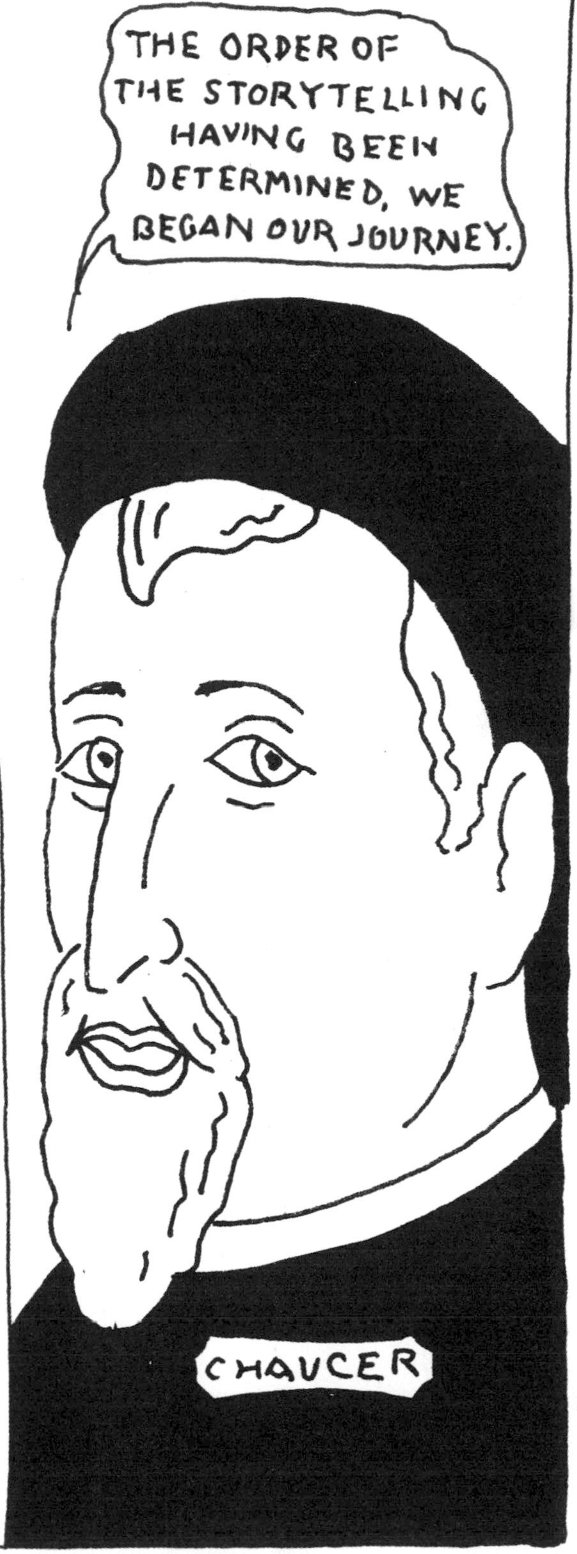
THE ORDER OF THE STORYTELLING HAVING BEEN DETERMINED, WE BEGAN OUR JOURNEY.
CHAUCER

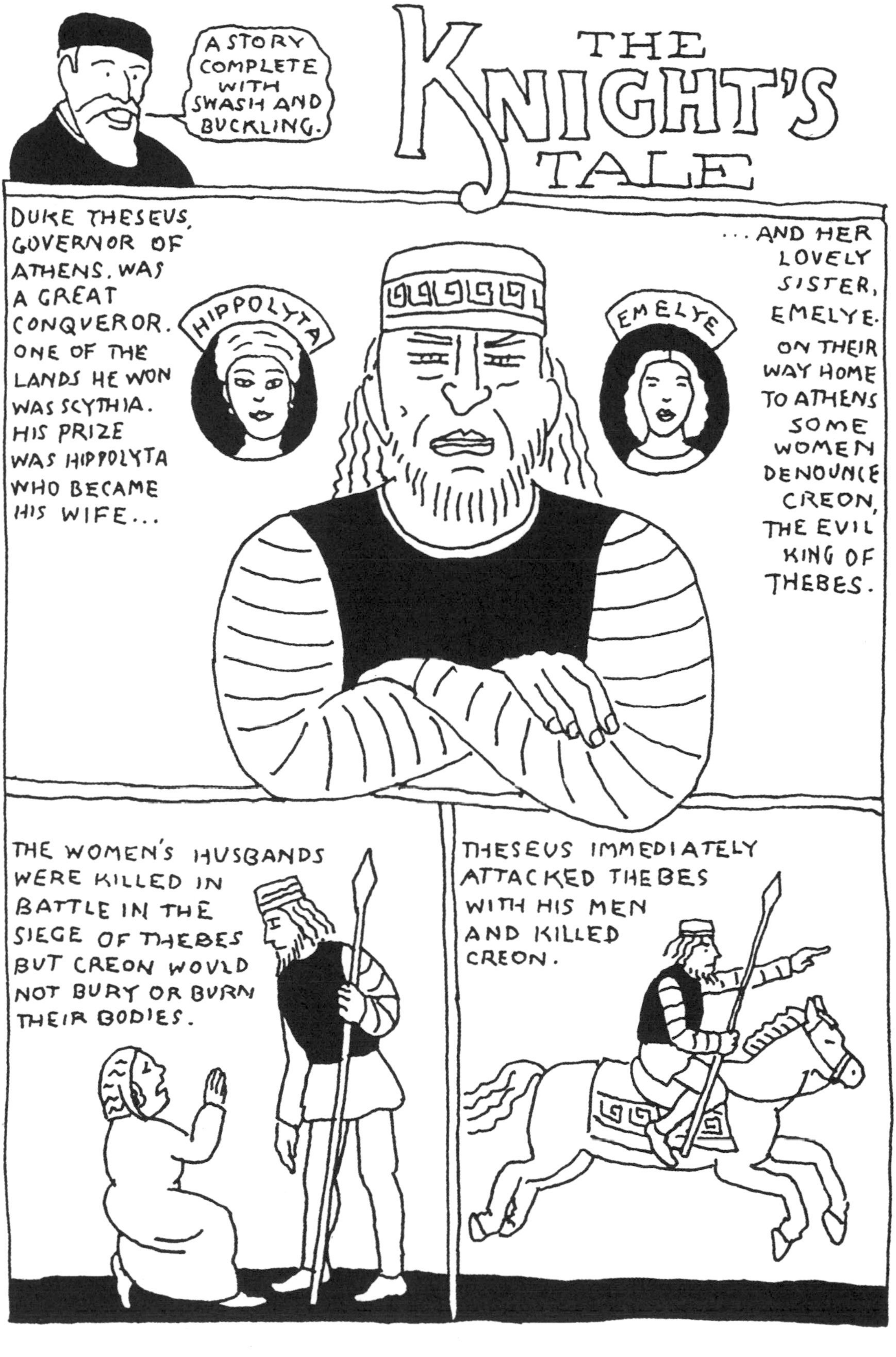
A STORY COMPLETE WITH SWASH AND BUCKLING.
THE KNIGHT'S TALE
DUKE THESEUS, GOVERNOR OF ATHENS, WAS A GREAT CONQUEROR. ONE OF THE LANDS HE WON WAS SCYTHIA. HIS PRIZE WAS HIPPOLYTA WHO BECAME HIS WIFE...
HIPPOLYTA
EMELYE
...AND HER LOVELY SISTER, EMELYE. ON THEIR WAY HOME TO ATHENS SOME WOMEN DENOUNCE CREON, THE EVIL KING OF THEBES.
THE WOMEN'S HUSBANDS WERE KILLED IN BATTLE IN THE SIEGE OF THEBES BUT CREON WOULD NOT BURY OR BURN THEIR BODIES.
THESEUS IMMEDIATELY ATTACKED THEBES WITH HIS MEN AND KILLED CREON.

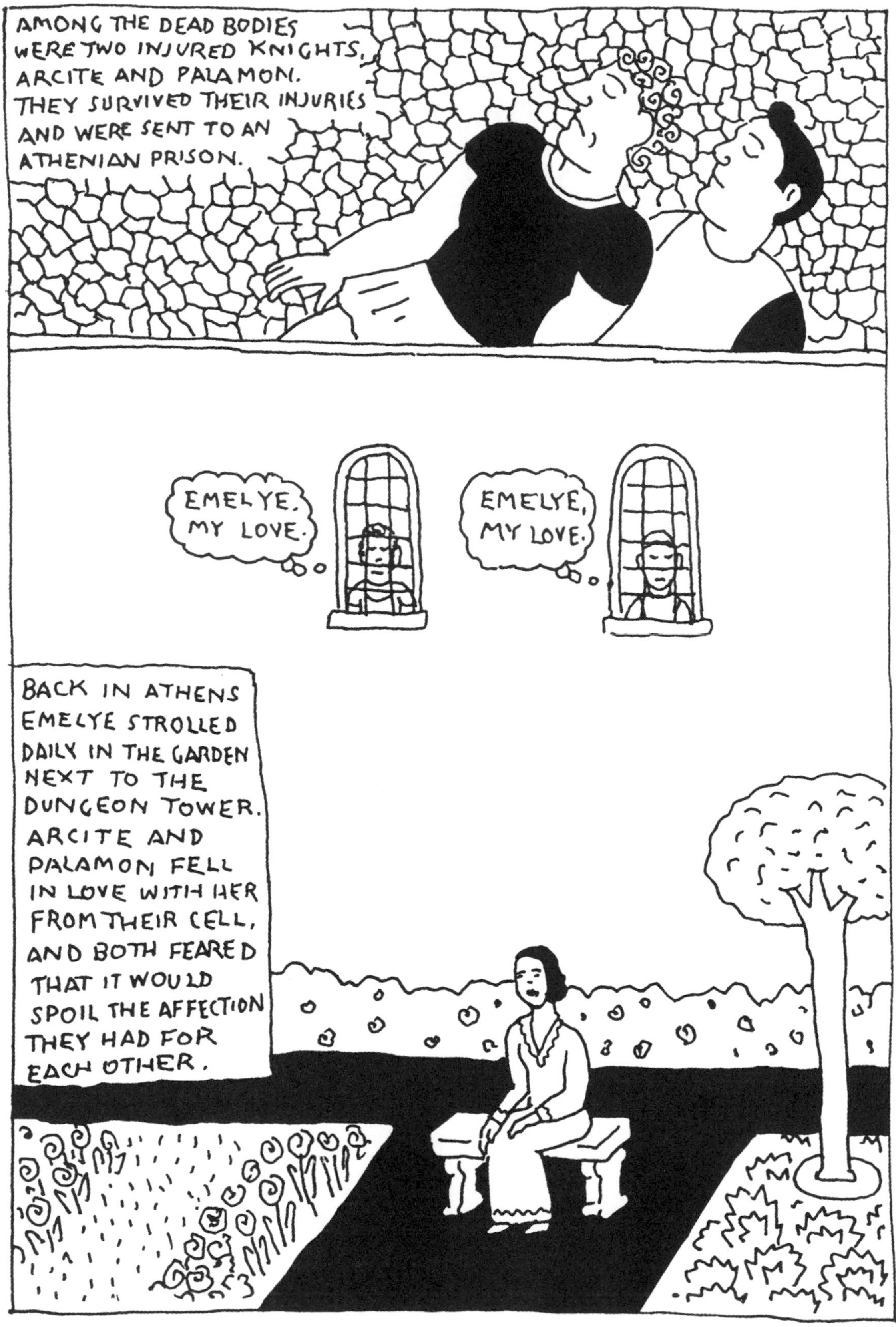
AMONG THE DEAD BODIES WERE TWO INJURED KNIGHTS, ARCITE AND PALAMON. THEY SURVIVED THEIR INJURIES AND WERE SENT TO AN ATHENIAN PRISON.
EMELYE, MY LOVE.
EMELYE, MY LOVE.
BACK IN ATHENS EMELYE STROLLED DAILY IN THE GARDEN NEXT TO THE DUNGEON TOWER. ARCITE AND PALAMON FELL IN LOVE WITH HER FROM THEIR CELL, AND BOTH FEARED THAT IT WOULD SPOIL THE AFFECTION THEY HAD FOR EACH OTHER.

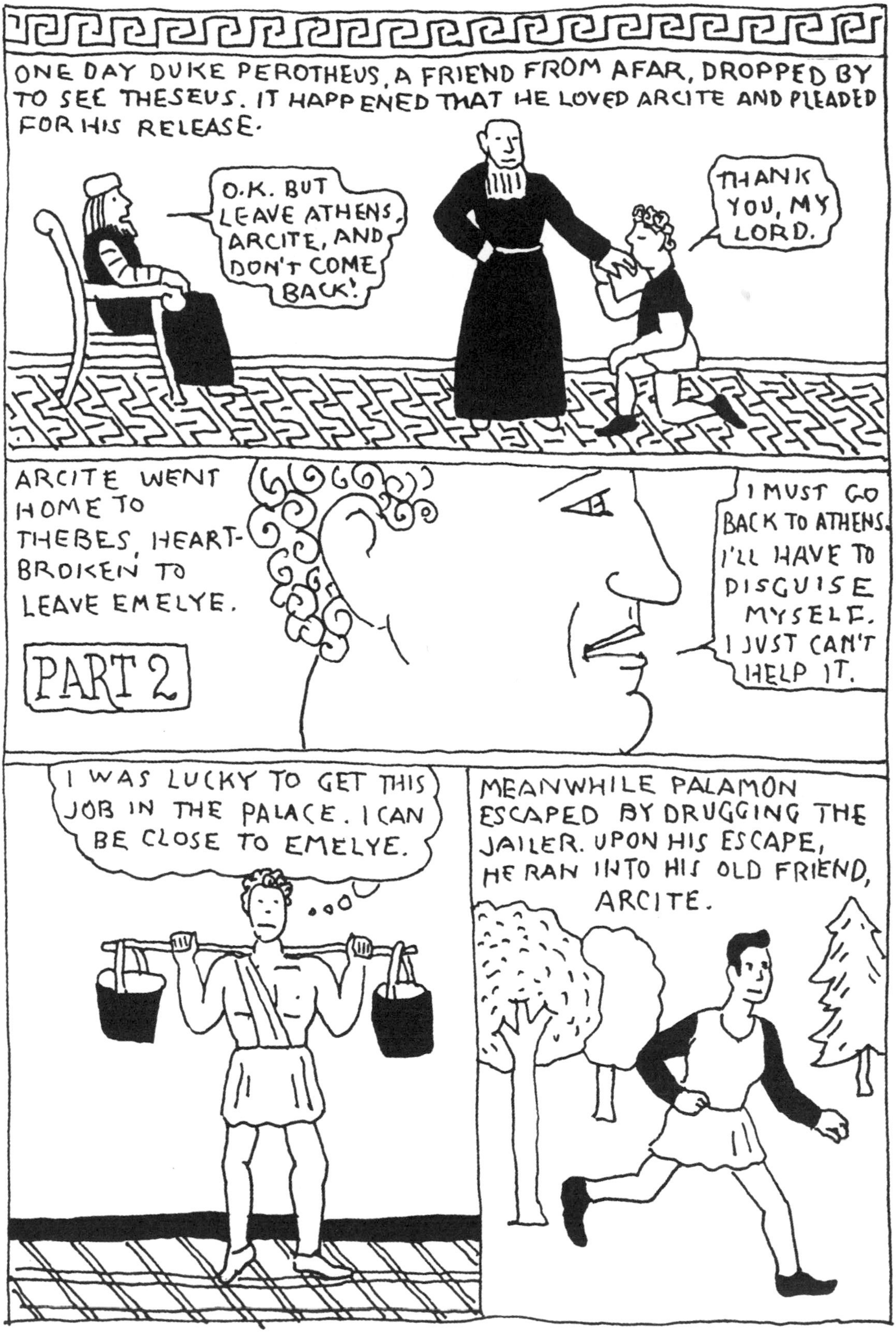
ONE DAY DUKE PEROTHEUS, A FRIEND FROM AFAR, DROPPED BY TO SEE THESEUS. IT HAPPENED THAT HE LOVED ARCITE AND PLEADED FOR HIS RELEASE.
O.K. BUT LEAVE ATHENS, ARCITE, AND DON'T COME BACK!
THANK YOU, MY LORD.
ARCITE WENT HOME TO THEBES, HEART-BROKEN TO LEAVE EMELYE.
PART 2
I MUST GO BACK TO ATHENS. I'LL HAVE TO DISGUISE MYSELF. I JUST CAN'T HELP IT.
I WAS LUCKY TO GET THIS JOB IN THE PALACE. I CAN BE CLOSE TO EMELYE.
MEANWHILE PALAMON ESCAPED BY DRUGGING THE JAILER. UPON HIS ESCAPE, HE RAN INTO HIS OLD FRIEND, ARCITE.

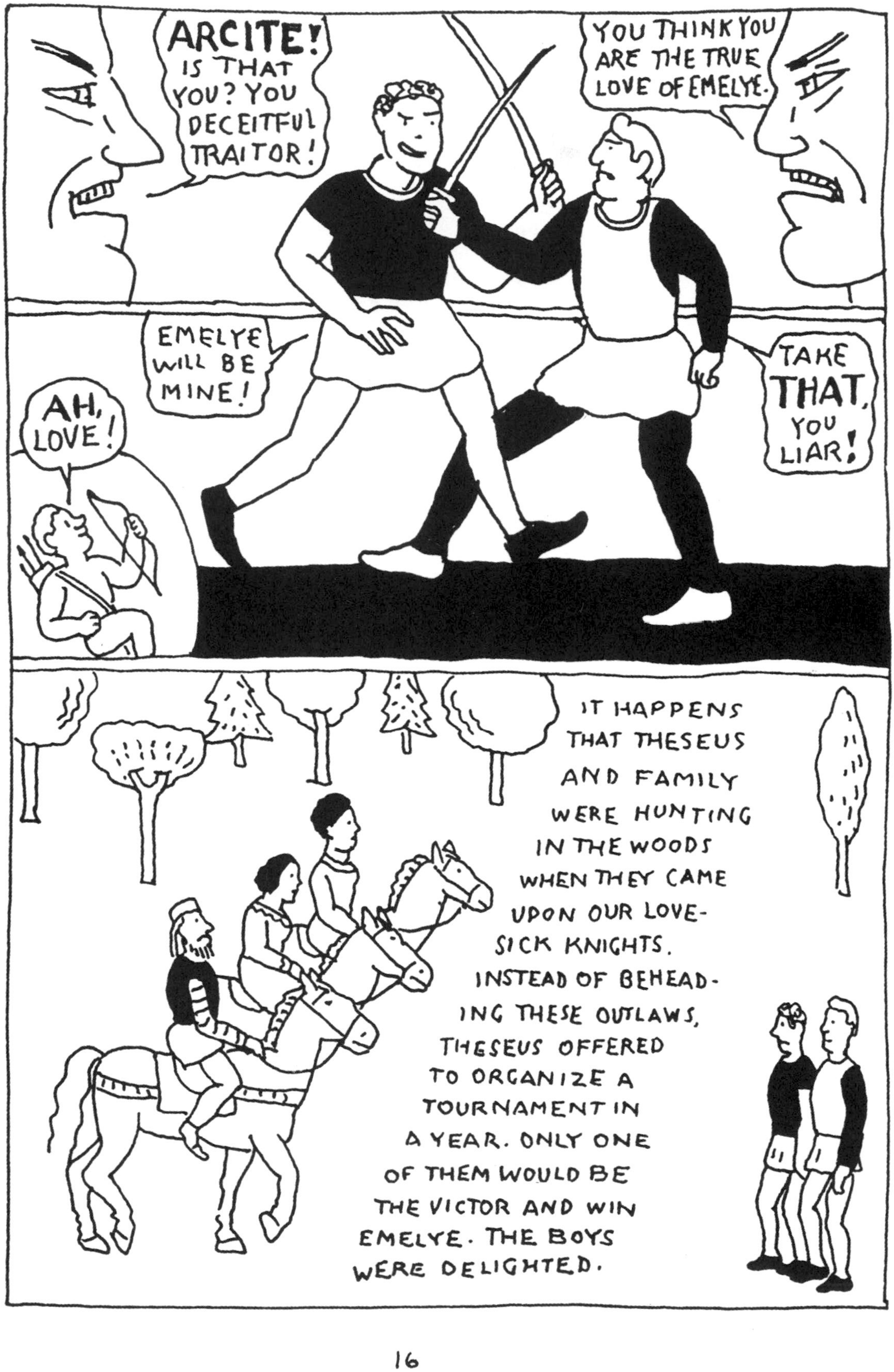
ARCITE! IS THAT YOU? YOU DECEITFUL TRAITOR!
YOU THINK YOU ARE THE TRUE LOVE OF EMELYE.
EMELYE WILL BE MINE!
TAKE THAT, YOU LIAR!
AH, LOVE!
IT HAPPENS THAT THESEUS AND FAMILY WERE HUNTING IN THE WOODS WHEN THEY CAME UPON OUR LOVE-SICK KNIGHTS. INSTEAD OF BEHEADING THESE OUTLAWS, THESEUS OFFERED TO ORGANIZE A TOURNAMENT IN A YEAR. ONLY ONE OF THEM WOULD BE THE VICTOR AND WIN EMELYE. THE BOYS WERE DELIGHTED.

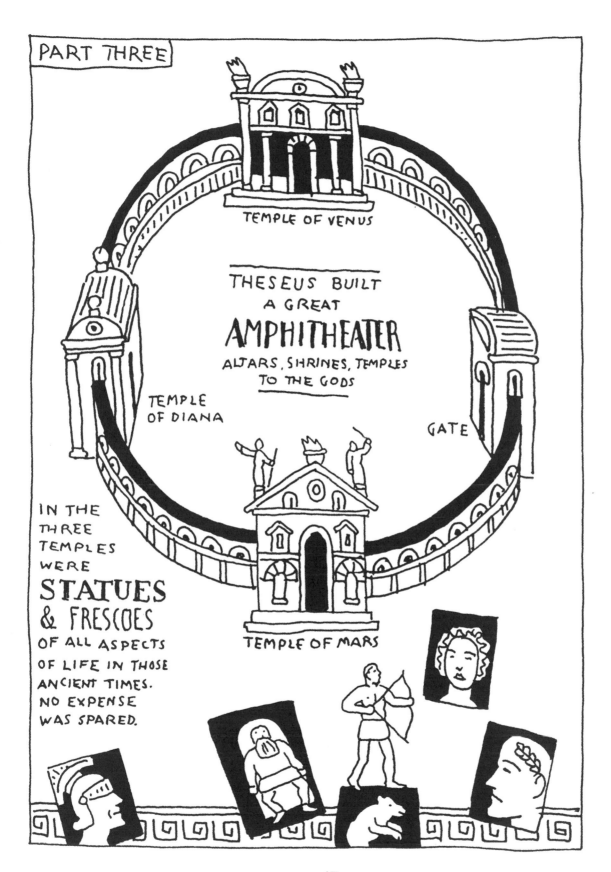

PART THREE

TEMPLE OF VENUS

THESEUS BUILT
A GREAT
AMPHITHEATER
ALTARS, SHRINES, TEMPLES
TO THE GODS

TEMPLE
OF DIANA

GATE

IN THE
THREE
TEMPLES
WERE
STATUES
& FRESCOES
OF ALL ASPECTS
OF LIFE IN THOSE
ANCIENT TIMES.
NO EXPENSE
WAS SPARED.

TEMPLE OF MARS

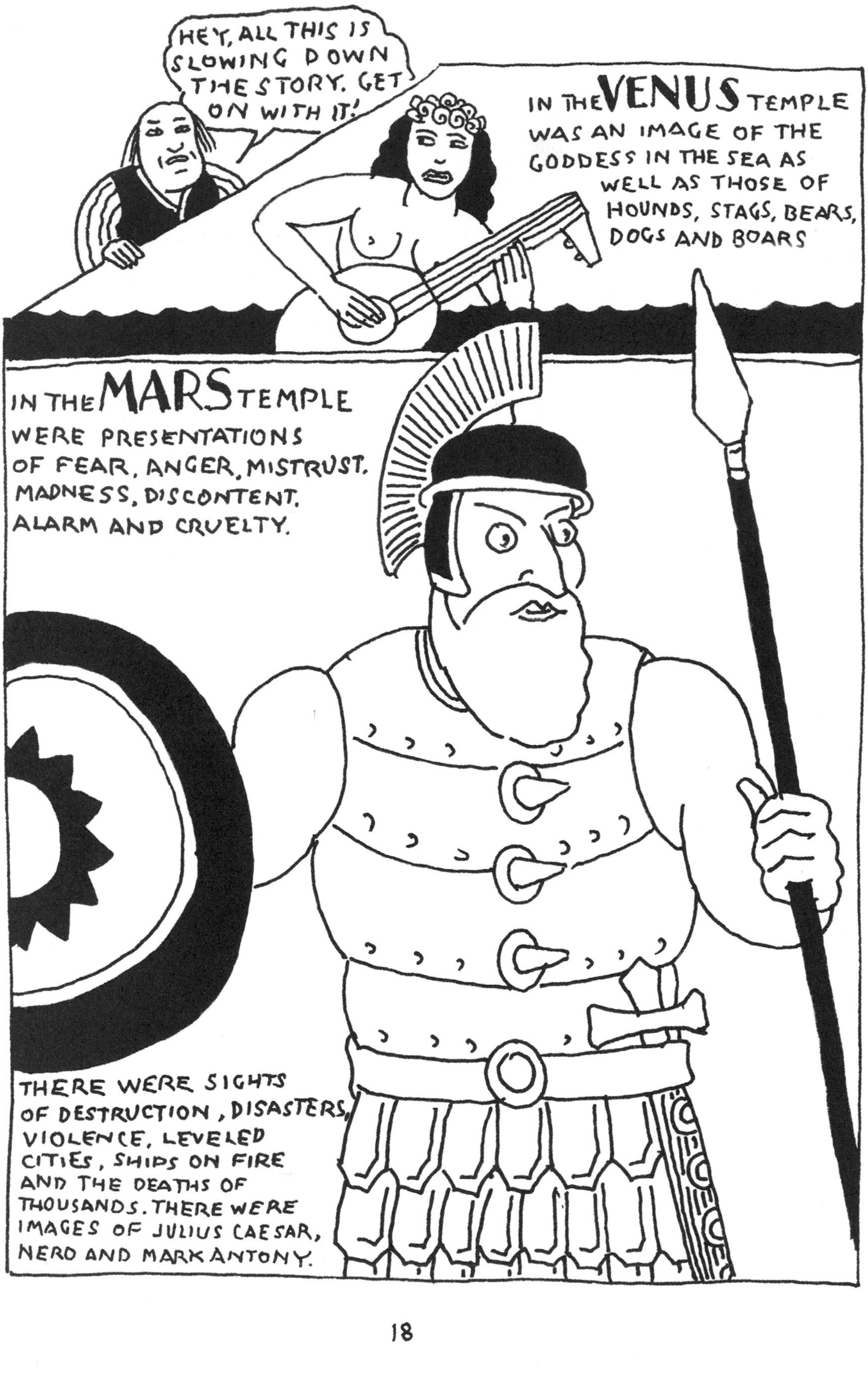
HEY, ALL THIS IS SLOWING DOWN THE STORY. GET ON WITH IT!
IN THE VENUS TEMPLE WAS AN IMAGE OF THE GODDESS IN THE SEA AS WELL AS THOSE OF HOUNDS, STAGS, BEARS, DOGS AND BOARS
IN THE MARS TEMPLE WERE PRESENTATIONS OF FEAR, ANGER, MISTRUST. MADNESS, DISCONTENT. ALARM AND CRUELTY.
THERE WERE SIGHTS OF DESTRUCTION, DISASTERS, VIOLENCE, LEVELED CITIES, SHIPS ON FIRE AND THE DEATHS OF THOUSANDS. THERE WERE IMAGES OF JULIUS CAESAR, NERO AND MARK ANTONY.

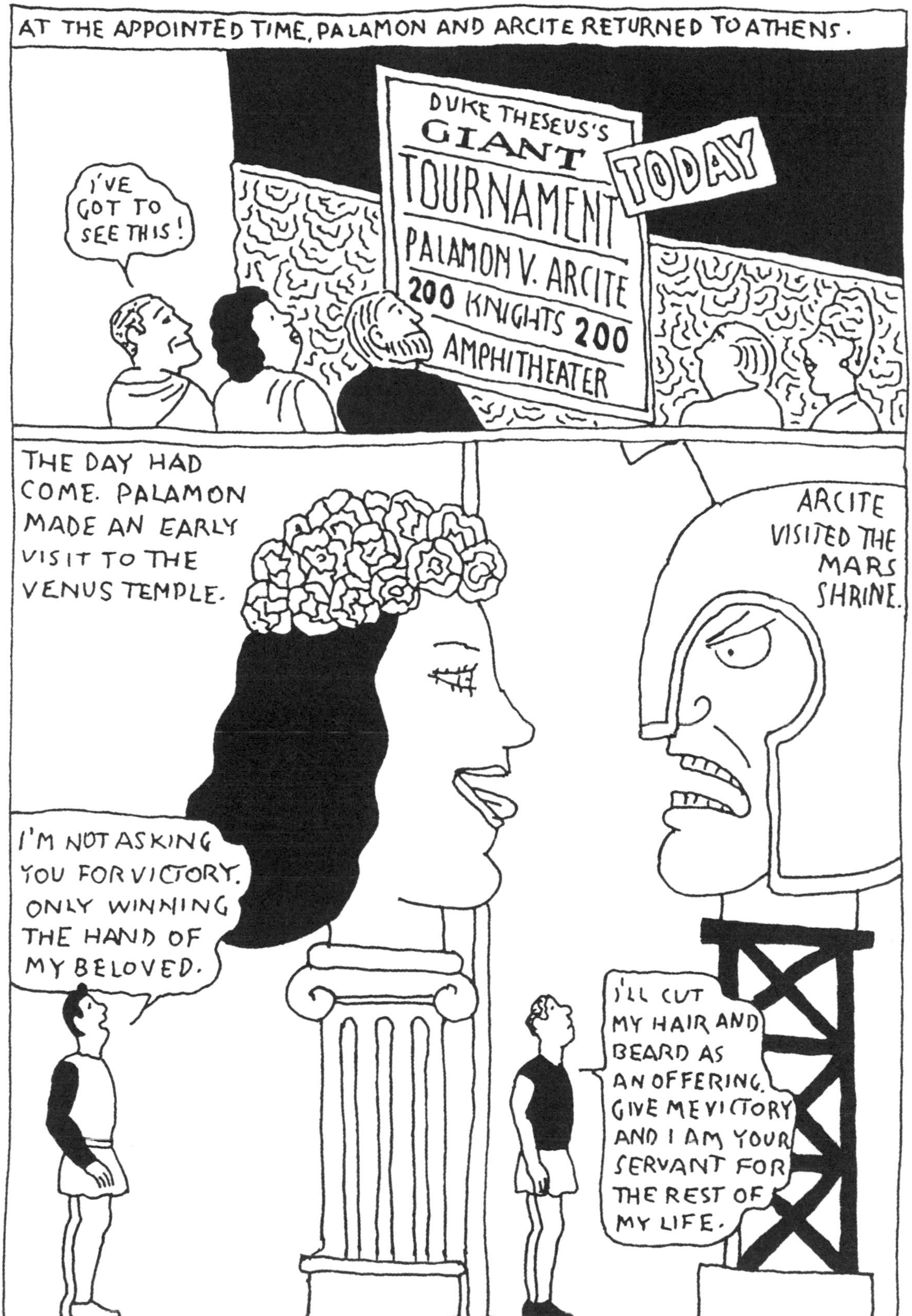
AT THE APPOINTED TIME, PALAMON AND ARCITE RETURNED TO ATHENS.
DUKE THESEUS'S GIANT TOURNAMENT PALAMON V. ARCITE 200 KNIGHTS 200 AMPHITHEATER
TODAY
I'VE GOT TO SEE THIS!
THE DAY HAD COME. PALAMON MADE AN EARLY VISIT TO THE VENUS TEMPLE.
ARCITE VISITED THE MARS SHRINE.
I'M NOT ASKING YOU FOR VICTORY. ONLY WINNING THE HAND OF MY BELOVED.
I'LL CUT MY HAIR AND BEARD AS AN OFFERING. GIVE ME VICTORY AND I AM YOUR SERVANT FOR THE REST OF MY LIFE.

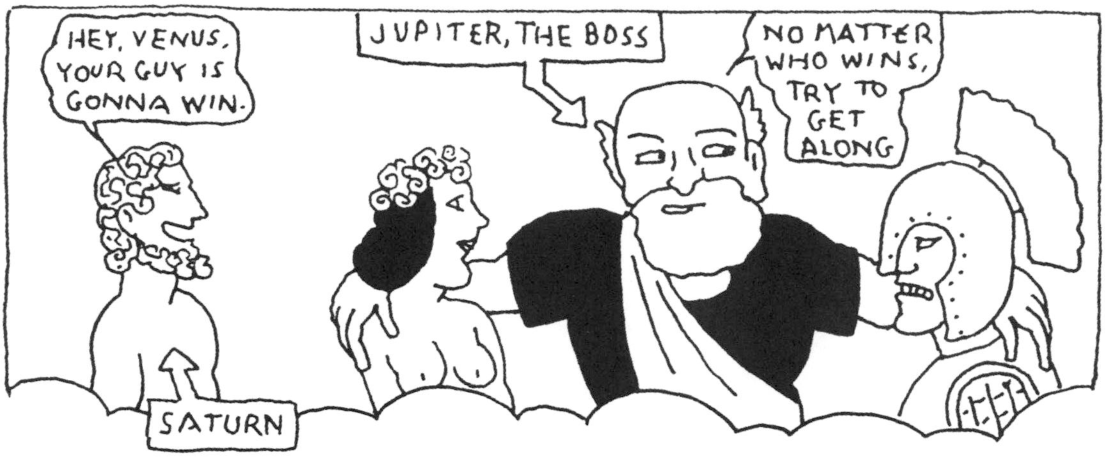
HEY, VENUS, YOUR GUY IS GONNA WIN.
JUPITER, THE BOSS
NO MATTER WHO WINS, TRY TO GET ALONG
SATURN

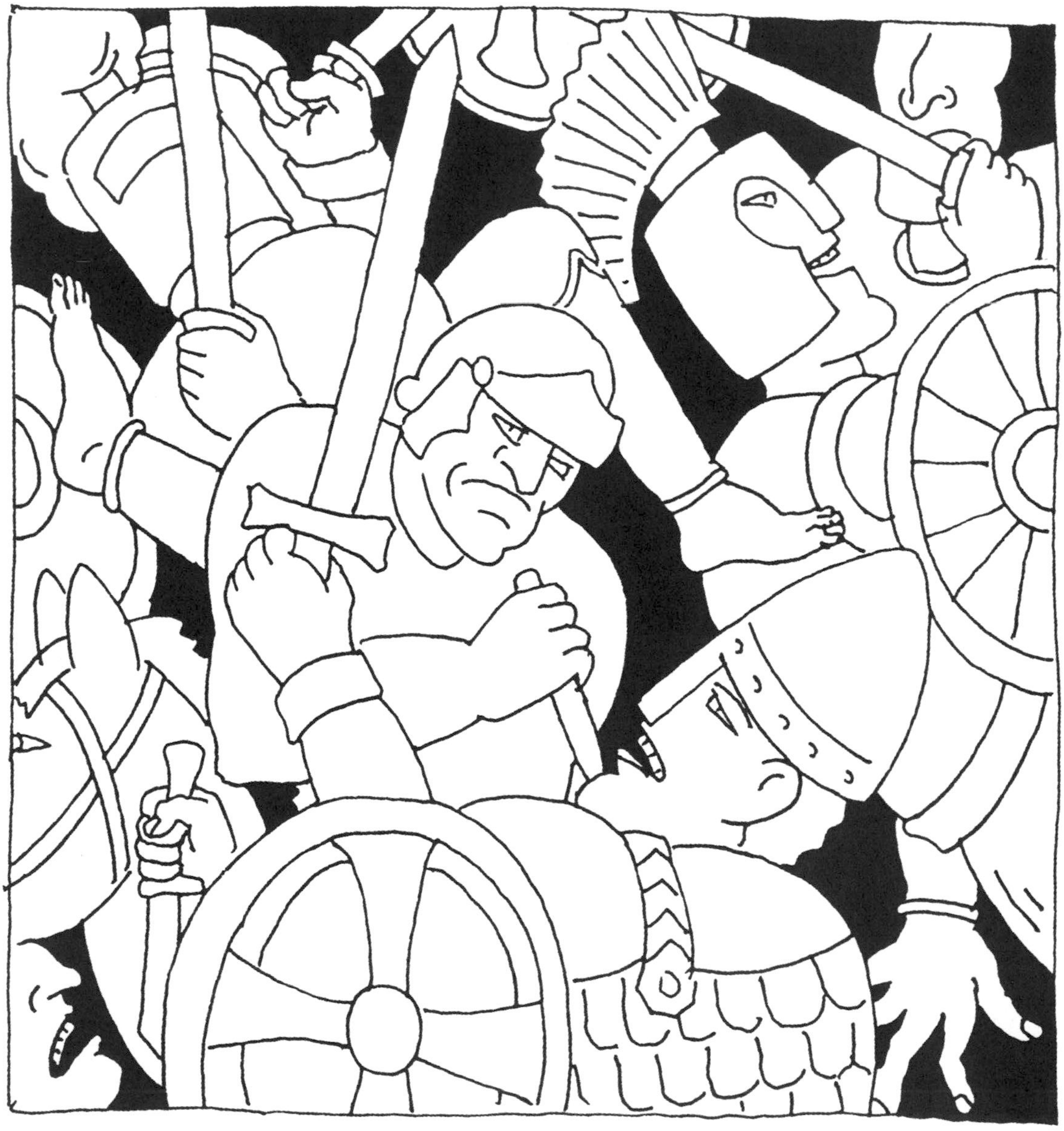

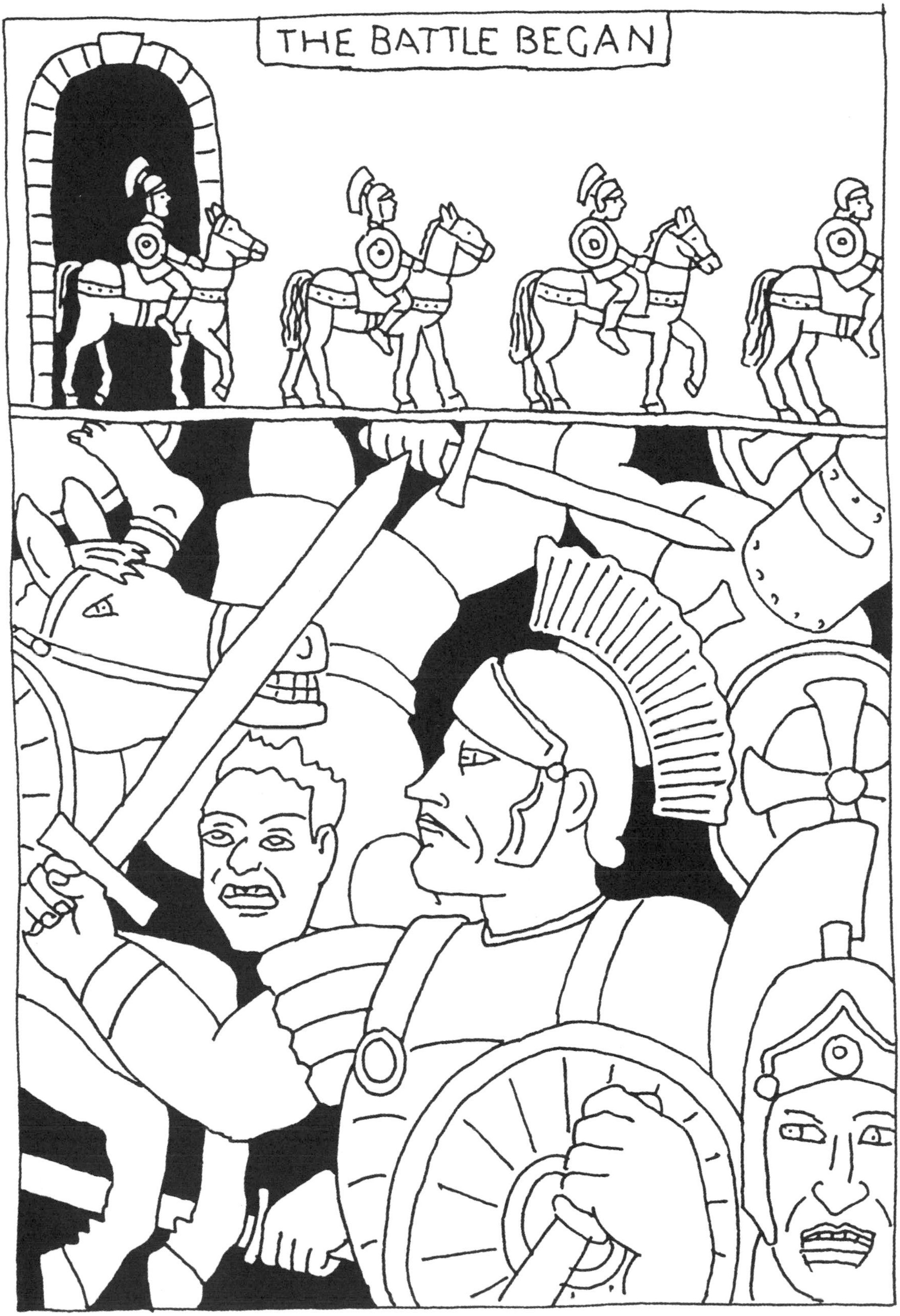
THE BATTLE BEGAN

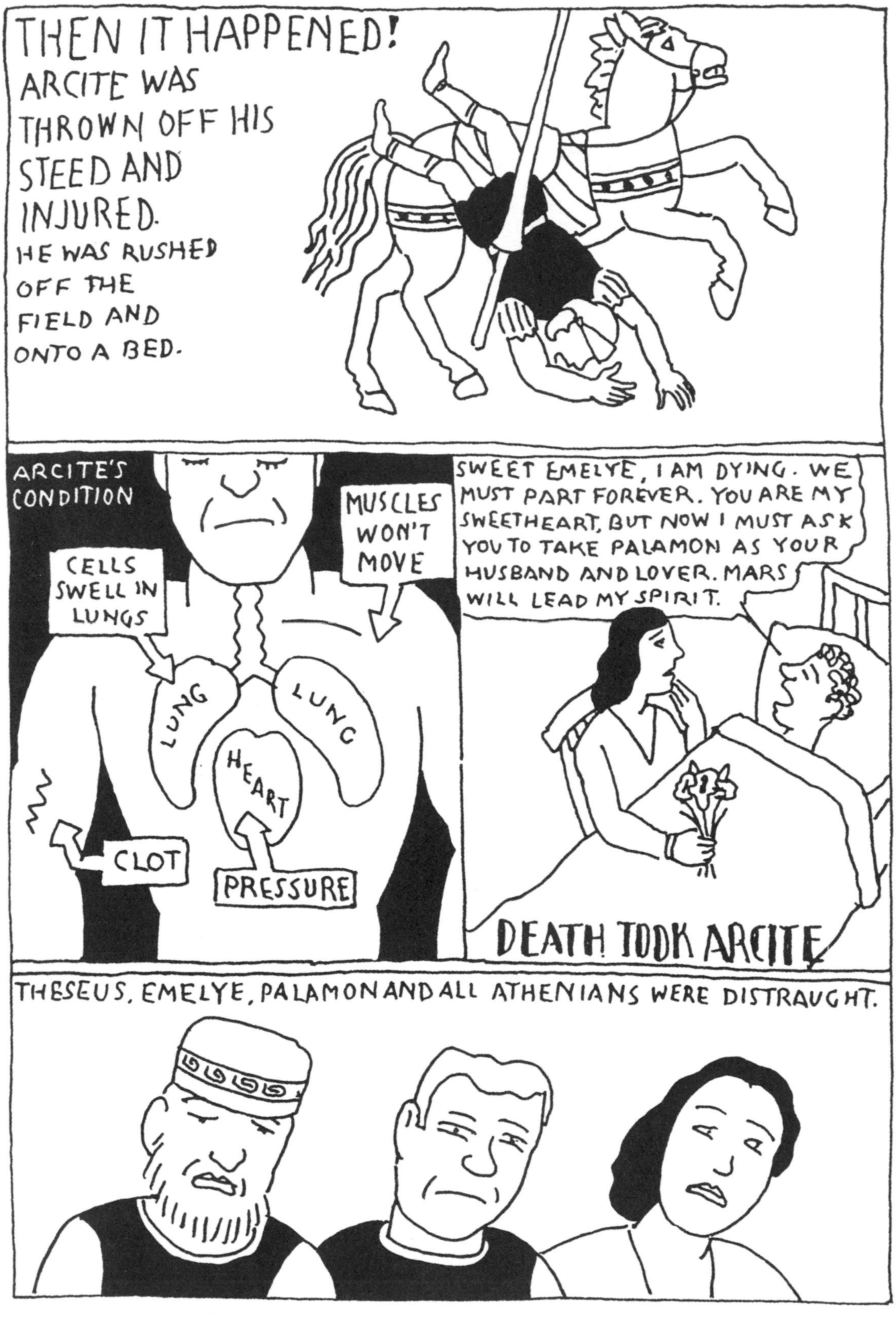

THEN IT HAPPENED!
ARCITE WAS THROWN OFF HIS STEED AND INJURED.
HE WAS RUSHED OFF THE FIELD AND ONTO A BED.
ARCITE'S CONDITION
MUSCLES WON'T MOVE
CELLS SWELL IN LUNGS
LUNG
LUNG
HEART
CLOT
PRESSURE
SWEET EMELYE, I AM DYING. WE MUST PART FOREVER. YOU ARE MY SWEETHEART, BUT NOW I MUST ASK YOU TO TAKE PALAMON AS YOUR HUSBAND AND LOVER. MARS WILL LEAD MY SPIRIT.
DEATH TOOK ARCITE
THESEUS, EMELYE, PALAMON AND ALL ATHENIANS WERE DISTRAUGHT.

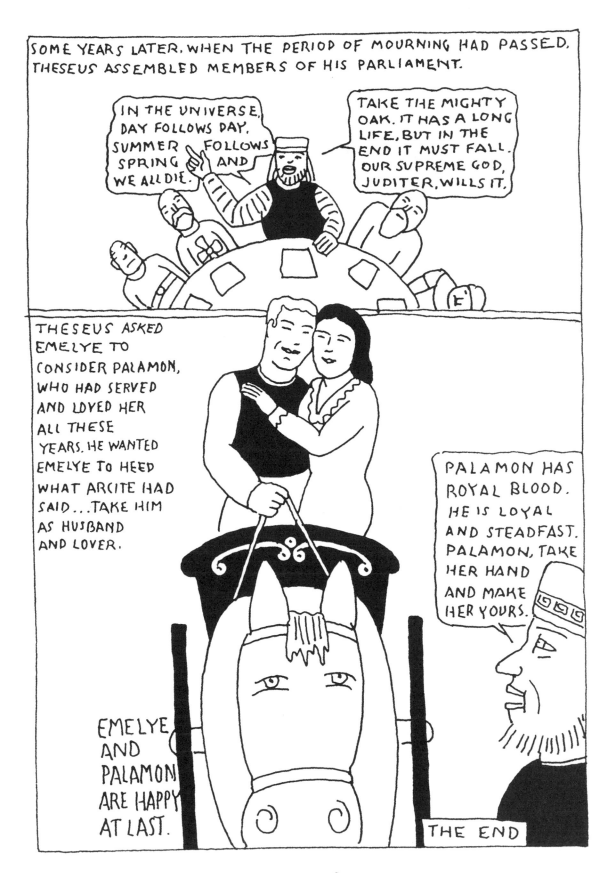

SOME YEARS LATER, WHEN THE PERIOD OF MOURNING HAD PASSED, THESEUS ASSEMBLED MEMBERS OF HIS PARLIAMENT.

IN THE UNIVERSE, DAY FOLLOWS DAY, SUMMER FOLLOWS SPRING AND WE ALL DIE.

TAKE THE MIGHTY OAK. IT HAS A LONG LIFE, BUT IN THE END IT MUST FALL. OUR SUPREME GOD, JUPITER, WILLS IT,

THESEUS ASKED EMELYE TO CONSIDER PALAMON, WHO HAD SERVED AND LOVED HER ALL THESE YEARS. HE WANTED EMELYE TO HEED WHAT ARCITE HAD SAID...TAKE HIM AS HUSBAND AND LOVER.

PALAMON HAS ROYAL BLOOD. HE IS LOYAL AND STEADFAST. PALAMON, TAKE HER HAND AND MAKE HER YOURS.

EMELYE AND PALAMON ARE HAPPY AT LAST.

THE END

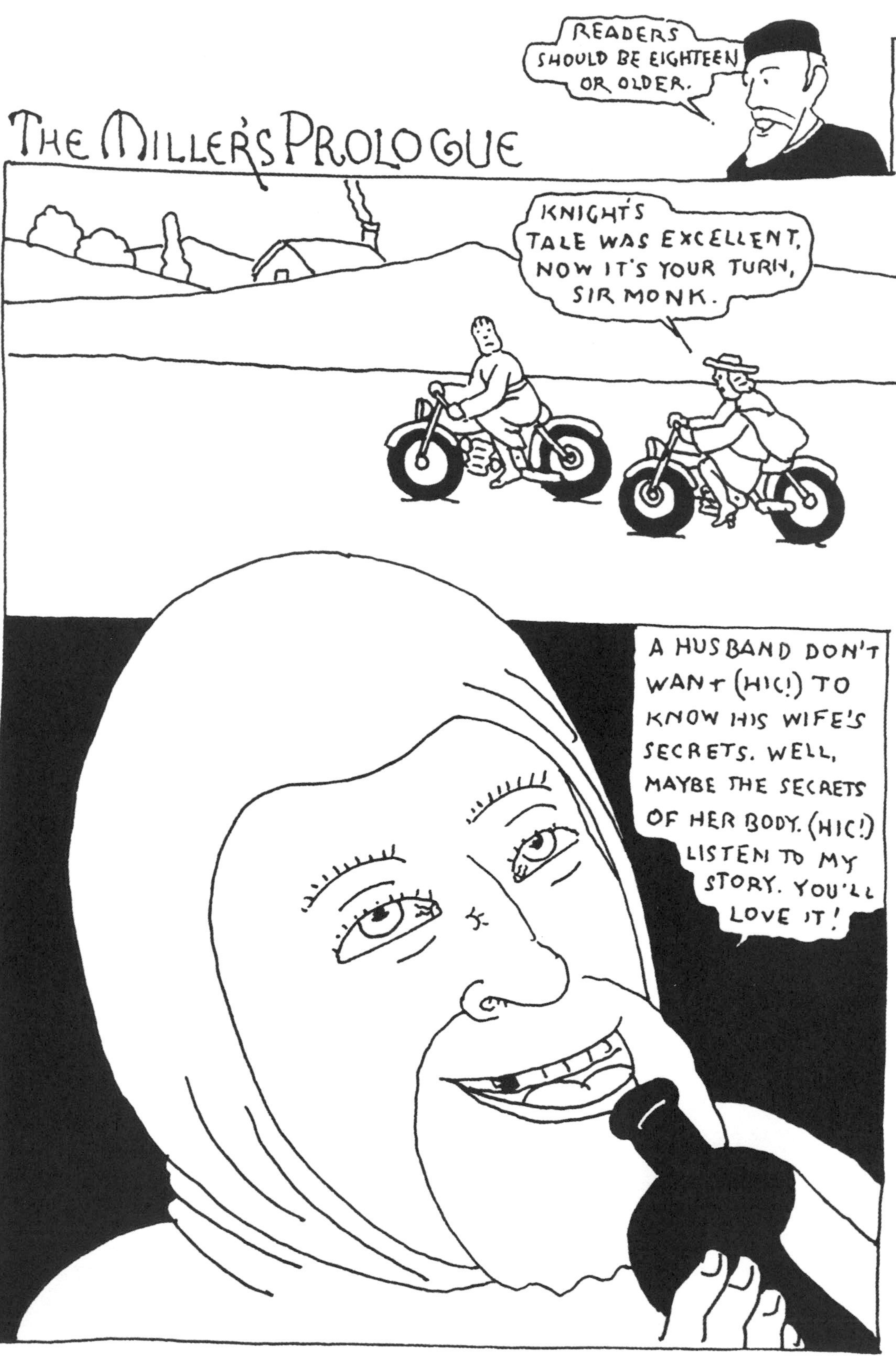
READERS SHOULD BE EIGHTEEN OR OLDER.
THE MILLER'S PROLOGUE
KNIGHT'S TALE WAS EXCELLENT, NOW IT'S YOUR TURN, SIR MONK.
A HUSBAND DON'T WANT (HIC!) TO KNOW HIS WIFE'S SECRETS. WELL, MAYBE THE SECRETS OF HER BODY. (HIC!) LISTEN TO MY STORY. YOU'LL LOVE IT!

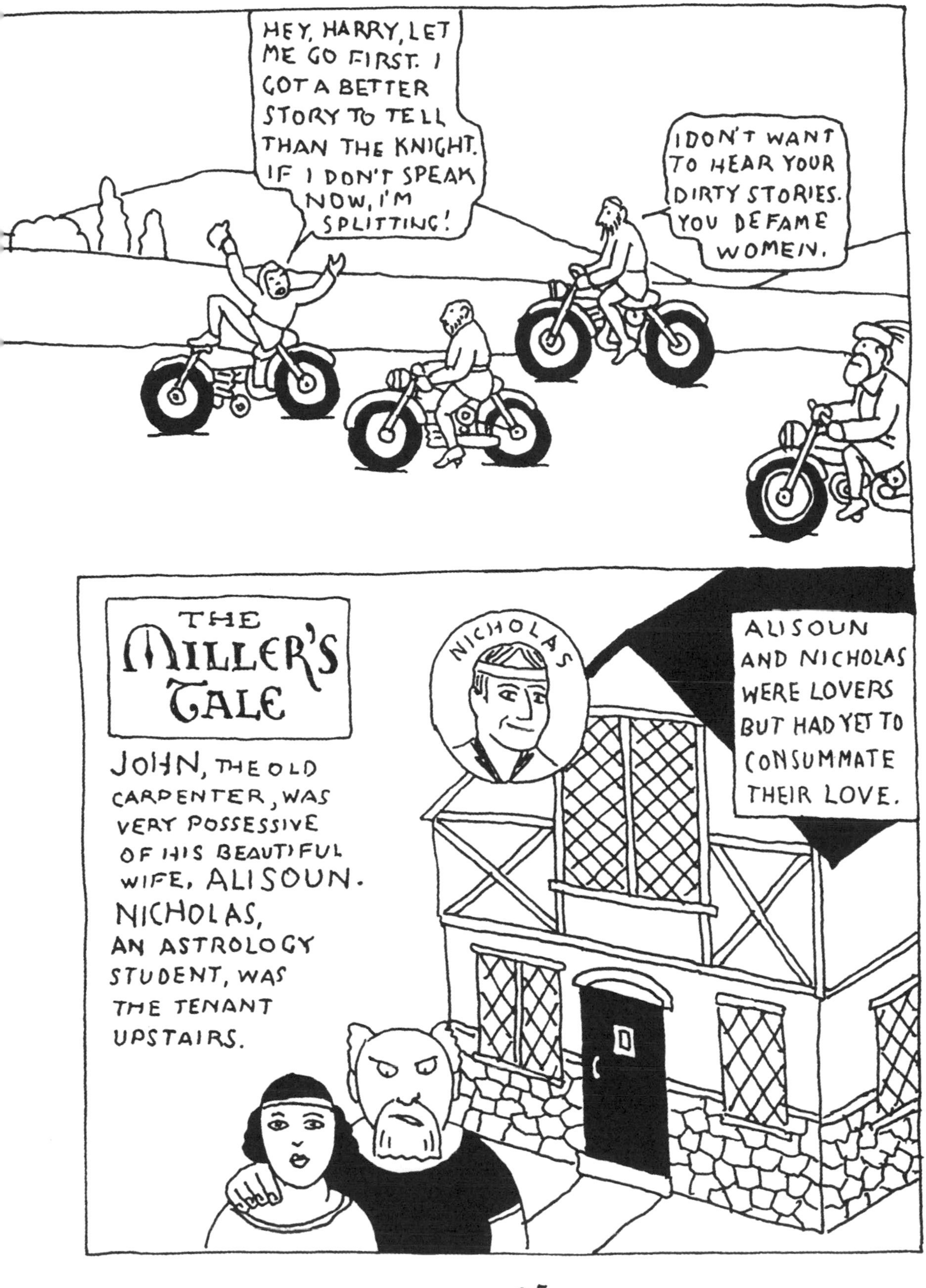
HEY, HARRY, LET ME GO FIRST. I GOT A BETTER STORY TO TELL THAN THE KNIGHT. IF I DON'T SPEAK NOW, I'M SPLITTING!
I DON'T WANT TO HEAR YOUR DIRTY STORIES. YOU DEFAME WOMEN.
THE MILLER'S TALE
JOHN, THE OLD CARPENTER, WAS VERY POSSESSIVE OF HIS BEAUTIFUL WIFE, ALISOUN. NICHOLAS, AN ASTROLOGY STUDENT, WAS THE TENANT UPSTAIRS.
NICHOLAS
ALISOUN AND NICHOLAS WERE LOVERS BUT HAD YET TO CONSUMMATE THEIR LOVE.

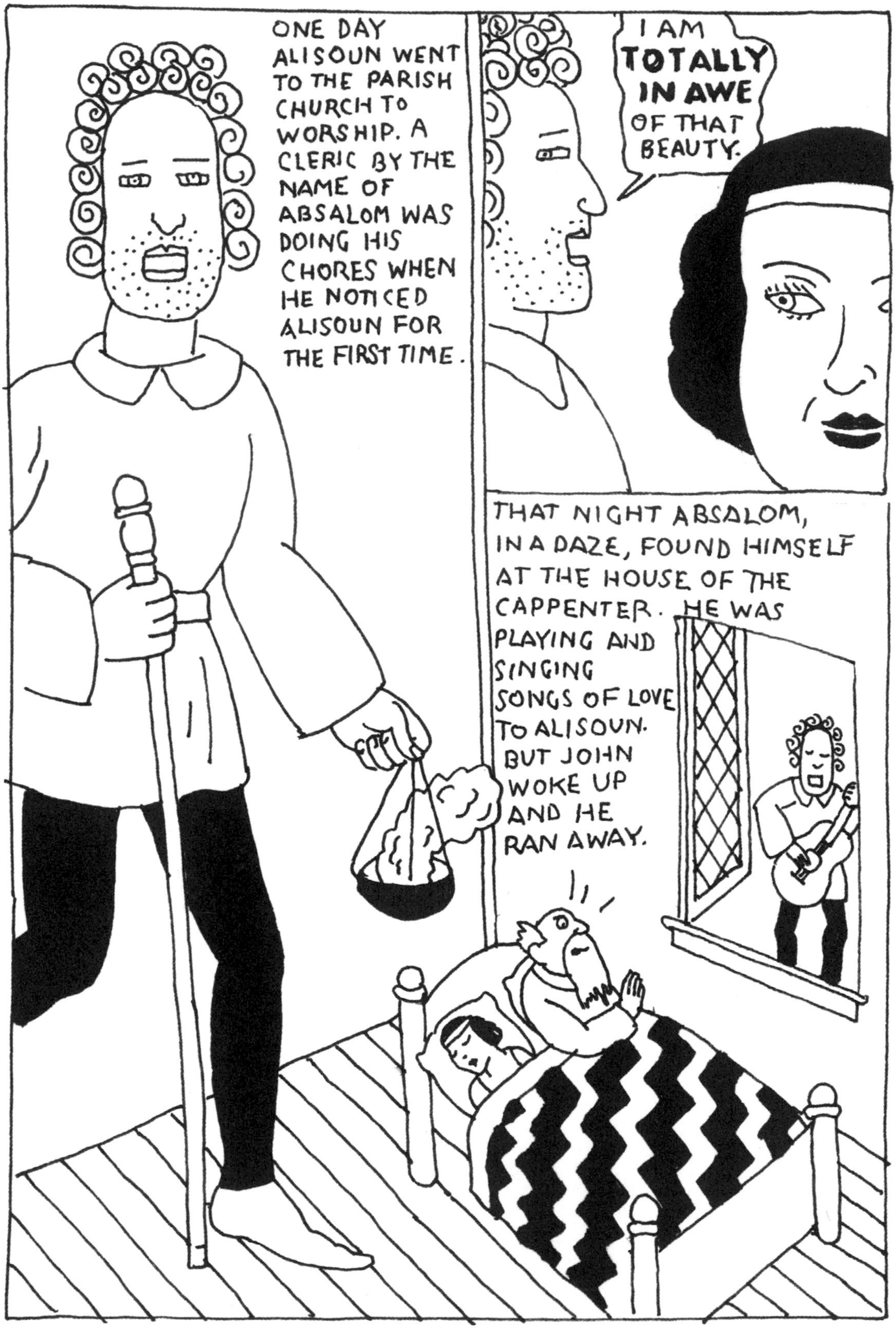
ONE DAY ALISOUN WENT TO THE PARISH CHURCH TO WORSHIP. A CLERIC BY THE NAME OF ABSALOM WAS DOING HIS CHORES WHEN HE NOTICED ALISOUN FOR THE FIRST TIME.
I AM **TOTALLY IN AWE** OF THAT BEAUTY.
THAT NIGHT ABSALOM, IN A DAZE, FOUND HIMSELF AT THE HOUSE OF THE CARPENTER. HE WAS PLAYING AND SINGING SONGS OF LOVE TO ALISOUN. BUT JOHN WOKE UP AND HE RAN AWAY.

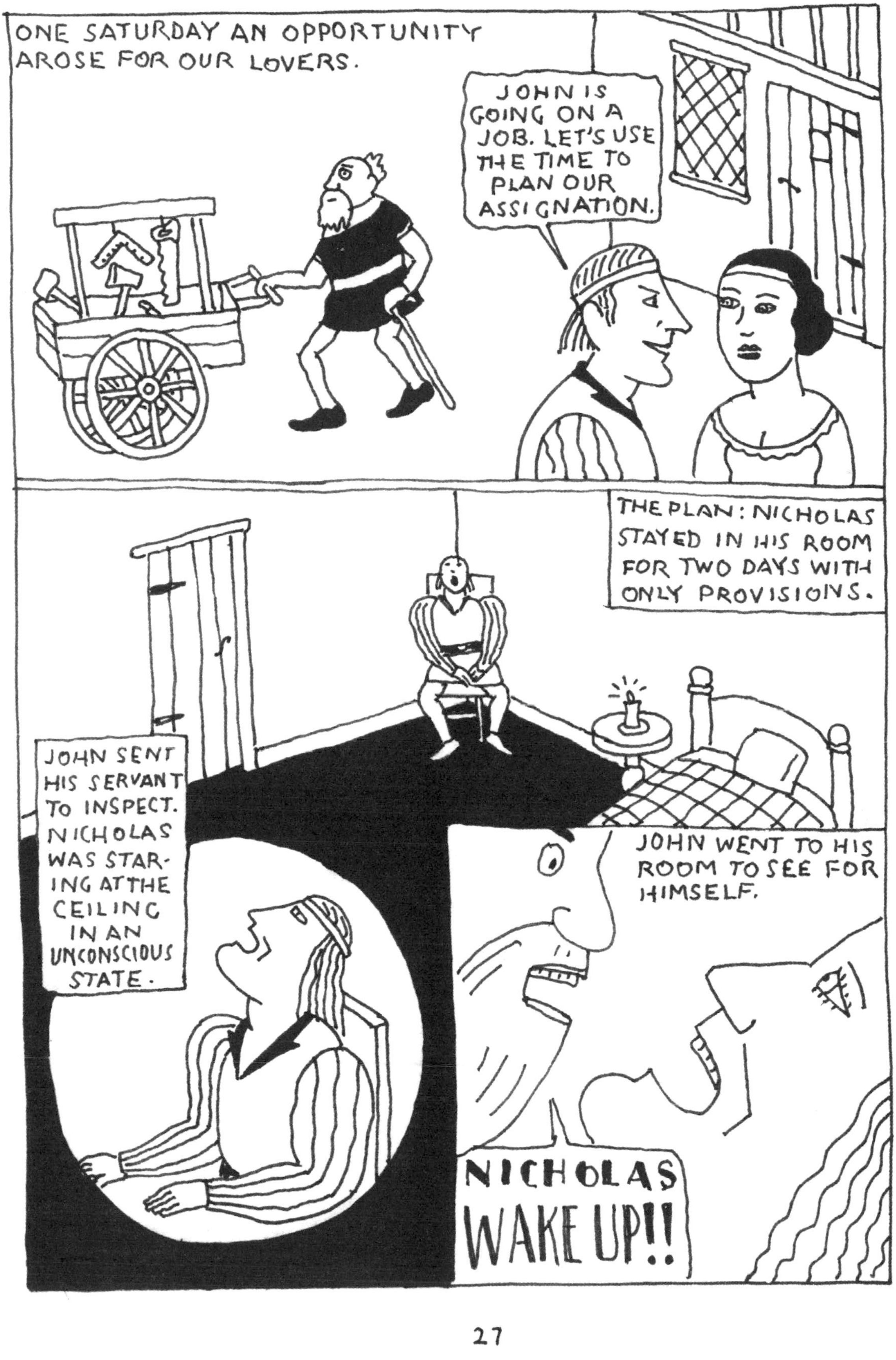
ONE SATURDAY AN OPPORTUNITY AROSE FOR OUR LOVERS.
JOHN IS GOING ON A JOB. LET'S USE THE TIME TO PLAN OUR ASSIGNATION.
THE PLAN: NICHOLAS STAYED IN HIS ROOM FOR TWO DAYS WITH ONLY PROVISIONS.
JOHN SENT HIS SERVANT TO INSPECT. NICHOLAS WAS STARING AT THE CEILING IN AN UNCONSCIOUS STATE.
JOHN WENT TO HIS ROOM TO SEE FOR HIMSELF.
NICHOLAS WAKE UP!!

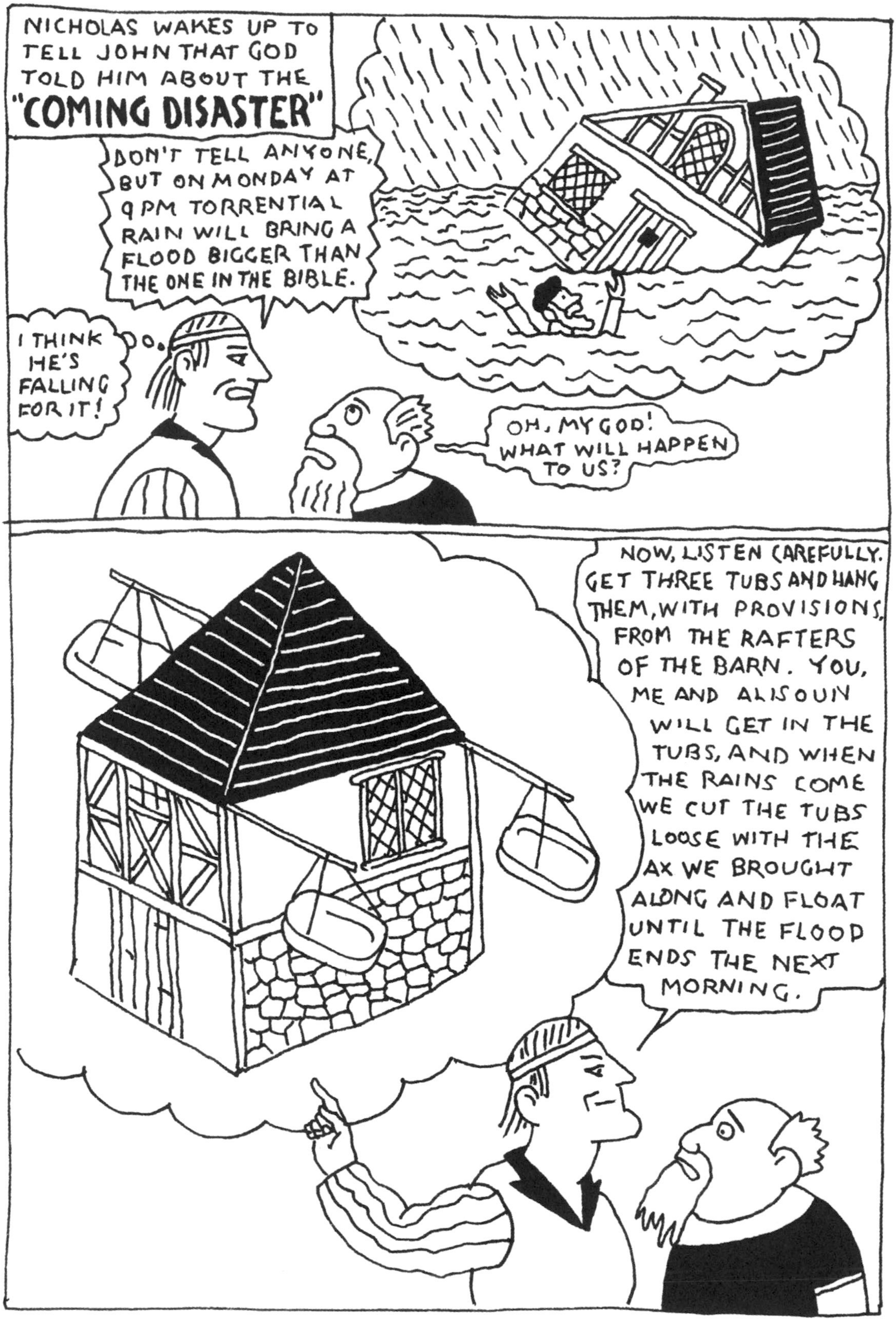
NICHOLAS WAKES UP TO TELL JOHN THAT GOD TOLD HIM ABOUT THE "COMING DISASTER"
DON'T TELL ANYONE, BUT ON MONDAY AT 9 PM TORRENTIAL RAIN WILL BRING A FLOOD BIGGER THAN THE ONE IN THE BIBLE.
I THINK HE'S FALLING FOR IT!
OH, MY GOD! WHAT WILL HAPPEN TO US?
NOW, LISTEN CAREFULLY. GET THREE TUBS AND HANG THEM, WITH PROVISIONS, FROM THE RAFTERS OF THE BARN. YOU, ME AND ALISOUN WILL GET IN THE TUBS, AND WHEN THE RAINS COME WE CUT THE TUBS LOOSE WITH THE AX WE BROUGHT ALONG AND FLOAT UNTIL THE FLOOD ENDS THE NEXT MORNING.

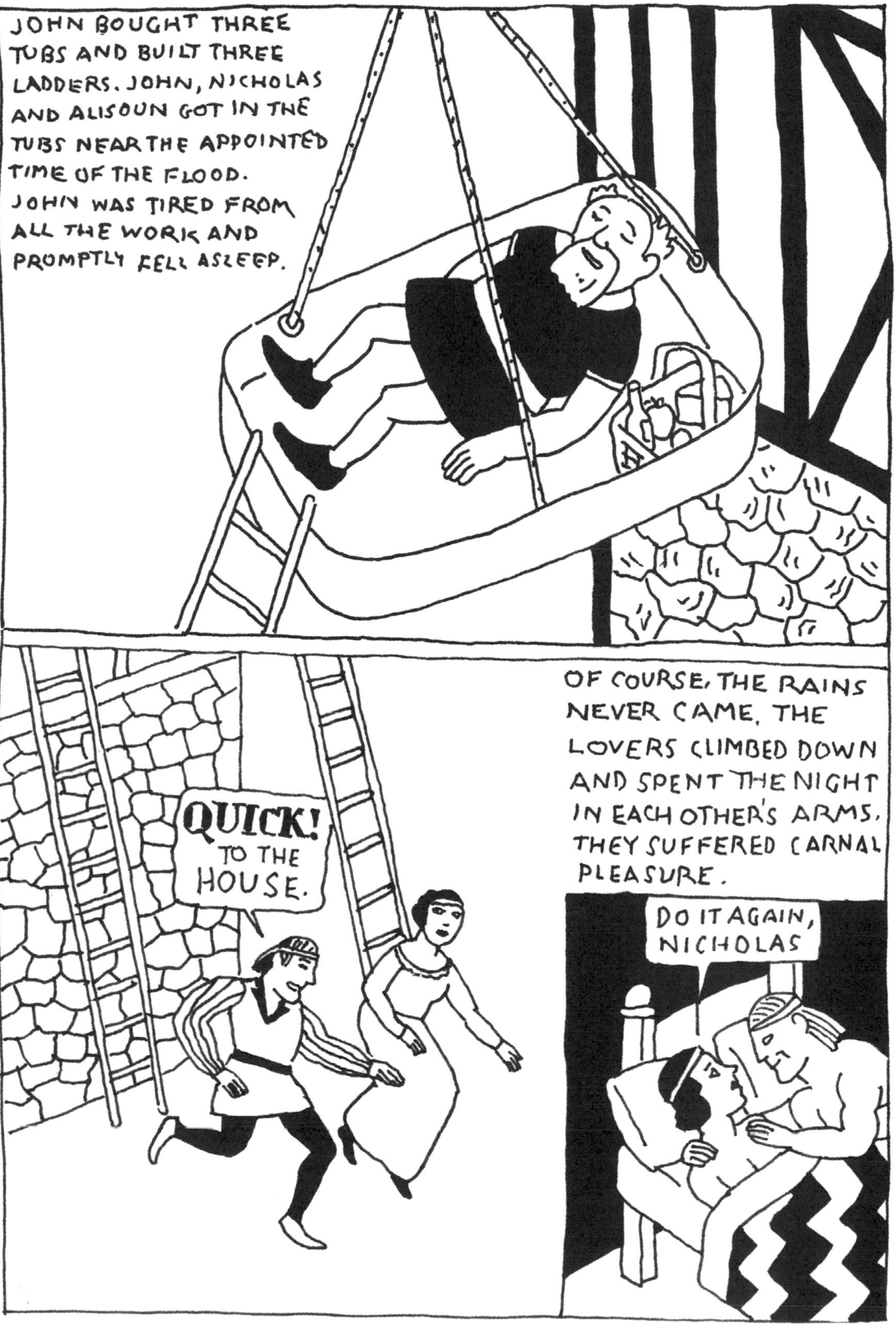
JOHN BOUGHT THREE TUBS AND BUILT THREE LADDERS. JOHN, NICHOLAS AND ALISOUN GOT IN THE TUBS NEAR THE APPOINTED TIME OF THE FLOOD. JOHN WAS TIRED FROM ALL THE WORK AND PROMPTLY FELL ASLEEP.
QUICK! TO THE HOUSE.
OF COURSE, THE RAINS NEVER CAME. THE LOVERS CLIMBED DOWN AND SPENT THE NIGHT IN EACH OTHER'S ARMS. THEY SUFFERED CARNAL PLEASURE.
DO IT AGAIN, NICHOLAS

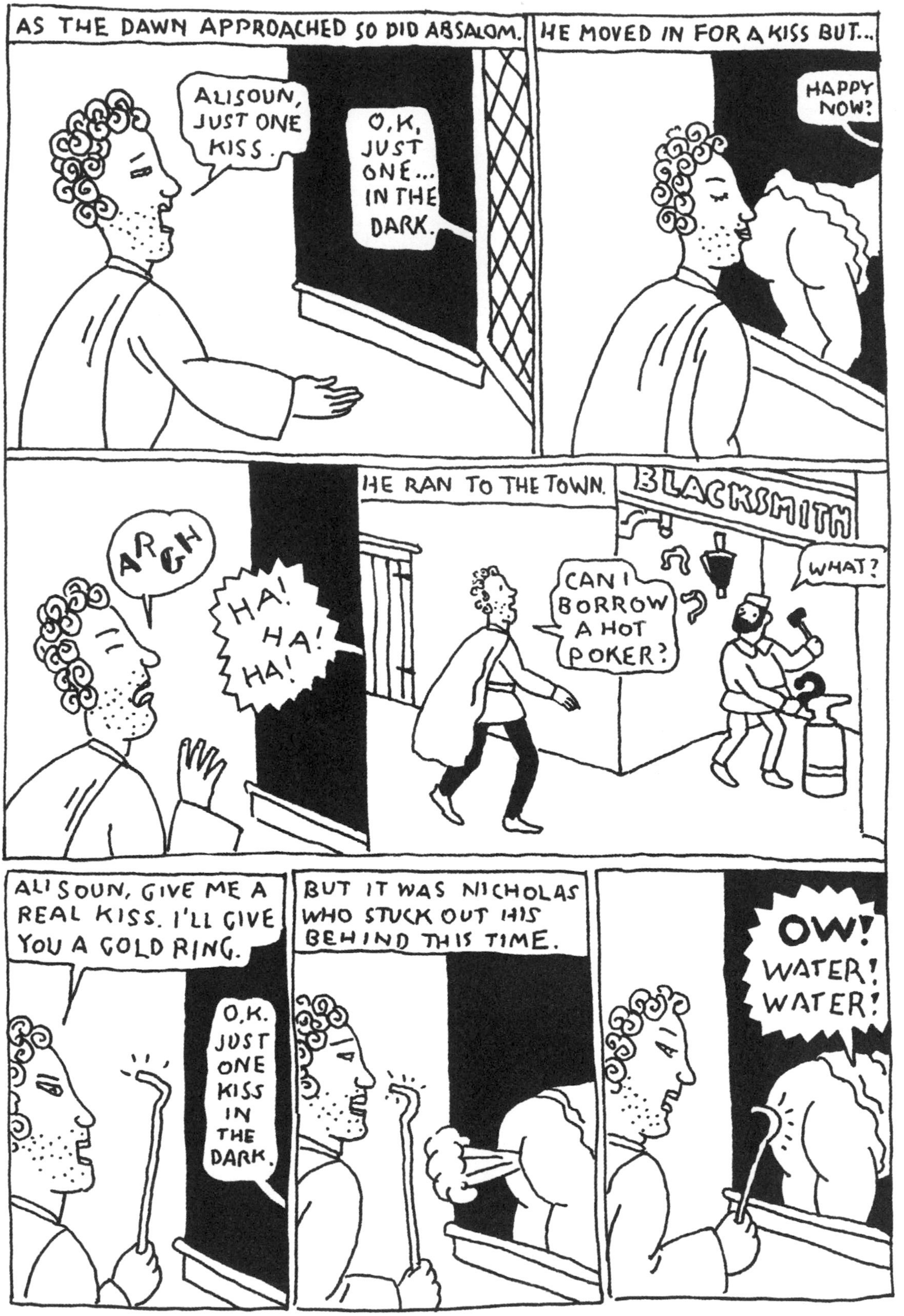
AS THE DAWN APPROACHED SO DID ABSALOM.
ALISOUN, JUST ONE KISS.
O.K, JUST ONE... IN THE DARK.
HE MOVED IN FOR A KISS BUT...
HAPPY NOW?
ARGH
HA! HA! HA!
HE RAN TO THE TOWN.
BLACKSMITH
CAN I BORROW A HOT POKER?
WHAT?
ALISOUN, GIVE ME A REAL KISS. I'LL GIVE YOU A GOLD RING.
O.K. JUST ONE KISS IN THE DARK.
BUT IT WAS NICHOLAS WHO STUCK OUT HIS BEHIND THIS TIME.
OW! WATER! WATER!

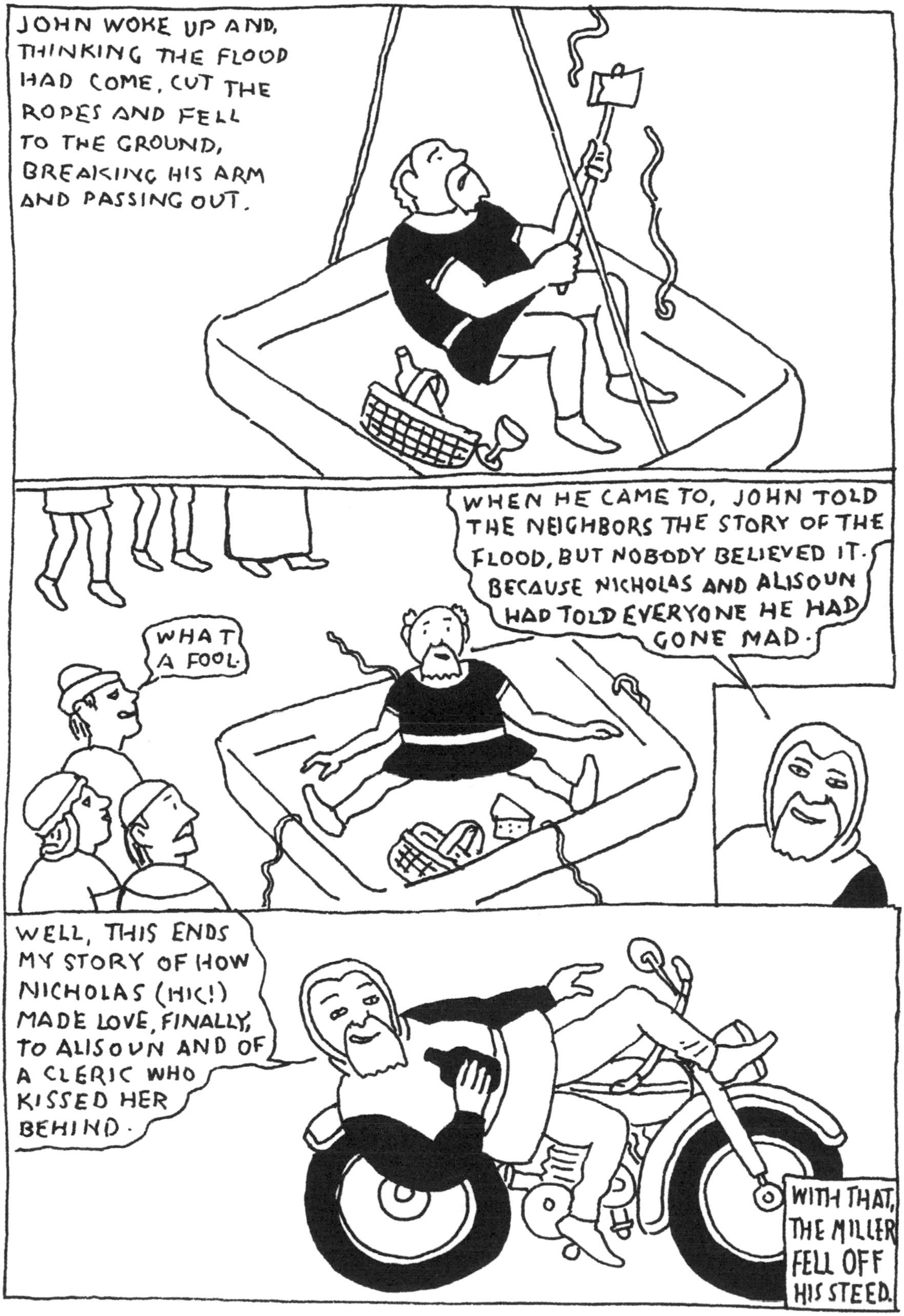
JOHN WOKE UP AND, THINKING THE FLOOD HAD COME, CUT THE ROPES AND FELL TO THE GROUND, BREAKING HIS ARM AND PASSING OUT.
WHEN HE CAME TO, JOHN TOLD THE NEIGHBORS THE STORY OF THE FLOOD, BUT NOBODY BELIEVED IT. BECAUSE NICHOLAS AND ALISOUN HAD TOLD EVERYONE HE HAD GONE MAD.
WHAT A FOOL.
WELL, THIS ENDS MY STORY OF HOW NICHOLAS (HIC!) MADE LOVE, FINALLY, TO ALISOUN AND OF A CLERIC WHO KISSED HER BEHIND.
WITH THAT, THE MILLER FELL OFF HIS STEED.

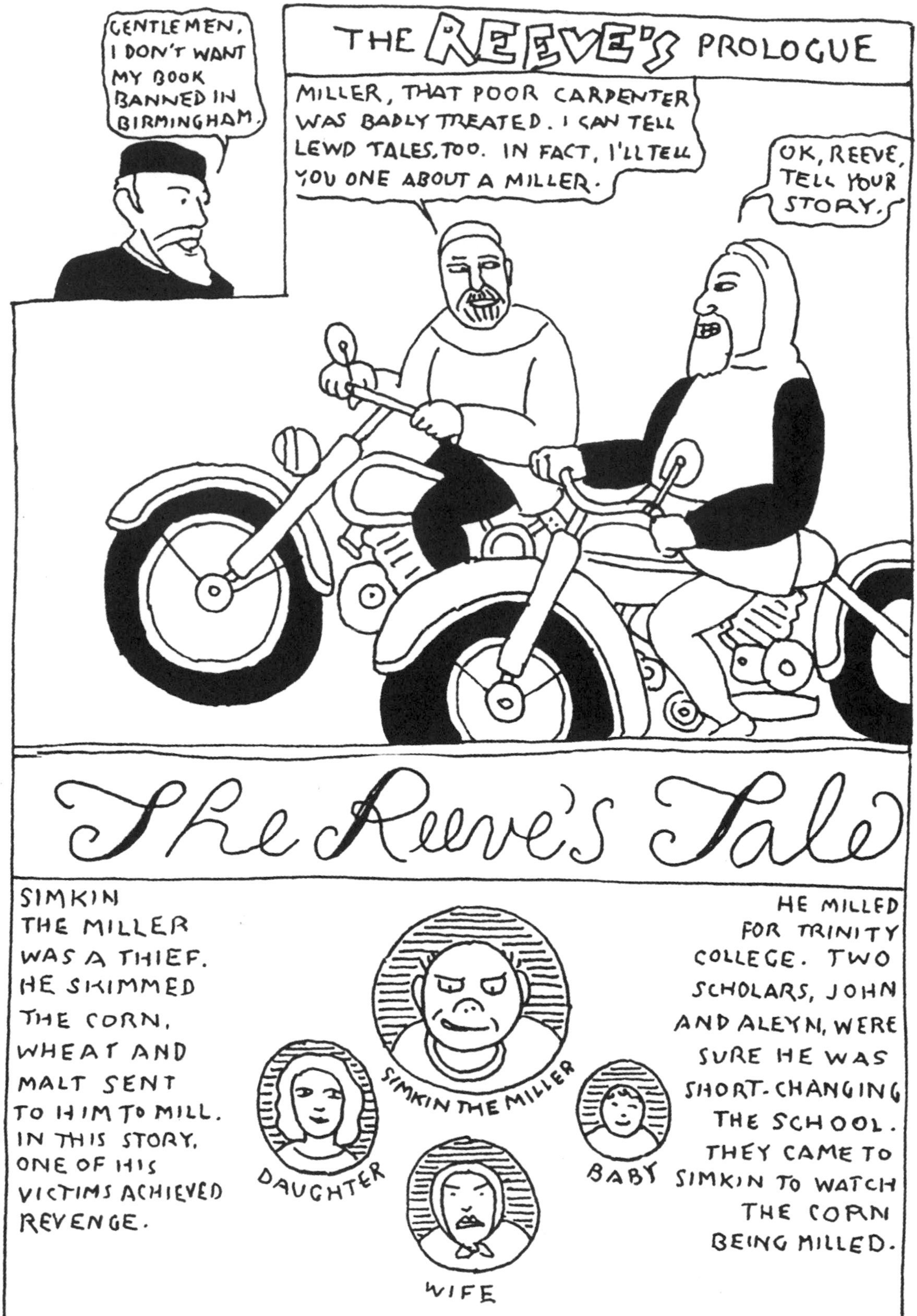
GENTLEMEN, I DON'T WANT MY BOOK BANNED IN BIRMINGHAM.
THE REEVE'S PROLOGUE
MILLER, THAT POOR CARPENTER WAS BADLY TREATED. I CAN TELL LEWD TALES, TOO. IN FACT, I'LL TELL YOU ONE ABOUT A MILLER.
OK, REEVE, TELL YOUR STORY.
The Reeve's Tale
SIMKIN THE MILLER WAS A THIEF. HE SKIMMED THE CORN, WHEAT AND MALT SENT TO HIM TO MILL. IN THIS STORY, ONE OF HIS VICTIMS ACHIEVED REVENGE.
SIMKIN THE MILLER
DAUGHTER
BABY
WIFE
HE MILLED FOR TRINITY COLLEGE. TWO SCHOLARS, JOHN AND ALEYN, WERE SURE HE WAS SHORT-CHANGING THE SCHOOL. THEY CAME TO SIMKIN TO WATCH THE CORN BEING MILLED.

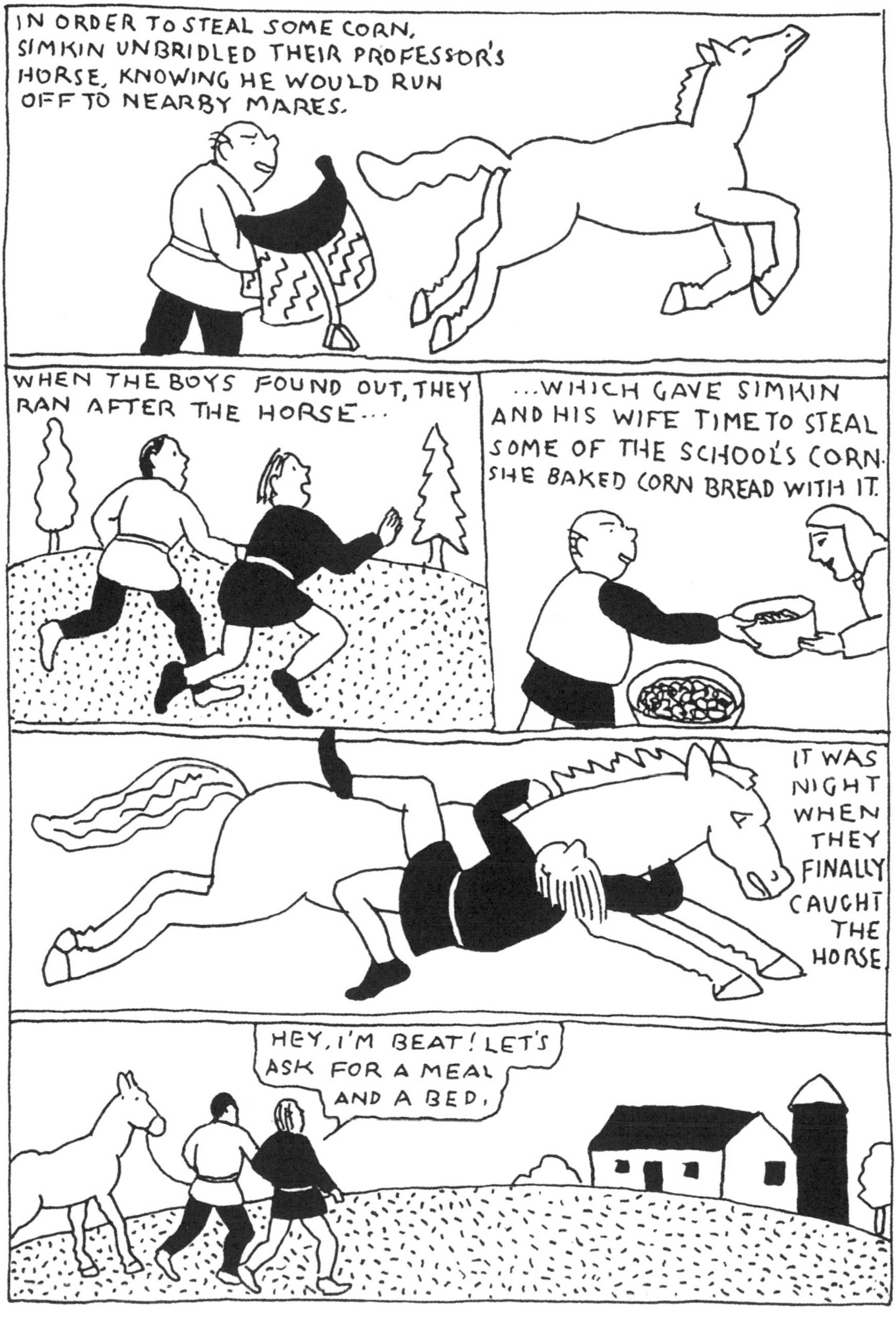
IN ORDER TO STEAL SOME CORN, SIMKIN UNBRIDLED THEIR PROFESSOR'S HORSE, KNOWING HE WOULD RUN OFF TO NEARBY MARES.
WHEN THE BOYS FOUND OUT, THEY RAN AFTER THE HORSE...
...WHICH GAVE SIMKIN AND HIS WIFE TIME TO STEAL SOME OF THE SCHOOL'S CORN. SHE BAKED CORN BREAD WITH IT.
IT WAS NIGHT WHEN THEY FINALLY CAUGHT THE HORSE
HEY, I'M BEAT! LET'S ASK FOR A MEAL AND A BED.

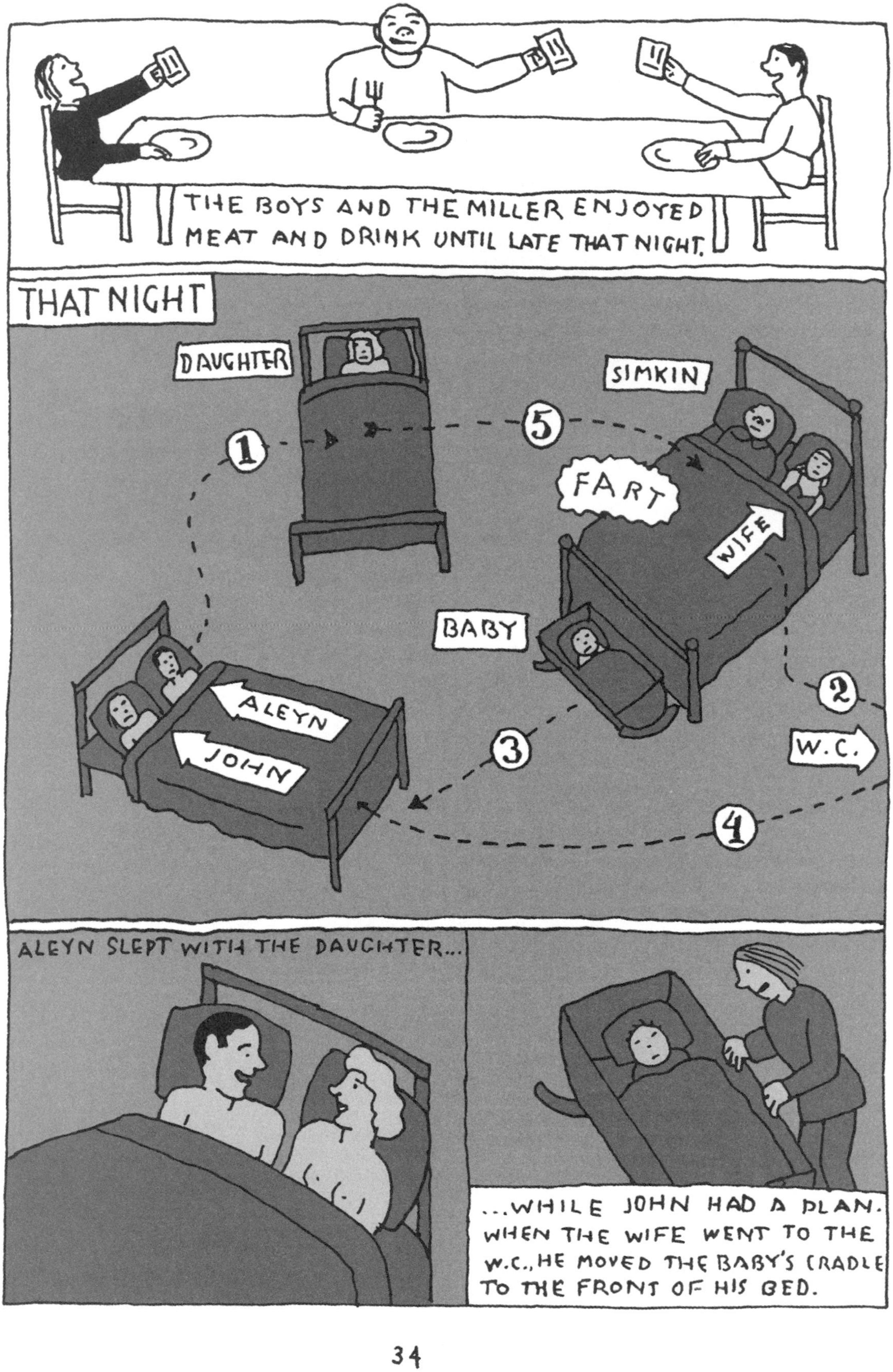
THE BOYS AND THE MILLER ENJOYED MEAT AND DRINK UNTIL LATE THAT NIGHT.
THAT NIGHT
DAUGHTER
SIMKIN
1
5
FART
WIFE
BABY
2
ALEYN
JOHN
3
W.C.
4
ALEYN SLEPT WITH THE DAUGHTER...
...WHILE JOHN HAD A PLAN. WHEN THE WIFE WENT TO THE W.C., HE MOVED THE BABY'S CRADLE TO THE FRONT OF HIS BED.

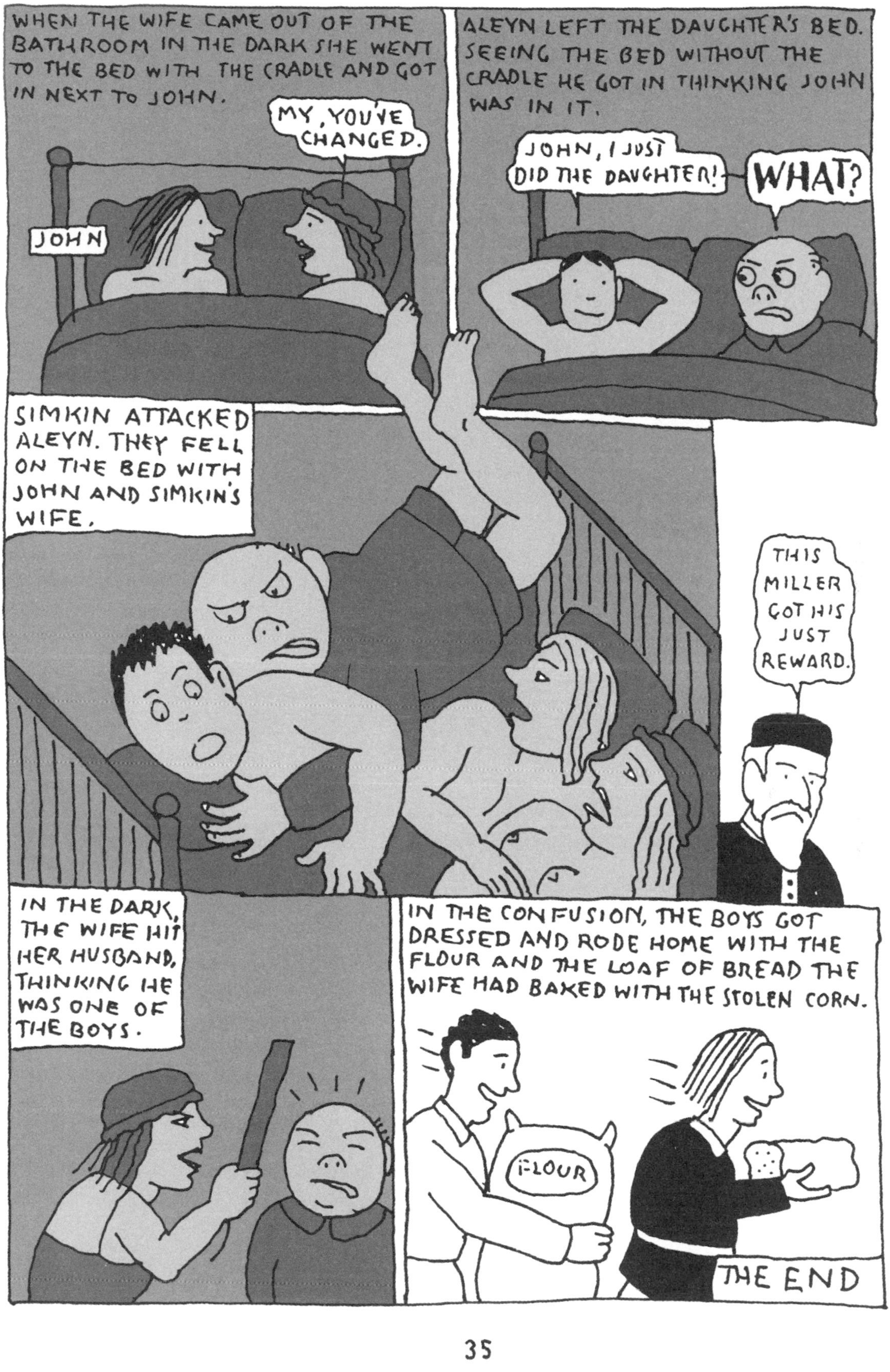
WHEN THE WIFE CAME OUT OF THE BATHROOM IN THE DARK SHE WENT TO THE BED WITH THE CRADLE AND GOT IN NEXT TO JOHN.
MY, YOU'VE CHANGED.
JOHN
ALEYN LEFT THE DAUGHTER'S BED. SEEING THE BED WITHOUT THE CRADLE HE GOT IN THINKING JOHN WAS IN IT.
JOHN, I JUST DID THE DAUGHTER!
WHAT?
SIMKIN ATTACKED ALEYN. THEY FELL ON THE BED WITH JOHN AND SIMKIN'S WIFE.
THIS MILLER GOT HIS JUST REWARD.
IN THE DARK, THE WIFE HIT HER HUSBAND, THINKING HE WAS ONE OF THE BOYS.
IN THE CONFUSION, THE BOYS GOT DRESSED AND RODE HOME WITH THE FLOUR AND THE LOAF OF BREAD THE WIFE HAD BAKED WITH THE STOLEN CORN.
FLOUR
THE END

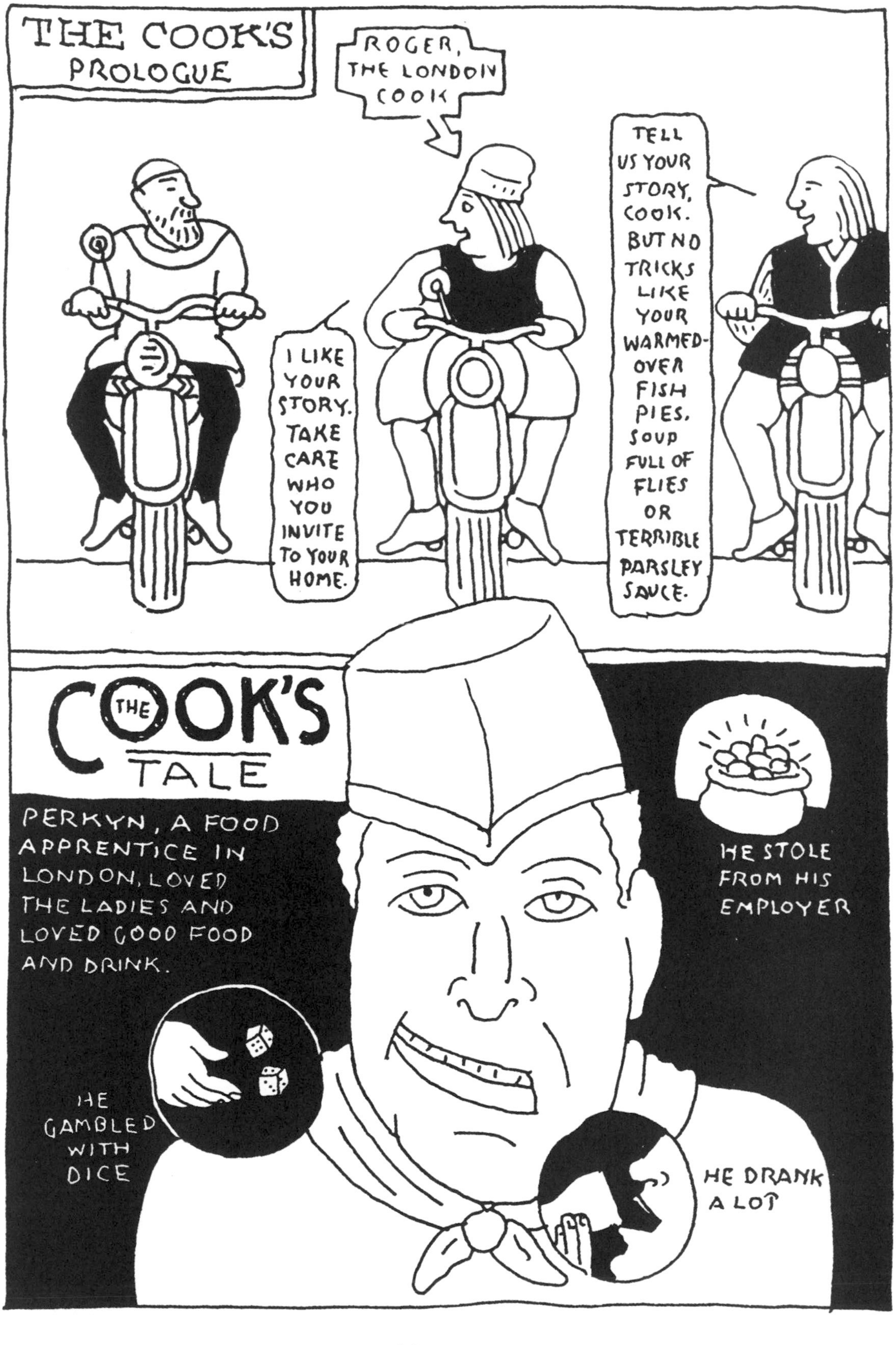
THE COOK'S PROLOGUE
ROGER, THE LONDON COOK
I LIKE YOUR STORY. TAKE CARE WHO YOU INVITE TO YOUR HOME.
TELL US YOUR STORY, COOK. BUT NO TRICKS LIKE YOUR WARMED-OVER FISH PIES, SOUP FULL OF FLIES OR TERRIBLE PARSLEY SAUCE.
THE COOK'S TALE
PERKYN, A FOOD APPRENTICE IN LONDON, LOVED THE LADIES AND LOVED GOOD FOOD AND DRINK.
HE STOLE FROM HIS EMPLOYER
HE GAMBLED WITH DICE
HE DRANK A LOT

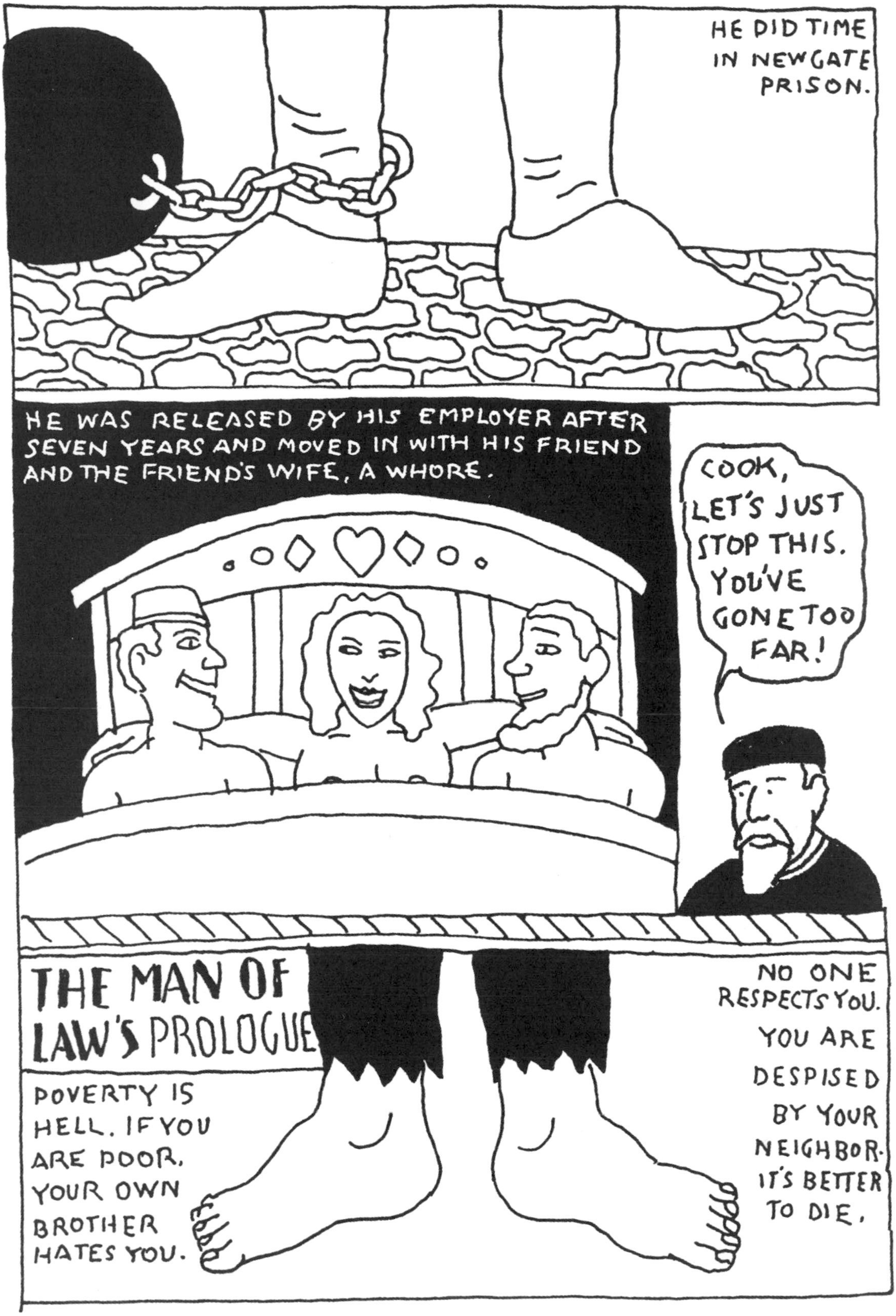
HE DID TIME IN NEWGATE PRISON.
HE WAS RELEASED BY HIS EMPLOYER AFTER SEVEN YEARS AND MOVED IN WITH HIS FRIEND AND THE FRIEND'S WIFE, A WHORE.
COOK, LET'S JUST STOP THIS. YOU'VE GONE TOO FAR!
THE MAN OF LAW'S PROLOGUE
POVERTY IS HELL. IF YOU ARE POOR, YOUR OWN BROTHER HATES YOU.
NO ONE RESPECTS YOU. YOU ARE DESPISED BY YOUR NEIGHBOR. IT'S BETTER TO DIE.

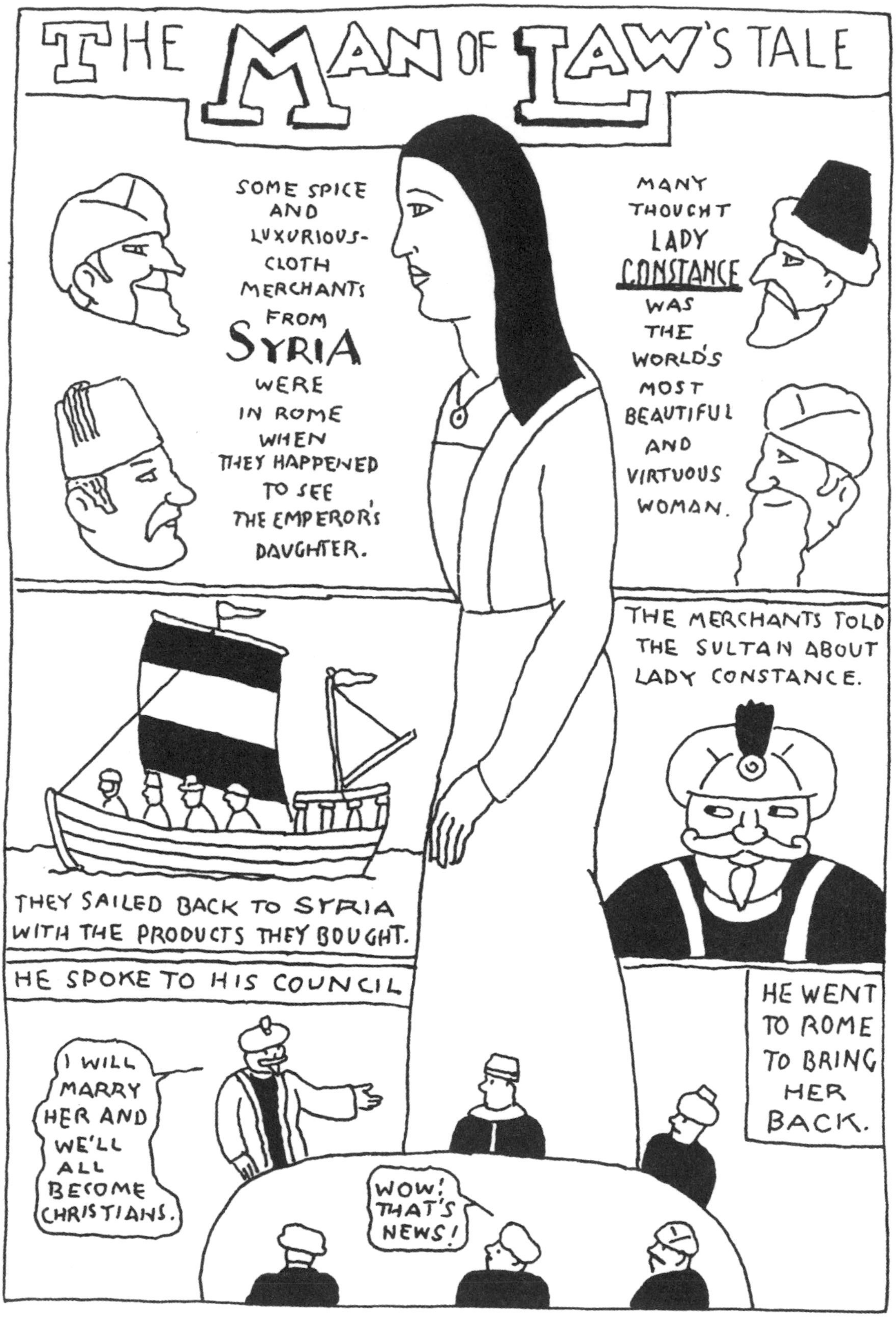
THE MAN OF LAW'S TALE
SOME SPICE AND LUXURIOUS-CLOTH MERCHANTS FROM SYRIA WERE IN ROME WHEN THEY HAPPENED TO SEE THE EMPEROR'S DAUGHTER.
MANY THOUGHT LADY CONSTANCE WAS THE WORLD'S MOST BEAUTIFUL AND VIRTUOUS WOMAN.
THEY SAILED BACK TO SYRIA WITH THE PRODUCTS THEY BOUGHT.
THE MERCHANTS TOLD THE SULTAN ABOUT LADY CONSTANCE.
HE SPOKE TO HIS COUNCIL
I WILL MARRY HER AND WE'LL ALL BECOME CHRISTIANS.
WOW! THAT'S NEWS!
HE WENT TO ROME TO BRING HER BACK.

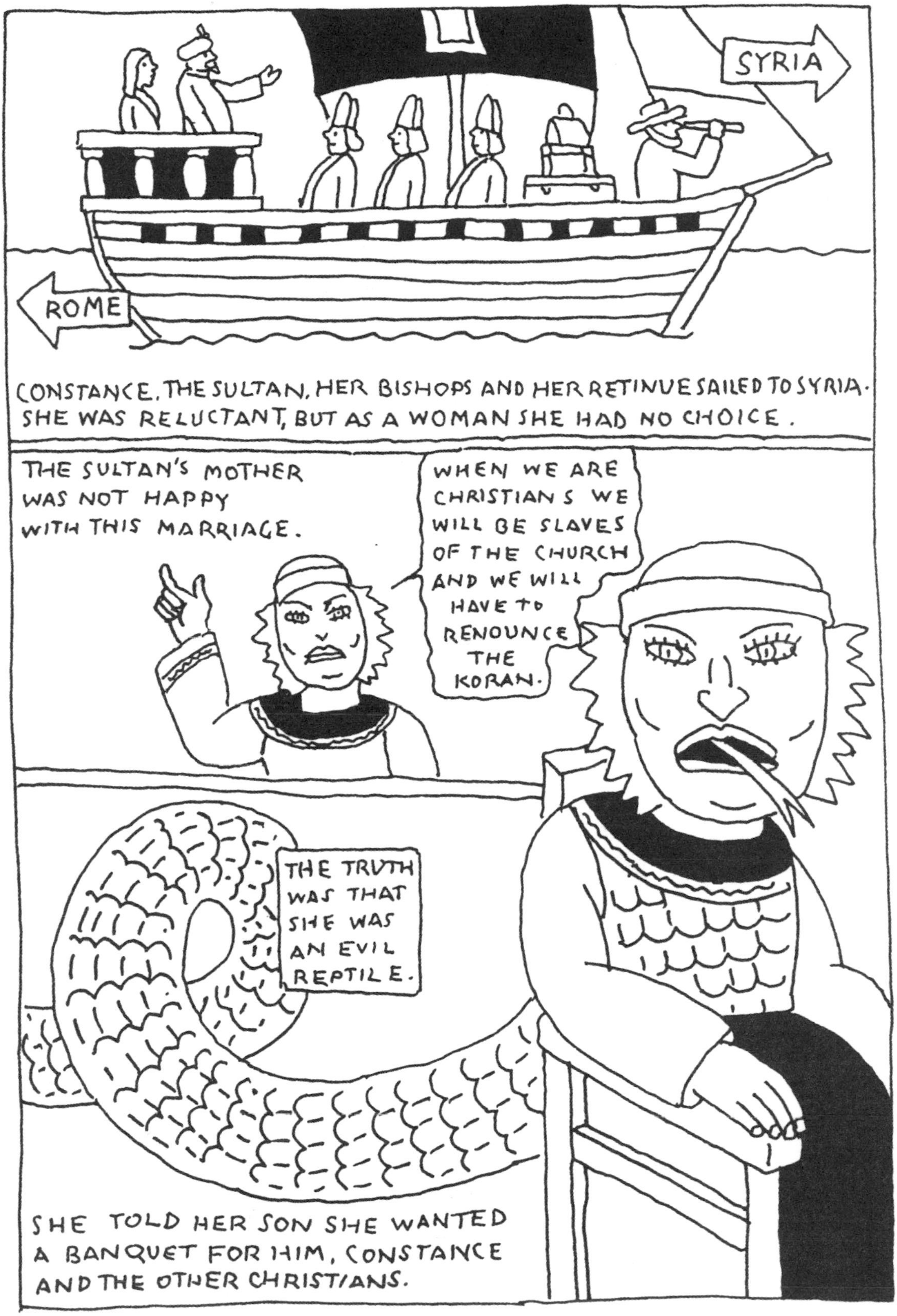
SYRIA
ROME
CONSTANCE, THE SULTAN, HER BISHOPS AND HER RETINUE SAILED TO SYRIA. SHE WAS RELUCTANT, BUT AS A WOMAN SHE HAD NO CHOICE.
THE SULTAN'S MOTHER WAS NOT HAPPY WITH THIS MARRIAGE.
WHEN WE ARE CHRISTIANS WE WILL BE SLAVES OF THE CHURCH AND WE WILL HAVE TO RENOUNCE THE KORAN.
THE TRUTH WAS THAT SHE WAS AN EVIL REPTILE.
SHE TOLD HER SON SHE WANTED A BANQUET FOR HIM, CONSTANCE AND THE OTHER CHRISTIANS.

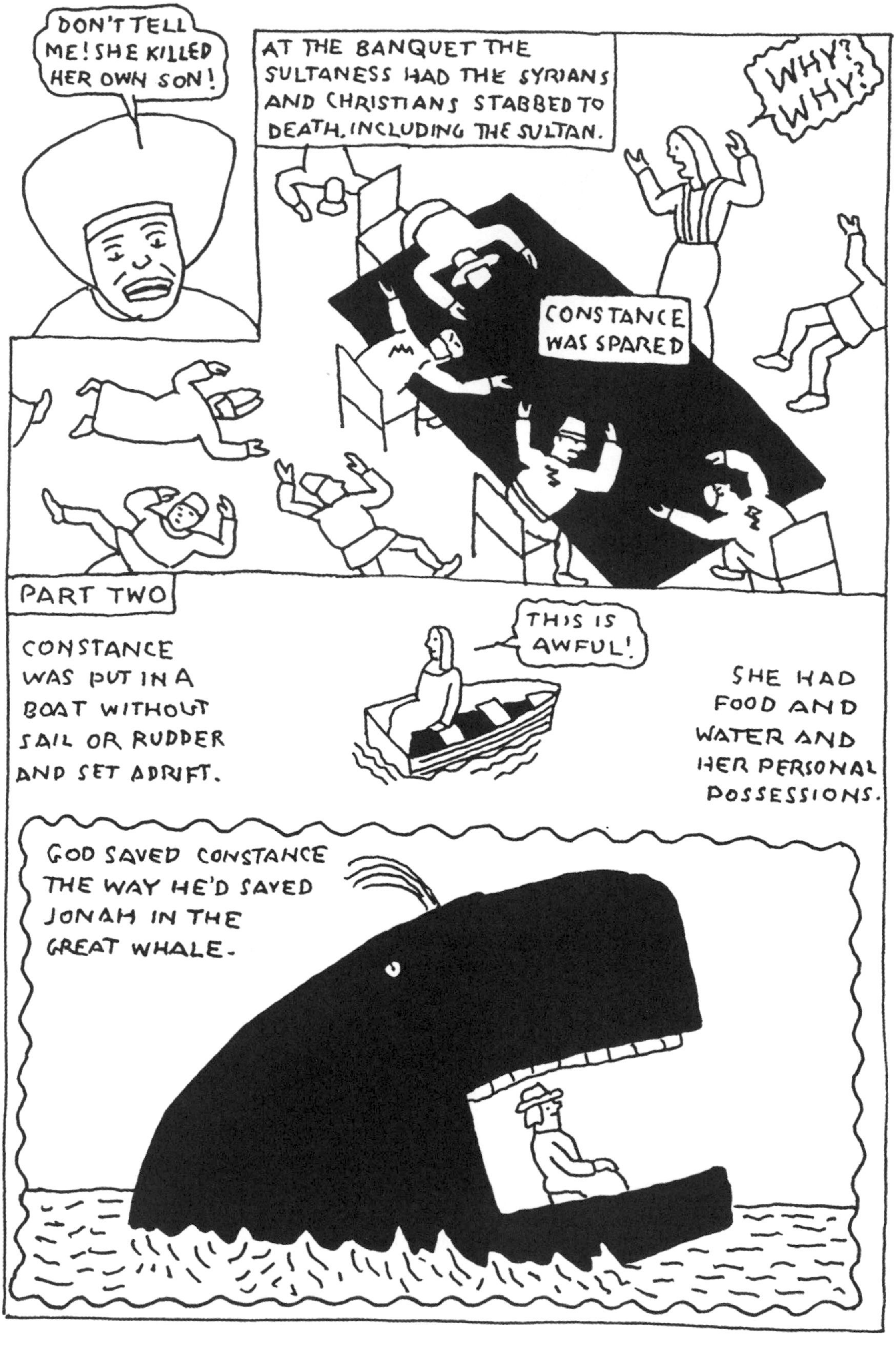
DON'T TELL ME! SHE KILLED HER OWN SON!
AT THE BANQUET THE SULTANESS HAD THE SYRIANS AND CHRISTIANS STABBED TO DEATH, INCLUDING THE SULTAN.
WHY? WHY?
CONSTANCE WAS SPARED
PART TWO
CONSTANCE WAS PUT IN A BOAT WITHOUT SAIL OR RUDDER AND SET ADRIFT.
THIS IS AWFUL!
SHE HAD FOOD AND WATER AND HER PERSONAL POSSESSIONS.
GOD SAVED CONSTANCE THE WAY HE'D SAVED JONAH IN THE GREAT WHALE.

AFTER YEARS IN THE OCEAN, SHE LANDED ON THE COAST OF NORTH-UMBERLAND, IN ENGLAND. THE GOVERNOR'S CASTLE WAS NEAR THE BEACH.

WEL-COME.

THE GOVERNOR AND HIS WIFE, HERMENGILD, TOOK CONSTANCE UNDER THEIR WINGS. THEY BECAME FOND OF HER.

CONSTANCE CONVERTED HER HOSTS FROM PAGANISM TO CHRISTIANITY. **I AM ANNOYED!**

SATAN FILLED A LOCAL KNIGHT WITH LUST FOR HER.

CONSTANCE WON'T PUT OUT! I'LL TEACH HER!

HE CREPT INTO HERMENGILD'S ROOM, KILLED HER AND LEFT THE DAGGER NEXT TO CONSTANCE.

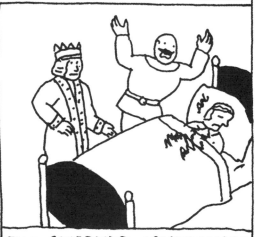

THE GOVERNOR, ACCOMPANIED BY KING ALLA, CAME HOME AND FOUND HIS WIFE DEAD.

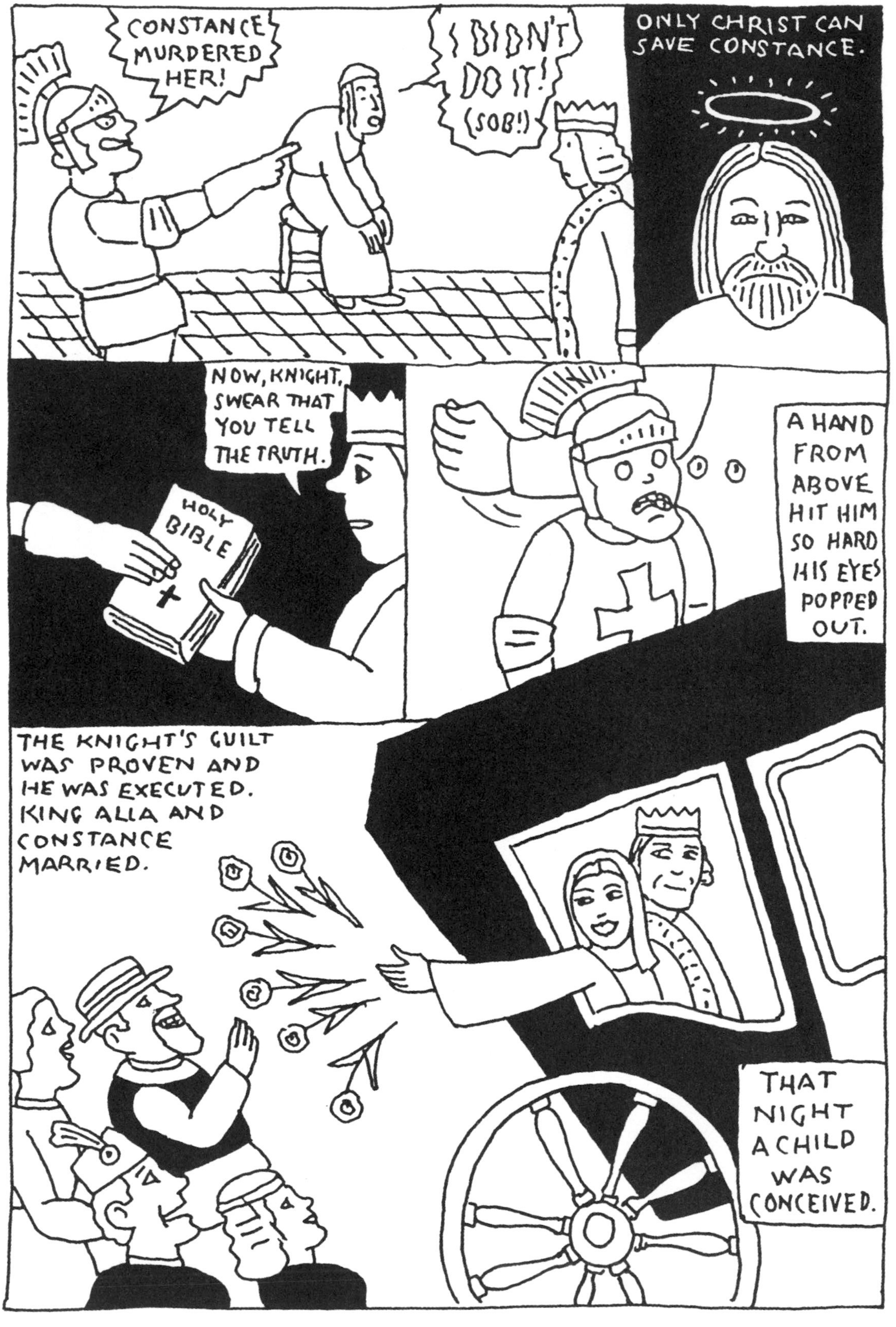
CONSTANCE MURDERED HER!
I DIDN'T DO IT! (SOB!)
ONLY CHRIST CAN SAVE CONSTANCE.
NOW, KNIGHT, SWEAR THAT YOU TELL THE TRUTH.
HOLY BIBLE
A HAND FROM ABOVE HIT HIM SO HARD HIS EYES POPPED OUT.
THE KNIGHT'S GUILT WAS PROVEN AND HE WAS EXECUTED. KING ALLA AND CONSTANCE MARRIED.
THAT NIGHT A CHILD WAS CONCEIVED.

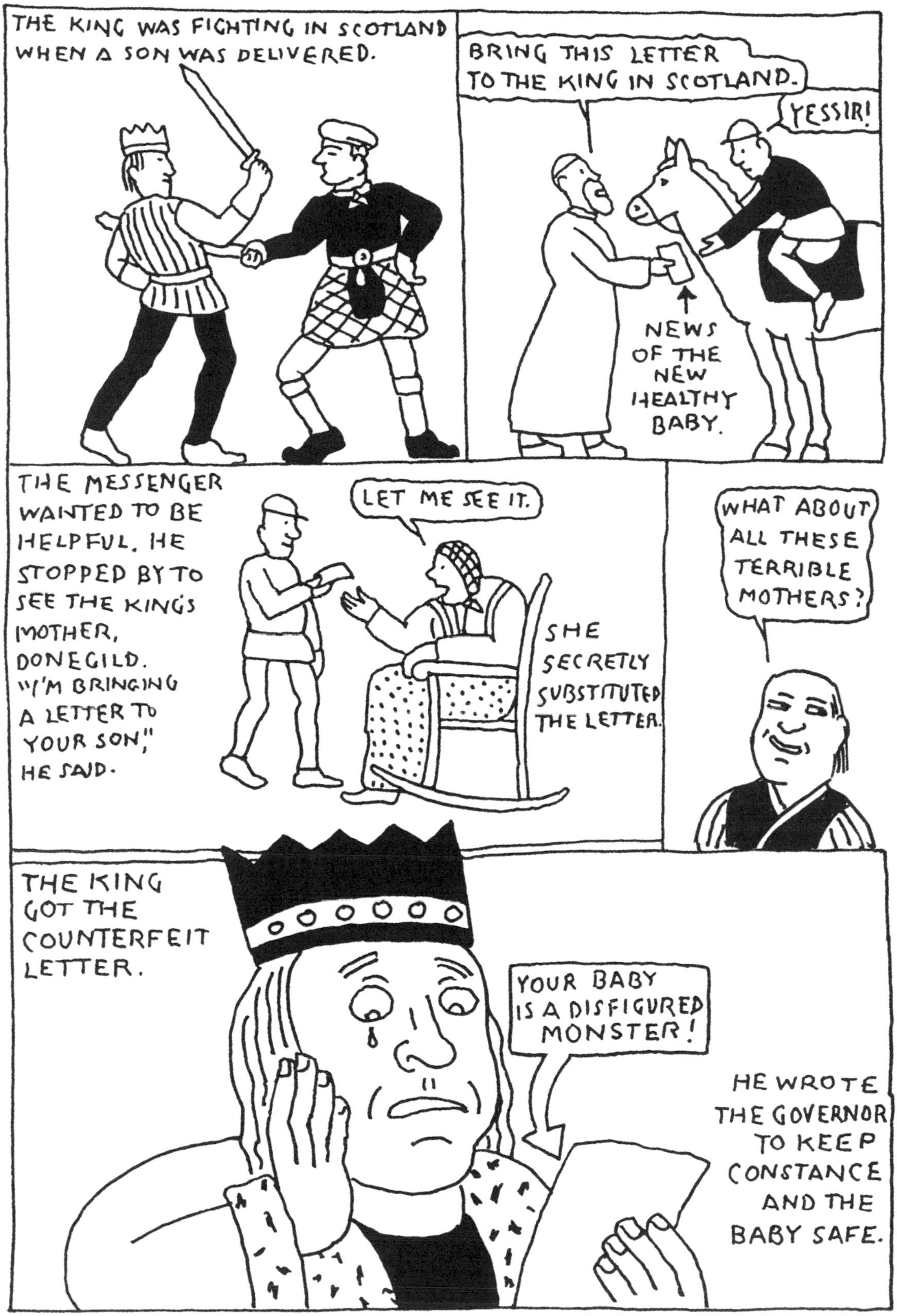
THE KING WAS FIGHTING IN SCOTLAND WHEN A SON WAS DELIVERED.
BRING THIS LETTER TO THE KING IN SCOTLAND.
YESSIR!
NEWS OF THE NEW HEALTHY BABY.
THE MESSENGER WANTED TO BE HELPFUL. HE STOPPED BY TO SEE THE KINGS MOTHER, DONEGILD. "I'M BRINGING A LETTER TO YOUR SON," HE SAID.
LET ME SEE IT.
SHE SECRETLY SUBSTITUTED THE LETTER.
WHAT ABOUT ALL THESE TERRIBLE MOTHERS?
THE KING GOT THE COUNTERFEIT LETTER.
YOUR BABY IS A DISFIGURED MONSTER!
HE WROTE THE GOVERNOR TO KEEP CONSTANCE AND THE BABY SAFE.

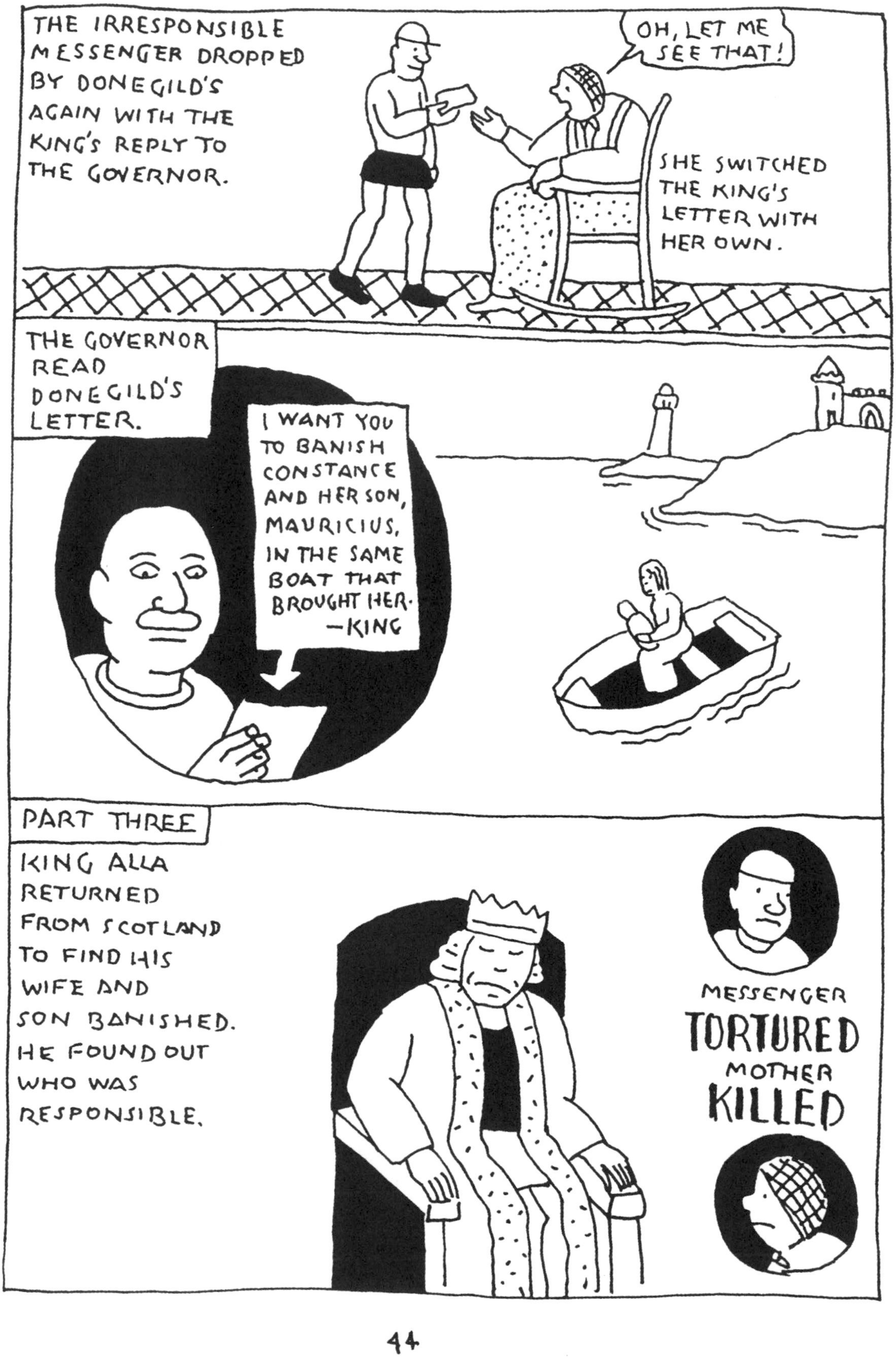
THE IRRESPONSIBLE MESSENGER DROPPED BY DONEGILD'S AGAIN WITH THE KING'S REPLY TO THE GOVERNOR.
OH, LET ME SEE THAT!
SHE SWITCHED THE KING'S LETTER WITH HER OWN.
THE GOVERNOR READ DONEGILD'S LETTER.
I WANT YOU TO BANISH CONSTANCE AND HER SON, MAURICIUS, IN THE SAME BOAT THAT BROUGHT HER. —KING
PART THREE
KING ALLA RETURNED FROM SCOTLAND TO FIND HIS WIFE AND SON BANISHED. HE FOUND OUT WHO WAS RESPONSIBLE.
MESSENGER TORTURED
MOTHER KILLED

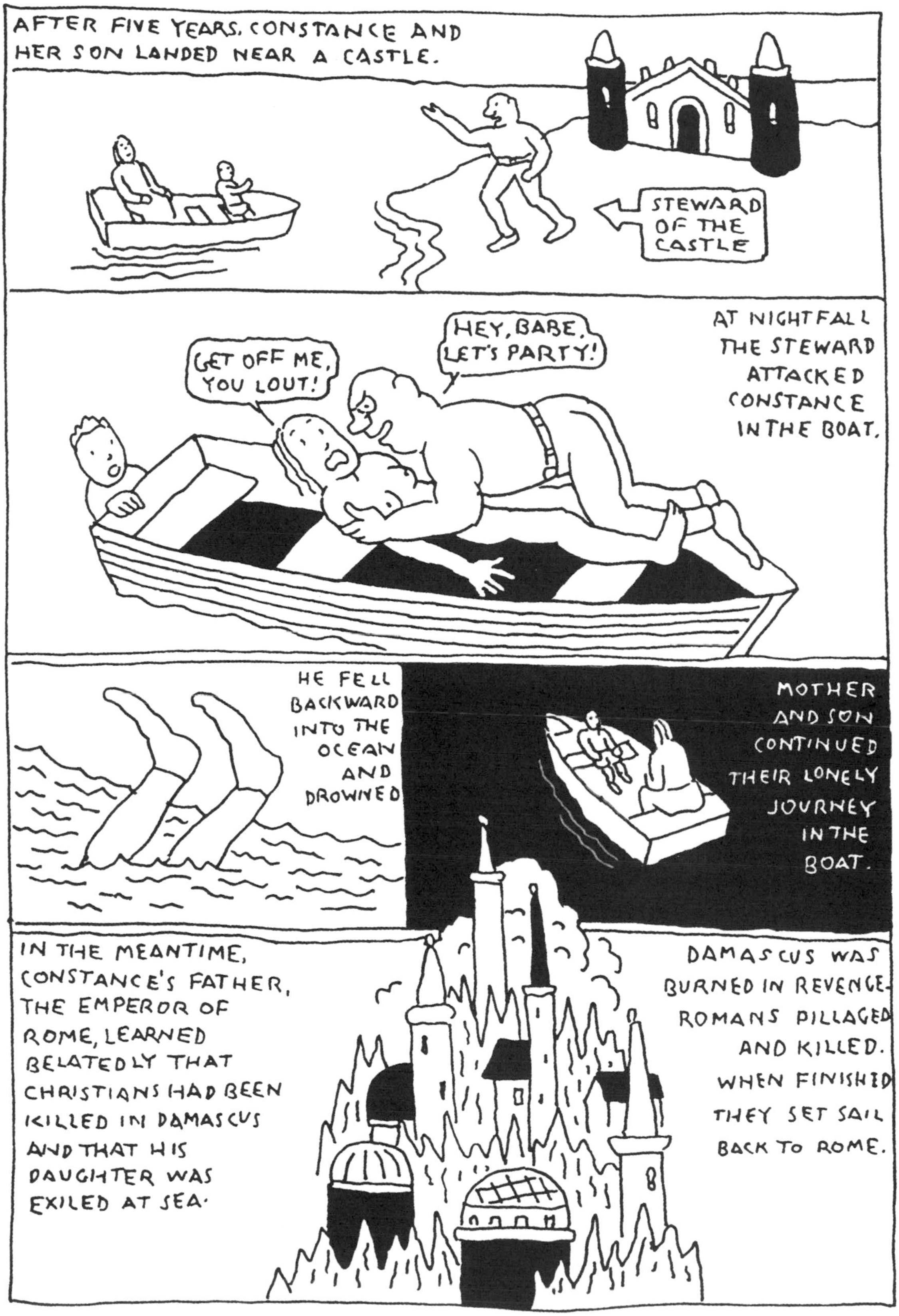
AFTER FIVE YEARS, CONSTANCE AND HER SON LANDED NEAR A CASTLE.
STEWARD OF THE CASTLE
AT NIGHTFALL THE STEWARD ATTACKED CONSTANCE IN THE BOAT.
GET OFF ME, YOU LOUT!
HEY, BABE, LET'S PARTY!
HE FELL BACKWARD INTO THE OCEAN AND DROWNED
MOTHER AND SON CONTINUED THEIR LONELY JOURNEY IN THE BOAT.
IN THE MEANTIME, CONSTANCE'S FATHER, THE EMPEROR OF ROME, LEARNED BELATEDLY THAT CHRISTIANS HAD BEEN KILLED IN DAMASCUS AND THAT HIS DAUGHTER WAS EXILED AT SEA.
DAMASCUS WAS BURNED IN REVENGE. ROMANS PILLAGED AND KILLED. WHEN FINISHED THEY SET SAIL BACK TO ROME.

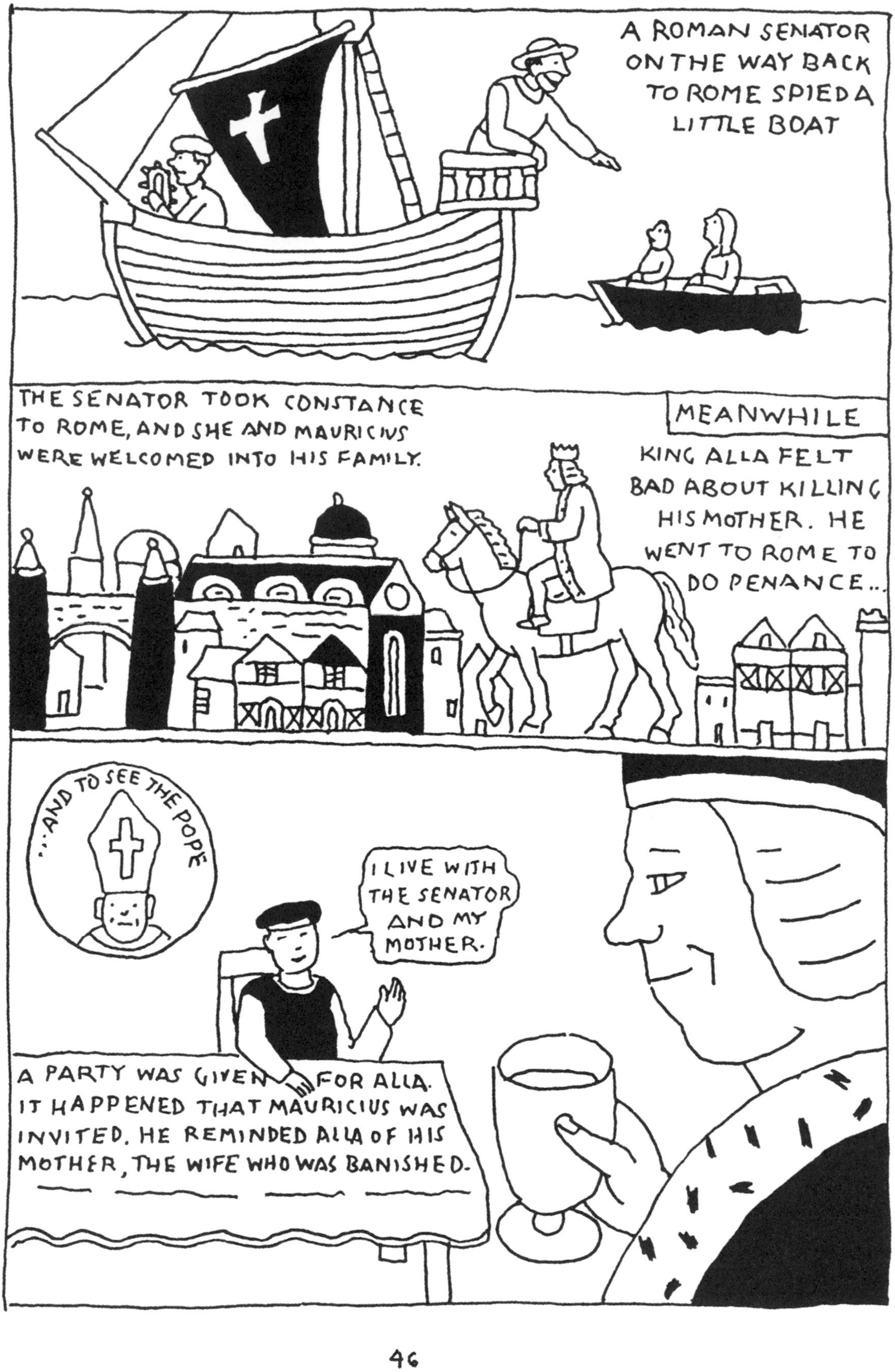
A ROMAN SENATOR ON THE WAY BACK TO ROME SPIED A LITTLE BOAT
THE SENATOR TOOK CONSTANCE TO ROME, AND SHE AND MAURICIUS WERE WELCOMED INTO HIS FAMILY.
MEANWHILE
KING ALLA FELT BAD ABOUT KILLING HIS MOTHER. HE WENT TO ROME TO DO PENANCE...
...AND TO SEE THE POPE
I LIVE WITH THE SENATOR AND MY MOTHER.
A PARTY WAS GIVEN FOR ALLA. IT HAPPENED THAT MAURICIUS WAS INVITED. HE REMINDED ALLA OF HIS MOTHER, THE WIFE WHO WAS BANISHED.

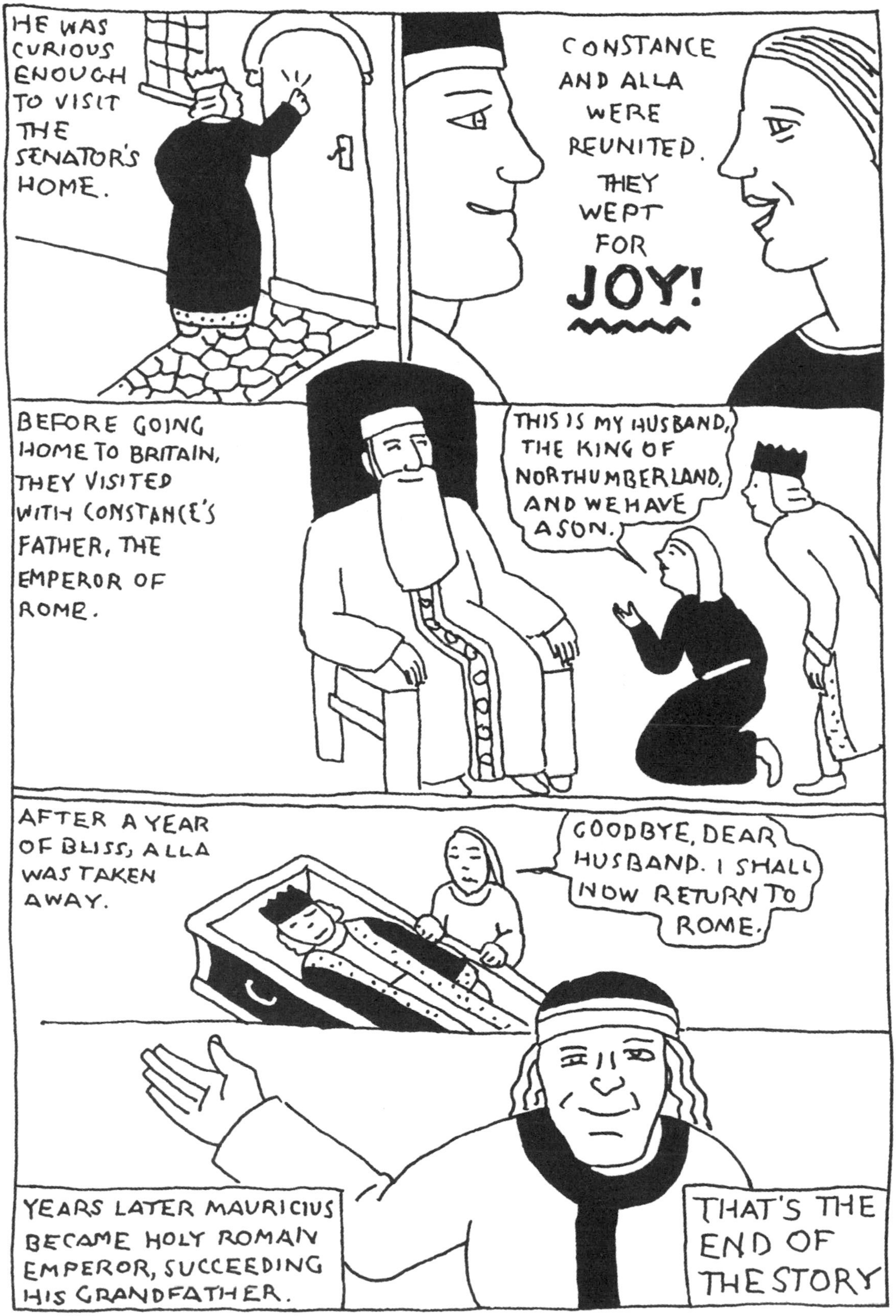
HE WAS CURIOUS ENOUGH TO VISIT THE SENATOR'S HOME.
CONSTANCE AND ALLA WERE REUNITED. THEY WEPT FOR JOY!
BEFORE GOING HOME TO BRITAIN, THEY VISITED WITH CONSTANCE'S FATHER, THE EMPEROR OF ROME.
THIS IS MY HUSBAND, THE KING OF NORTHUMBERLAND, AND WE HAVE A SON.
AFTER A YEAR OF BLISS, ALLA WAS TAKEN AWAY.
GOODBYE, DEAR HUSBAND. I SHALL NOW RETURN TO ROME.
YEARS LATER MAURICIUS BECAME HOLY ROMAN EMPEROR, SUCCEEDING HIS GRANDFATHER.
THAT'S THE END OF THE STORY

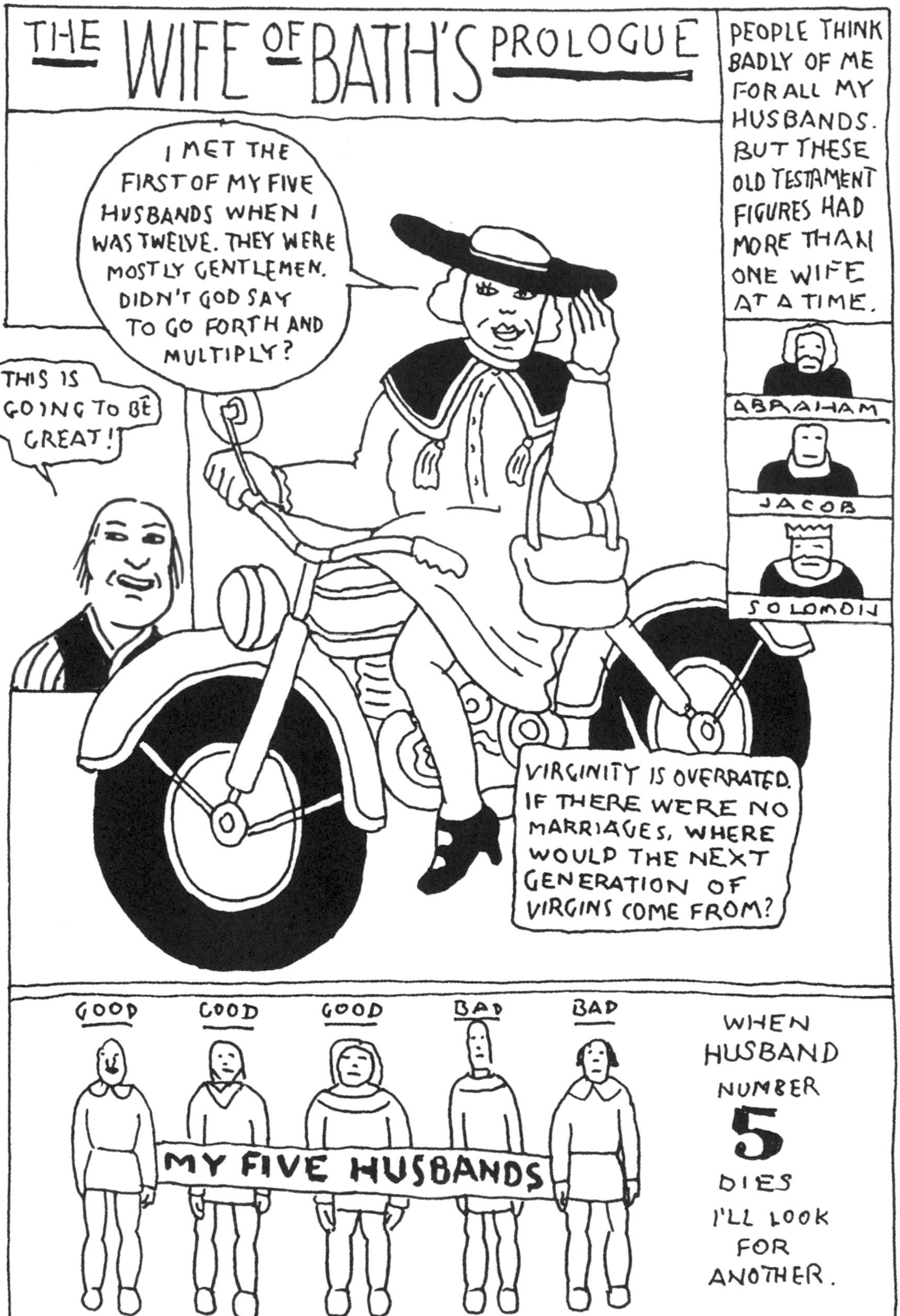
THE WIFE OF BATH'S PROLOGUE
PEOPLE THINK BADLY OF ME FOR ALL MY HUSBANDS. BUT THESE OLD TESTAMENT FIGURES HAD MORE THAN ONE WIFE AT A TIME.
ABRAHAM
JACOB
SOLOMON
I MET THE FIRST OF MY FIVE HUSBANDS WHEN I WAS TWELVE. THEY WERE MOSTLY GENTLEMEN. DIDN'T GOD SAY TO GO FORTH AND MULTIPLY?
THIS IS GOING TO BE GREAT!
VIRGINITY IS OVERRATED. IF THERE WERE NO MARRIAGES, WHERE WOULD THE NEXT GENERATION OF VIRGINS COME FROM?
GOOD
GOOD
GOOD
BAD
BAD
MY FIVE HUSBANDS
WHEN HUSBAND NUMBER 5 DIES I'LL LOOK FOR ANOTHER.

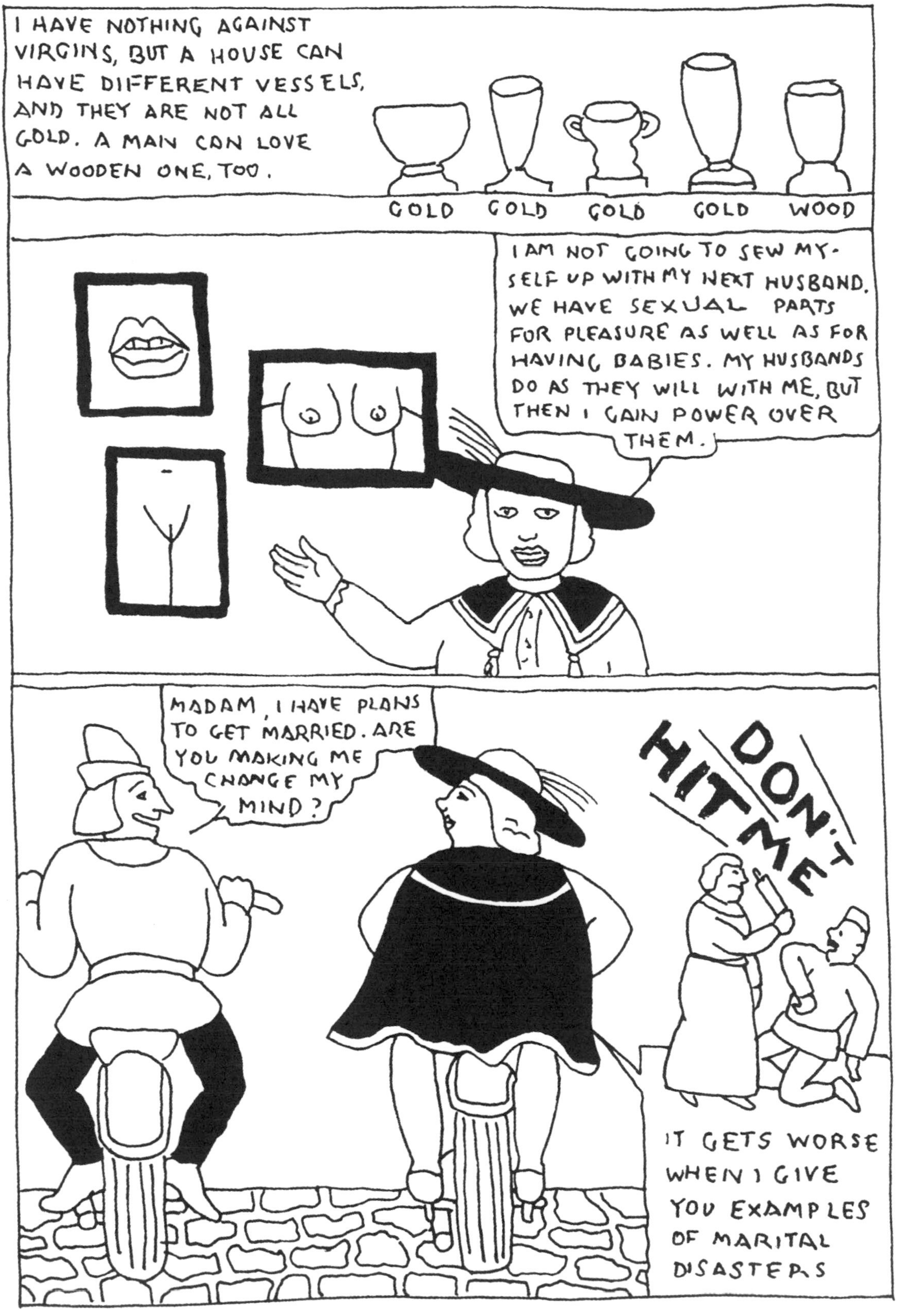

I HAVE NOTHING AGAINST VIRGINS, BUT A HOUSE CAN HAVE DIFFERENT VESSELS, AND THEY ARE NOT ALL GOLD. A MAN CAN LOVE A WOODEN ONE, TOO.
GOLD
GOLD
GOLD
GOLD
WOOD
I AM NOT GOING TO SEW MY-SELF UP WITH MY NEXT HUSBAND. WE HAVE SEXUAL PARTS FOR PLEASURE AS WELL AS FOR HAVING BABIES. MY HUSBANDS DO AS THEY WILL WITH ME, BUT THEN I GAIN POWER OVER THEM.
MADAM, I HAVE PLANS TO GET MARRIED. ARE YOU MAKING ME CHANGE MY MIND?
DON'T HIT ME
IT GETS WORSE WHEN I GIVE YOU EXAMPLES OF MARITAL DISASTERS

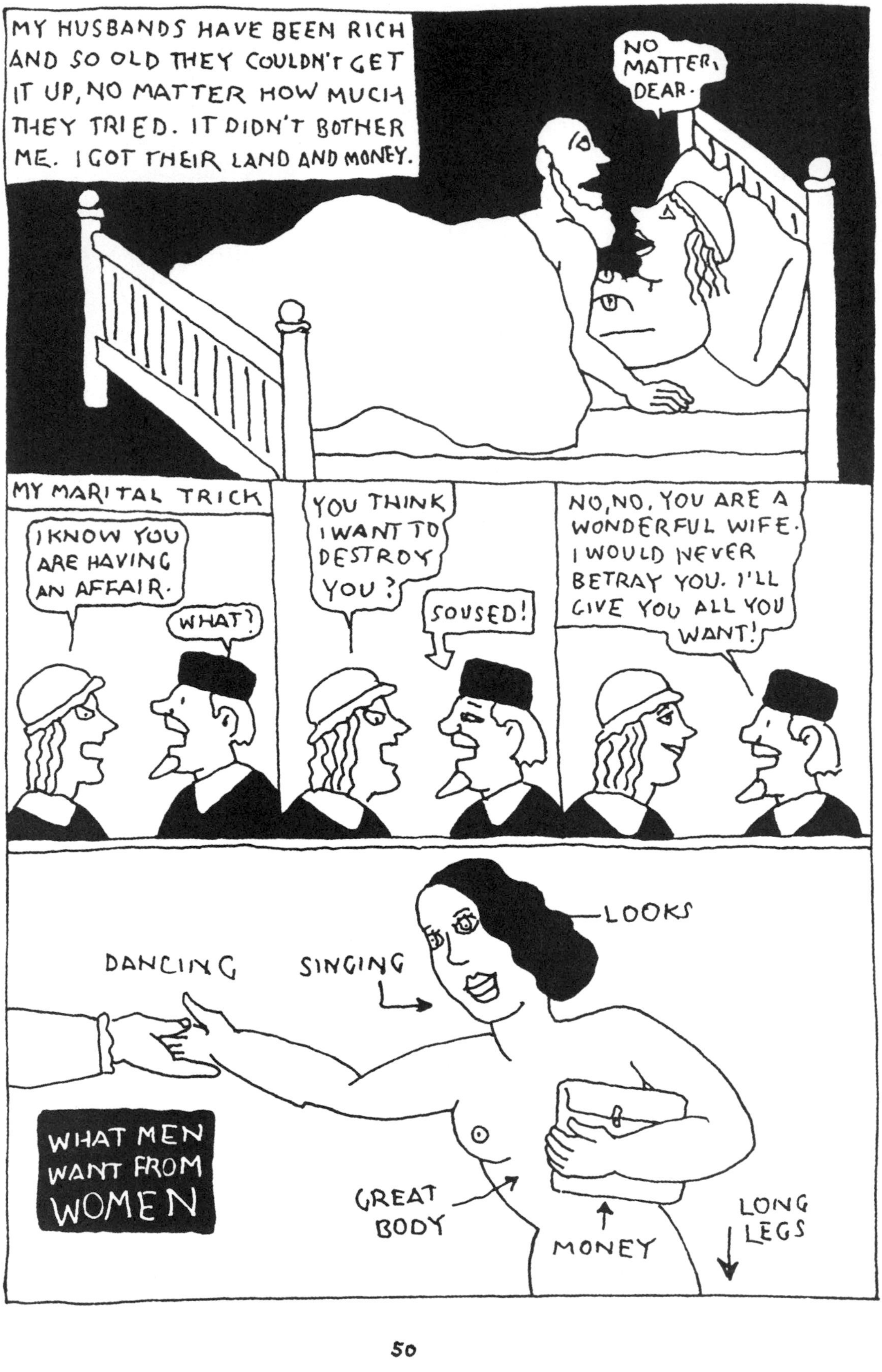

MY HUSBANDS HAVE BEEN RICH AND SO OLD THEY COULDN'T GET IT UP, NO MATTER HOW MUCH THEY TRIED. IT DIDN'T BOTHER ME. I GOT THEIR LAND AND MONEY.
NO MATTER, DEAR.
MY MARITAL TRICK
I KNOW YOU ARE HAVING AN AFFAIR.
WHAT?
YOU THINK I WANT TO DESTROY YOU?
SOUSED!
NO, NO. YOU ARE A WONDERFUL WIFE. I WOULD NEVER BETRAY YOU. I'LL GIVE YOU ALL YOU WANT!
LOOKS
DANCING
SINGING
WHAT MEN WANT FROM WOMEN
GREAT BODY
MONEY
LONG LEGS

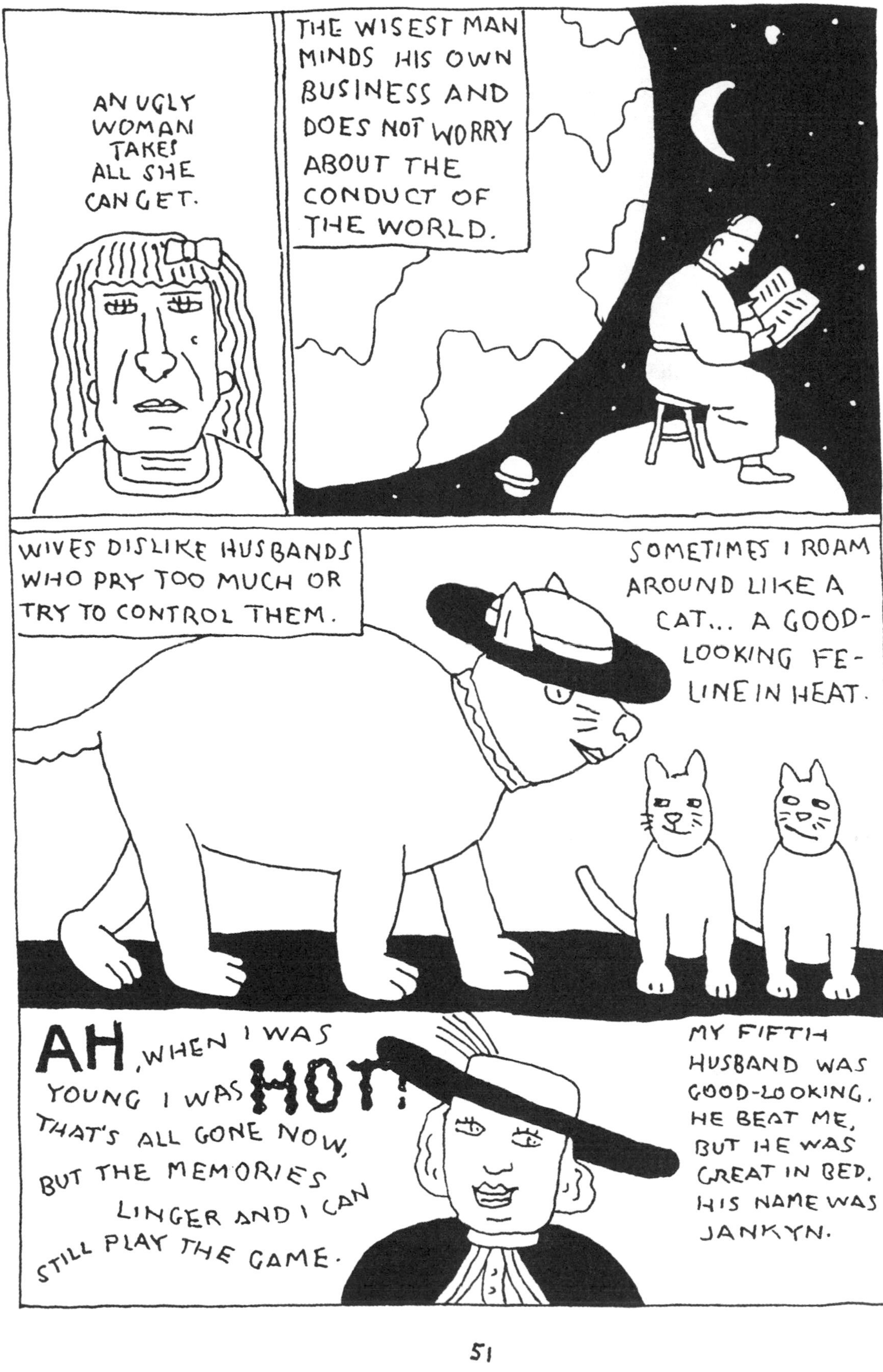
AN UGLY WOMAN TAKES ALL SHE CAN GET.
THE WISEST MAN MINDS HIS OWN BUSINESS AND DOES NOT WORRY ABOUT THE CONDUCT OF THE WORLD.
WIVES DISLIKE HUSBANDS WHO PRY TOO MUCH OR TRY TO CONTROL THEM.
SOMETIMES I ROAM AROUND LIKE A CAT... A GOOD-LOOKING FE-LINE IN HEAT.
AH, WHEN I WAS YOUNG I WAS HOT! THAT'S ALL GONE NOW, BUT THE MEMORIES LINGER AND I CAN STILL PLAY THE GAME.
MY FIFTH HUSBAND WAS GOOD-LOOKING. HE BEAT ME, BUT HE WAS GREAT IN BED. HIS NAME WAS JANKYN.

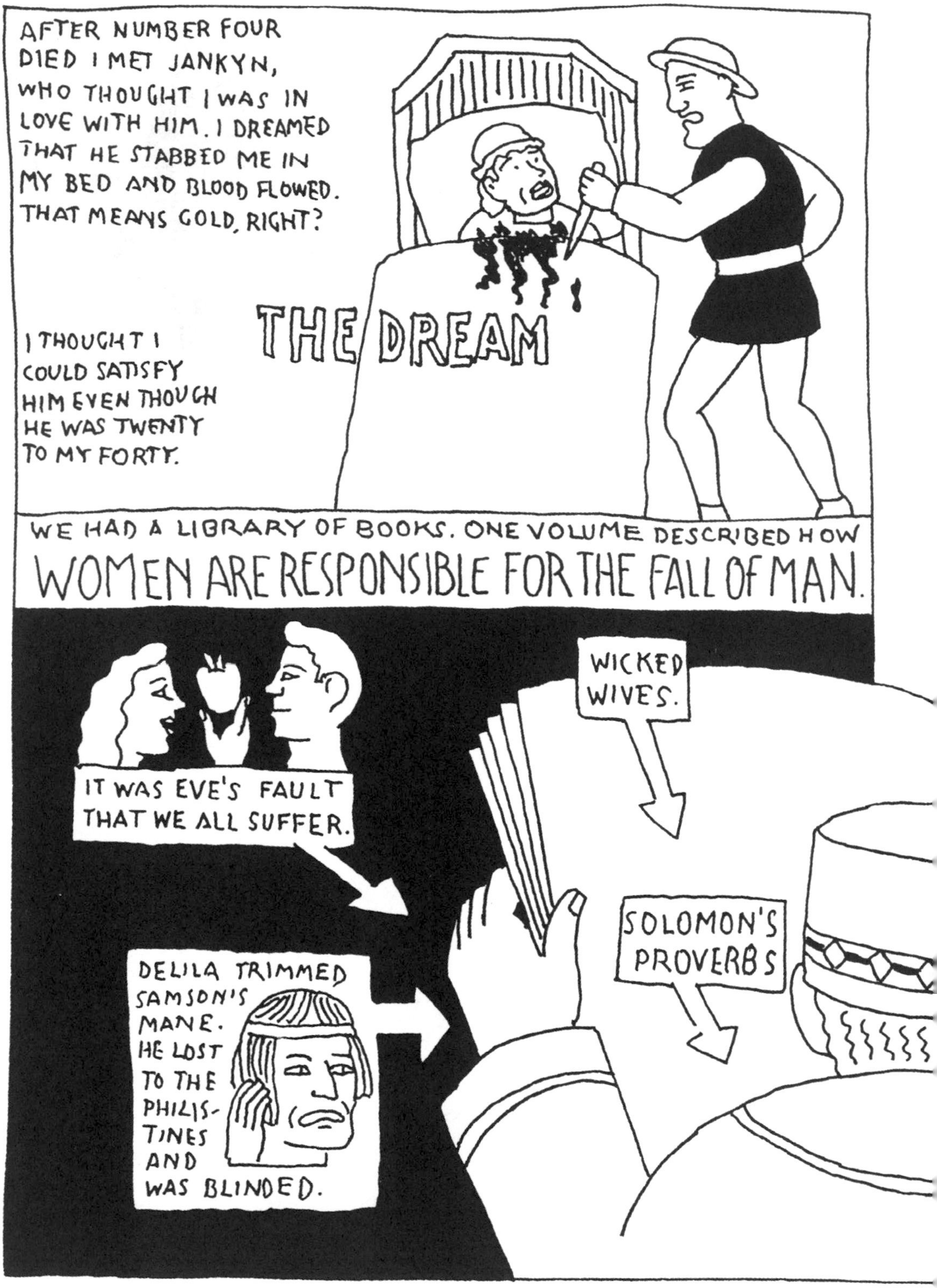
AFTER NUMBER FOUR DIED I MET JANKYN, WHO THOUGHT I WAS IN LOVE WITH HIM. I DREAMED THAT HE STABBED ME IN MY BED AND BLOOD FLOWED. THAT MEANS GOLD, RIGHT?
THE DREAM
I THOUGHT I COULD SATISFY HIM EVEN THOUGH HE WAS TWENTY TO MY FORTY.
WE HAD A LIBRARY OF BOOKS. ONE VOLUME DESCRIBED HOW
WOMEN ARE RESPONSIBLE FOR THE FALL OF MAN.
IT WAS EVE'S FAULT THAT WE ALL SUFFER.
WICKED WIVES.
DELILA TRIMMED SAMSON'S MANE. HE LOST TO THE PHILIS-TINES AND WAS BLINDED.
SOLOMON'S PROVERBS

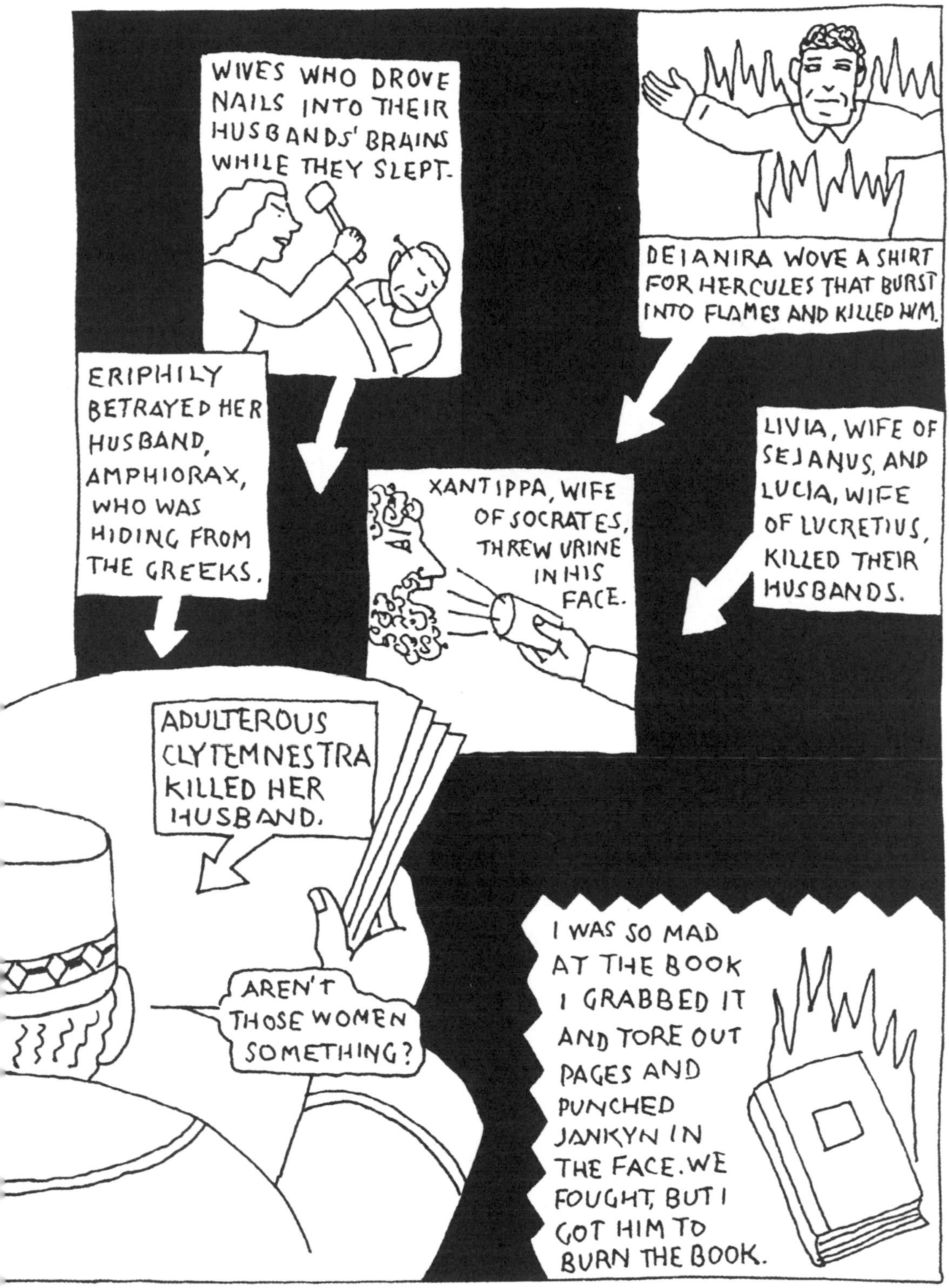
WIVES WHO DROVE NAILS INTO THEIR HUSBANDS' BRAINS WHILE THEY SLEPT.
DEIANIRA WOVE A SHIRT FOR HERCULES THAT BURST INTO FLAMES AND KILLED HIM.
ERIPHILY BETRAYED HER HUSBAND, AMPHIORAX, WHO WAS HIDING FROM THE GREEKS.
XANTIPPA, WIFE OF SOCRATES, THREW URINE IN HIS FACE.
LIVIA, WIFE OF SEJANUS, AND LUCIA, WIFE OF LUCRETIUS, KILLED THEIR HUSBANDS.
ADULTEROUS CLYTEMNESTRA KILLED HER HUSBAND.
AREN'T THOSE WOMEN SOMETHING?
I WAS SO MAD AT THE BOOK I GRABBED IT AND TORE OUT PAGES AND PUNCHED JANKYN IN THE FACE. WE FOUGHT, BUT I GOT HIM TO BURN THE BOOK.

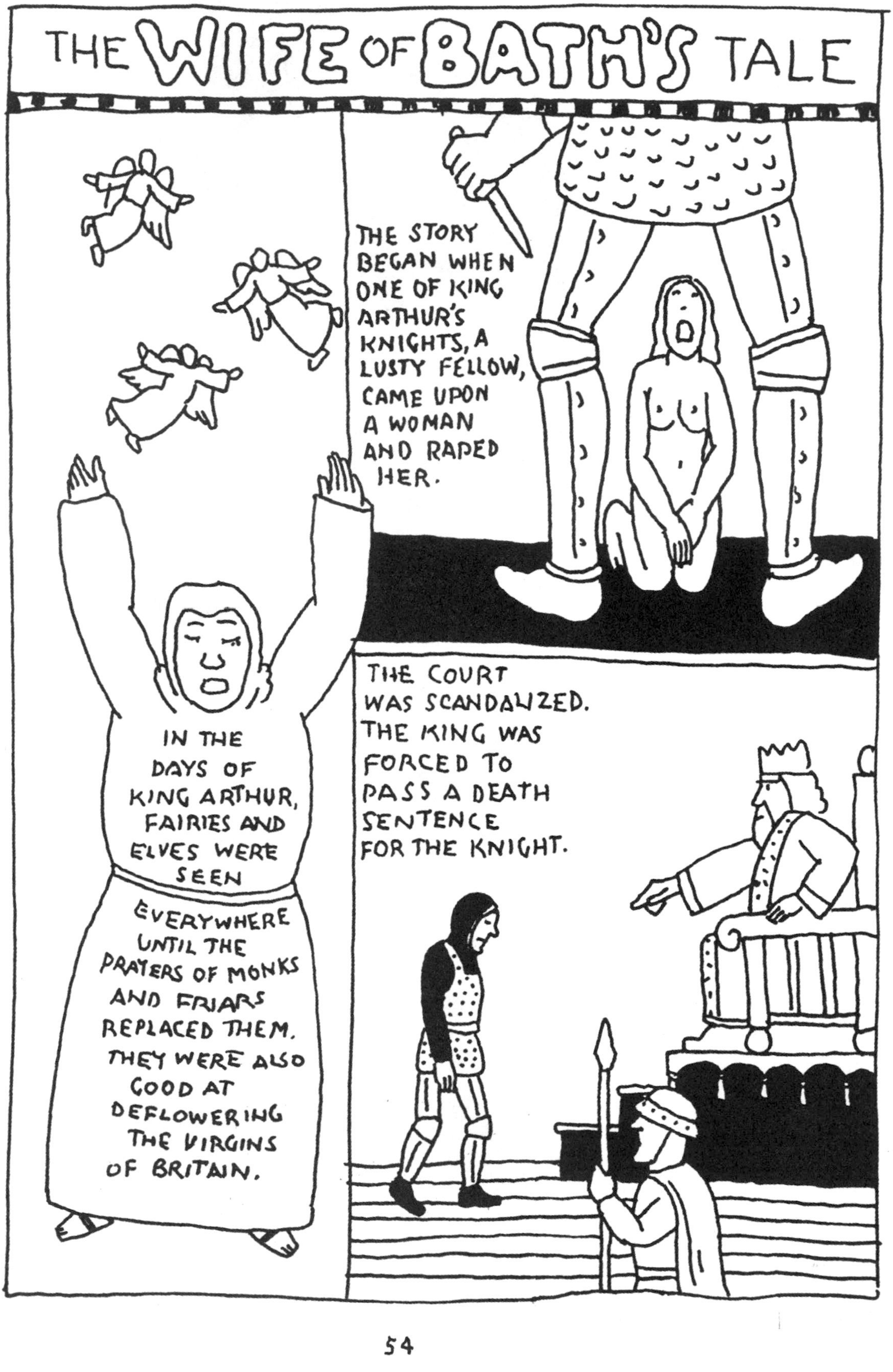
THE WIFE OF BATH'S TALE
IN THE DAYS OF KING ARTHUR, FAIRIES AND ELVES WERE SEEN
EVERYWHERE UNTIL THE PRAYERS OF MONKS AND FRIARS REPLACED THEM. THEY WERE ALSO GOOD AT DEFLOWERING THE VIRGINS OF BRITAIN.
THE STORY BEGAN WHEN ONE OF KING ARTHUR'S KNIGHTS, A LUSTY FELLOW, CAME UPON A WOMAN AND RAPED HER.
THE COURT WAS SCANDALIZED. THE KING WAS FORCED TO PASS A DEATH SENTENCE FOR THE KNIGHT.

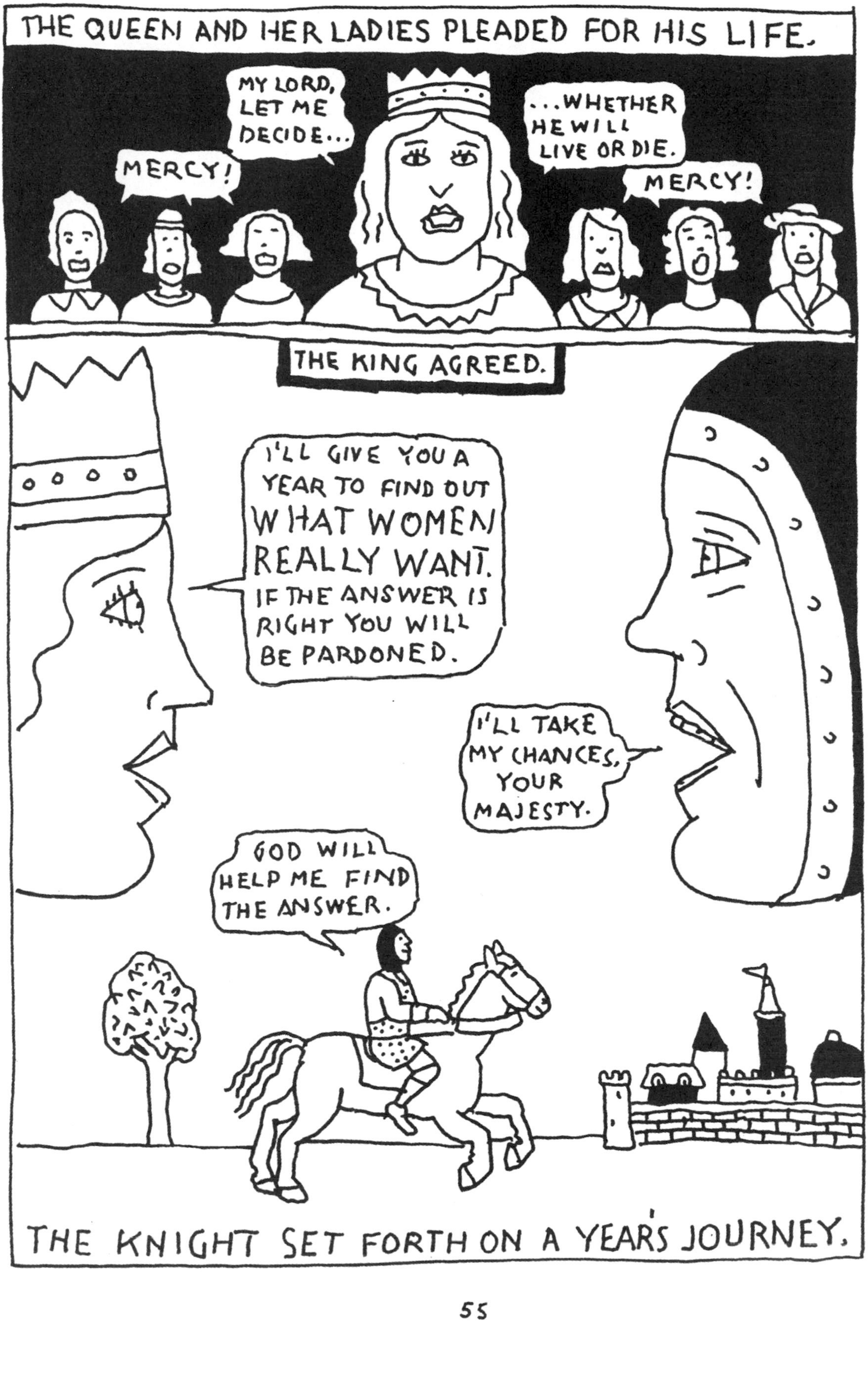
THE QUEEN AND HER LADIES PLEADED FOR HIS LIFE.
MERCY!
MY LORD, LET ME DECIDE...
...WHETHER HE WILL LIVE OR DIE.
MERCY!
THE KING AGREED.
I'LL GIVE YOU A YEAR TO FIND OUT WHAT WOMEN REALLY WANT. IF THE ANSWER IS RIGHT YOU WILL BE PARDONED.
I'LL TAKE MY CHANCES, YOUR MAJESTY.
GOD WILL HELP ME FIND THE ANSWER.
THE KNIGHT SET FORTH ON A YEAR'S JOURNEY.

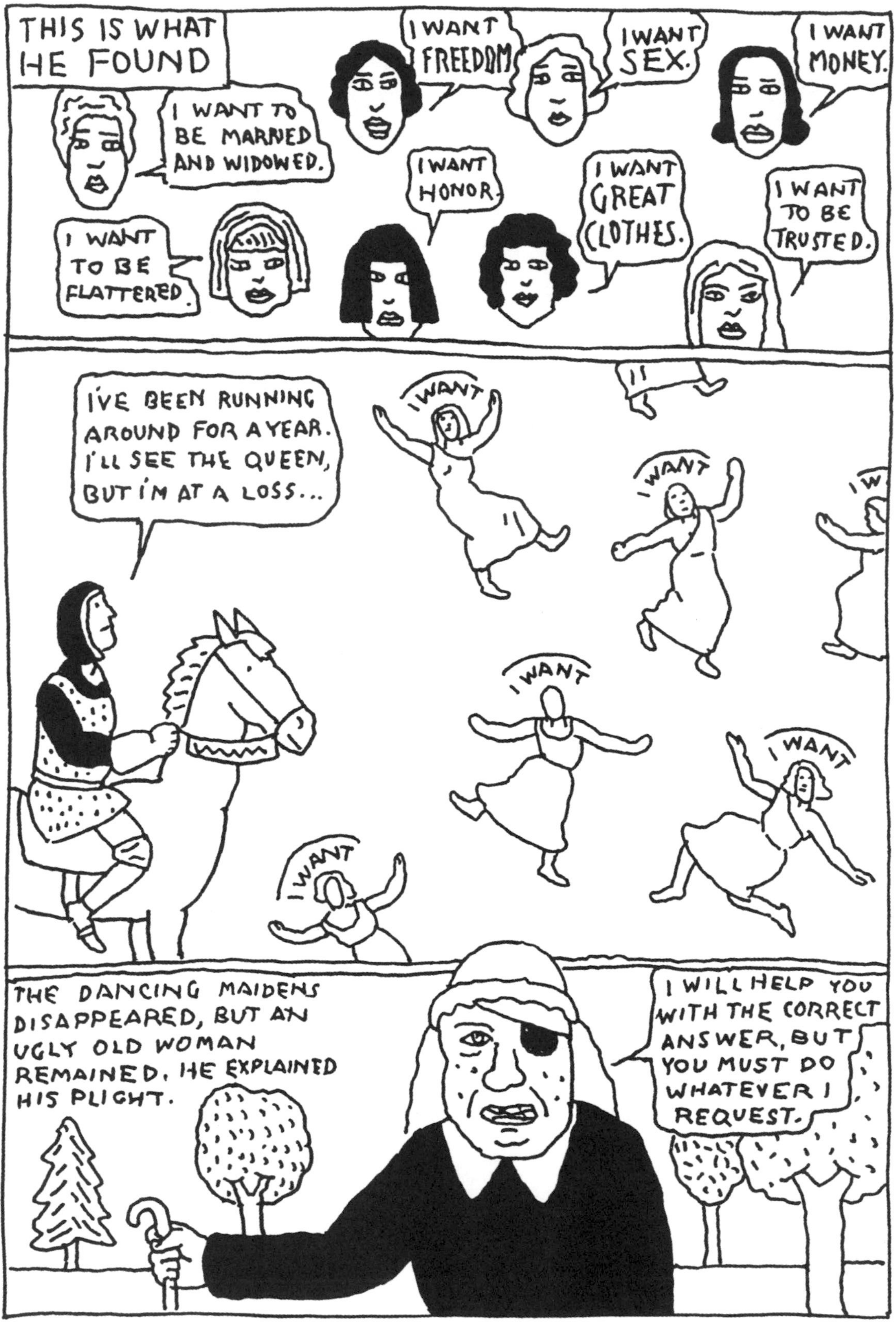
THIS IS WHAT HE FOUND
I WANT FREEDOM
I WANT SEX.
I WANT MONEY.
I WANT TO BE MARRIED AND WIDOWED.
I WANT HONOR.
I WANT GREAT CLOTHES.
I WANT TO BE TRUSTED.
I WANT TO BE FLATTERED.
I'VE BEEN RUNNING AROUND FOR A YEAR. I'LL SEE THE QUEEN, BUT I'M AT A LOSS...
I WANT
I WANT
I WANT
I WANT
I WANT
THE DANCING MAIDENS DISAPPEARED, BUT AN UGLY OLD WOMAN REMAINED. HE EXPLAINED HIS PLIGHT.
I WILL HELP YOU WITH THE CORRECT ANSWER, BUT YOU MUST DO WHATEVER I REQUEST.

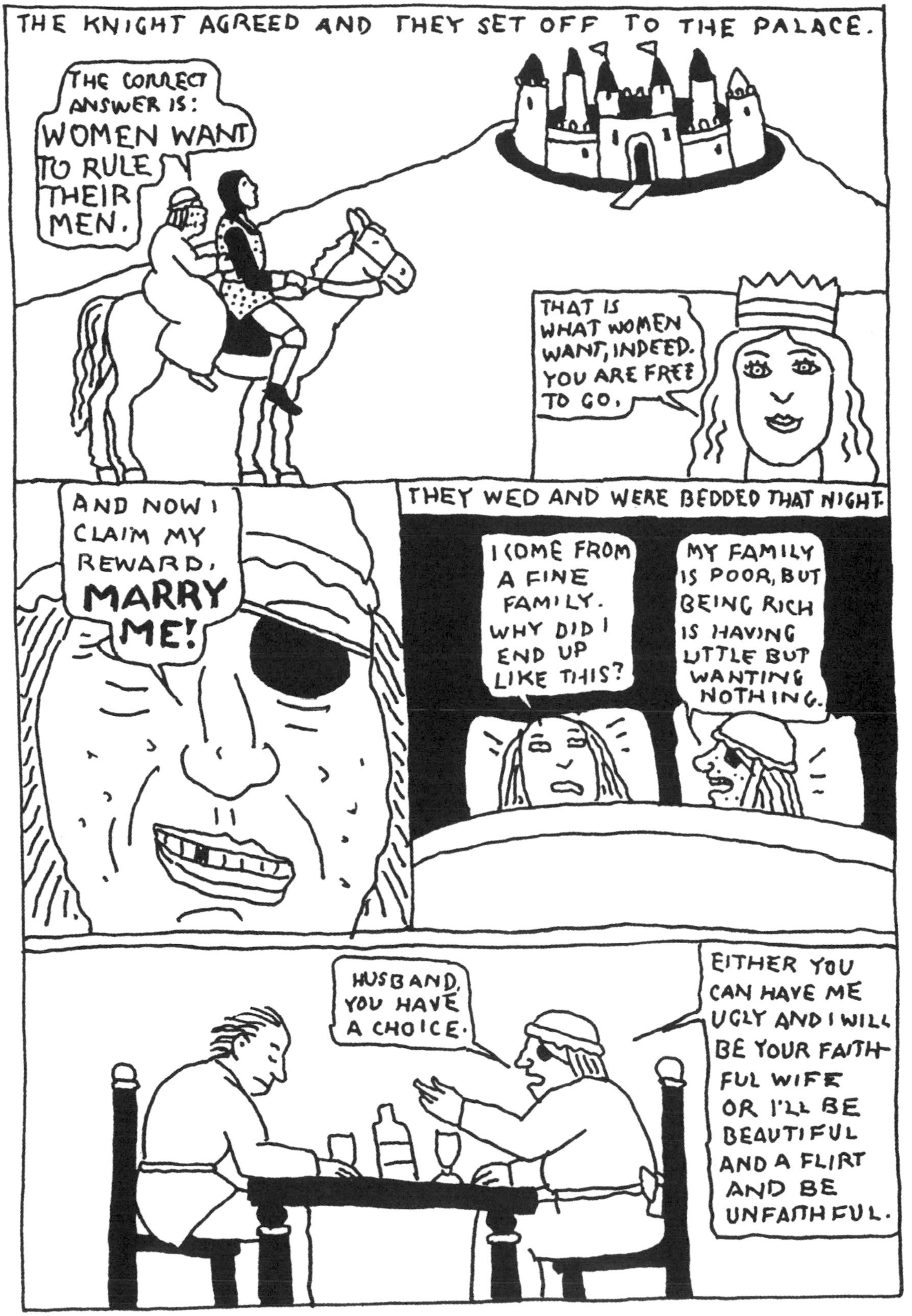
THE KNIGHT AGREED AND THEY SET OFF TO THE PALACE.
THE CORRECT ANSWER IS: WOMEN WANT TO RULE THEIR MEN.
THAT IS WHAT WOMEN WANT, INDEED. YOU ARE FREE TO GO.
AND NOW I CLAIM MY REWARD. MARRY ME!
THEY WED AND WERE BEDDED THAT NIGHT.
I COME FROM A FINE FAMILY. WHY DID I END UP LIKE THIS?
MY FAMILY IS POOR, BUT BEING RICH IS HAVING LITTLE BUT WANTING NOTHING.
HUSBAND, YOU HAVE A CHOICE.
EITHER YOU CAN HAVE ME UGLY AND I WILL BE YOUR FAITHFUL WIFE OR I'LL BE BEAUTIFUL AND A FLIRT AND BE UNFAITHFUL.

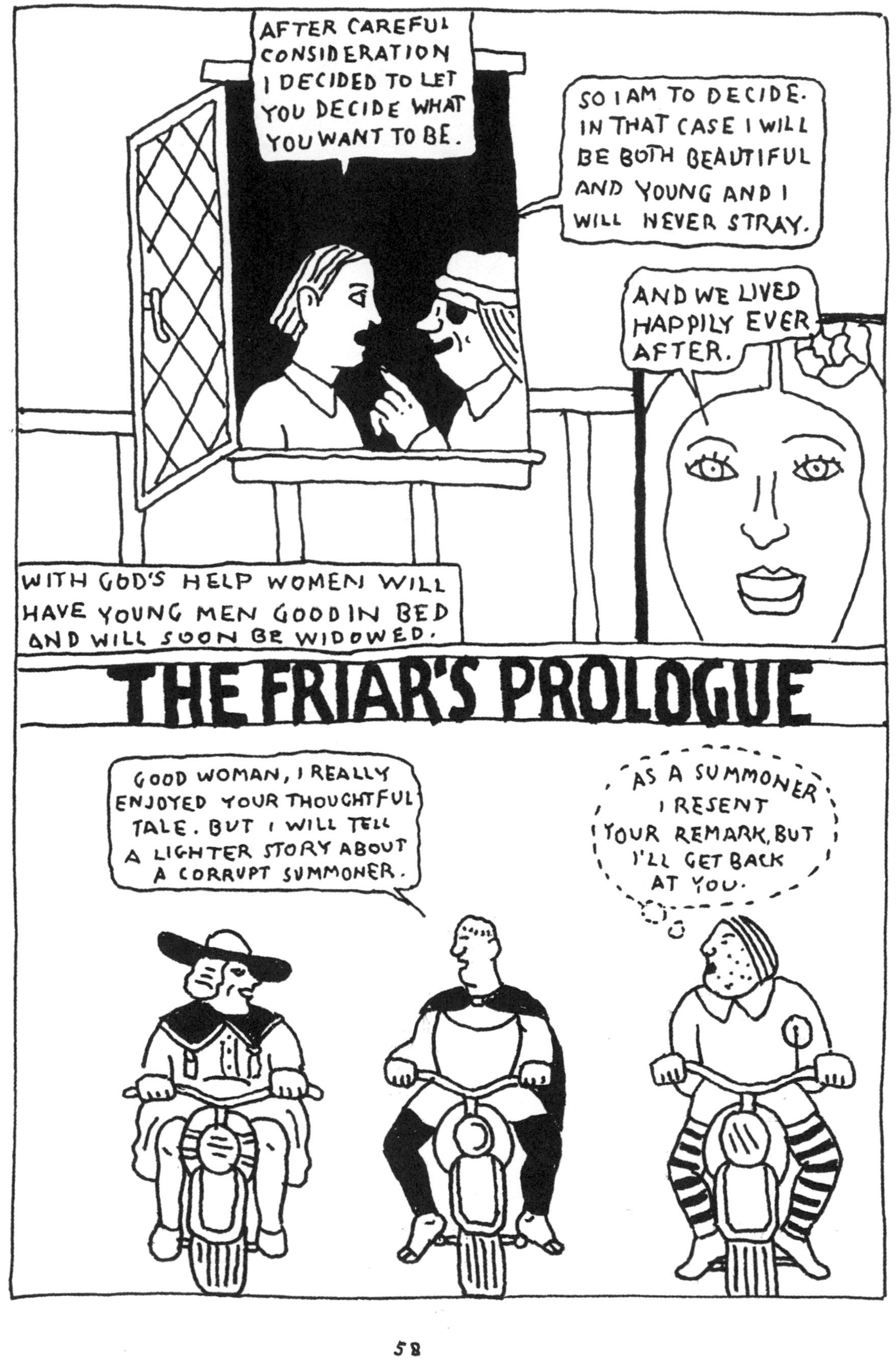
AFTER CAREFUL CONSIDERATION I DECIDED TO LET YOU DECIDE WHAT YOU WANT TO BE.
SO I AM TO DECIDE. IN THAT CASE I WILL BE BOTH BEAUTIFUL AND YOUNG AND I WILL NEVER STRAY.
AND WE LIVED HAPPILY EVER AFTER.
WITH GOD'S HELP WOMEN WILL HAVE YOUNG MEN GOOD IN BED AND WILL SOON BE WIDOWED.
THE FRIAR'S PROLOGUE
GOOD WOMAN, I REALLY ENJOYED YOUR THOUGHTFUL TALE. BUT I WILL TELL A LIGHTER STORY ABOUT A CORRUPT SUMMONER.
AS A SUMMONER I RESENT YOUR REMARK, BUT I'LL GET BACK AT YOU.

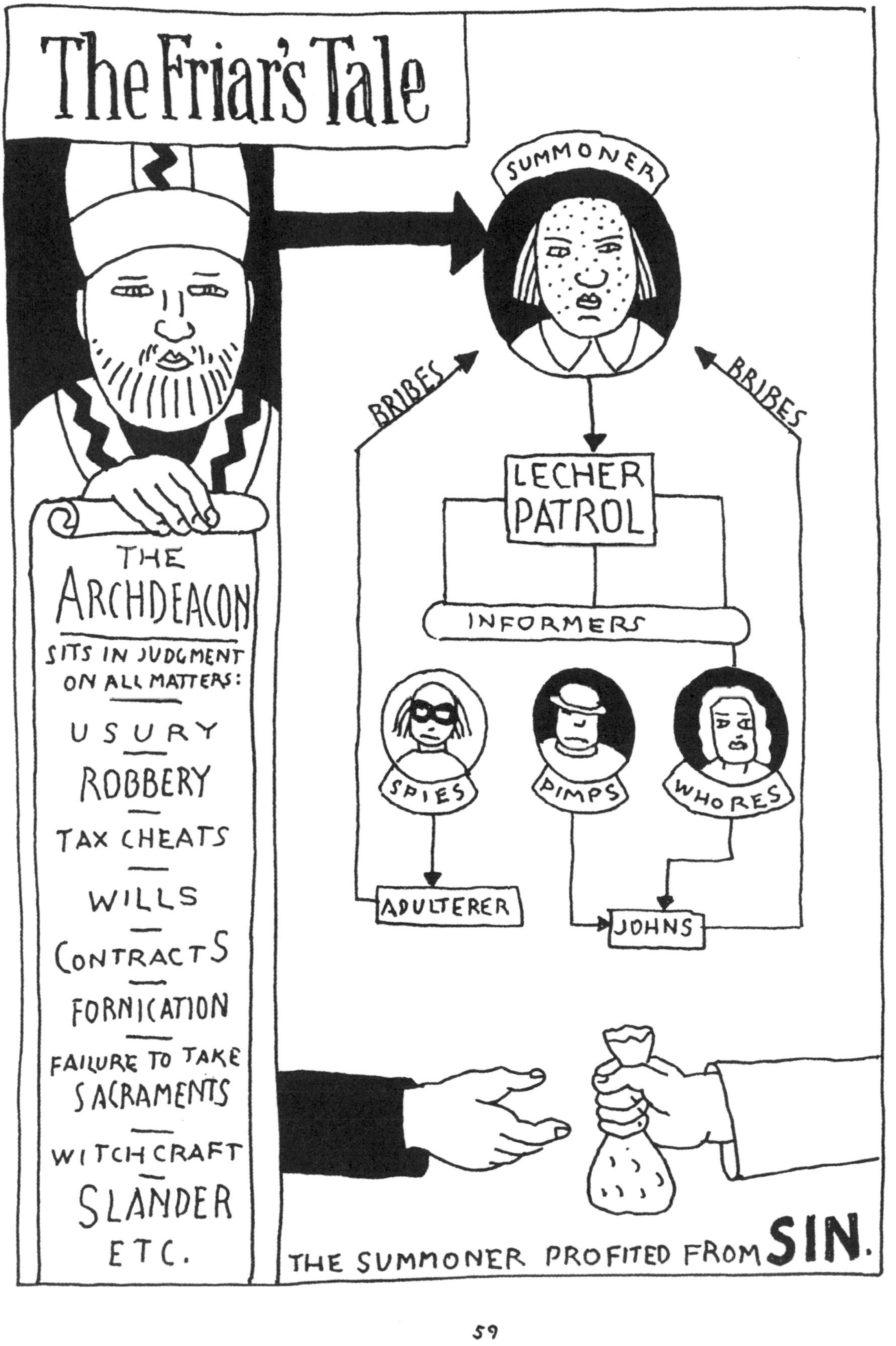
The Friar's Tale
SUMMONER
BRIBES
BRIBES
LECHER PATROL
INFORMERS
SPIES
PIMPS
WHORES
ADULTERER
JOHNS
THE ARCHDEACON
SITS IN JUDGMENT ON ALL MATTERS:
USURY
ROBBERY
TAX CHEATS
WILLS
CONTRACTS
FORNICATION
FAILURE TO TAKE SACRAMENTS
WITCHCRAFT
SLANDER
ETC.
THE SUMMONER PROFITED FROM SIN.

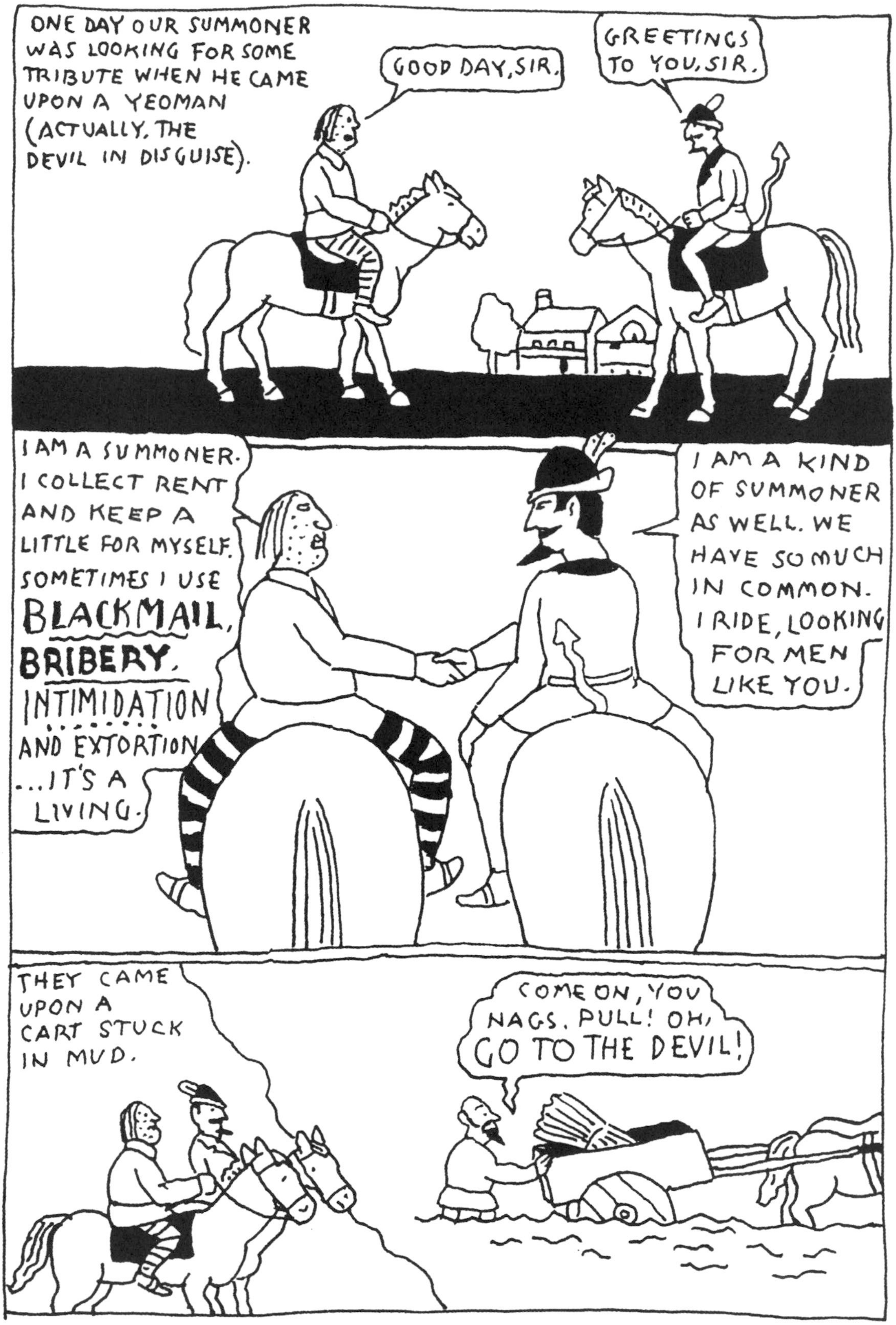
ONE DAY OUR SUMMONER WAS LOOKING FOR SOME TRIBUTE WHEN HE CAME UPON A YEOMAN (ACTUALLY, THE DEVIL IN DISGUISE).
GOOD DAY, SIR.
GREETINGS TO YOU, SIR.
I AM A SUMMONER. I COLLECT RENT AND KEEP A LITTLE FOR MYSELF. SOMETIMES I USE BLACKMAIL, BRIBERY, INTIMIDATION AND EXTORTION ...IT'S A LIVING.
I AM A KIND OF SUMMONER AS WELL. WE HAVE SO MUCH IN COMMON. I RIDE, LOOKING FOR MEN LIKE YOU.
THEY CAME UPON A CART STUCK IN MUD.
COME ON, YOU NAGS. PULL! OH, GO TO THE DEVIL!

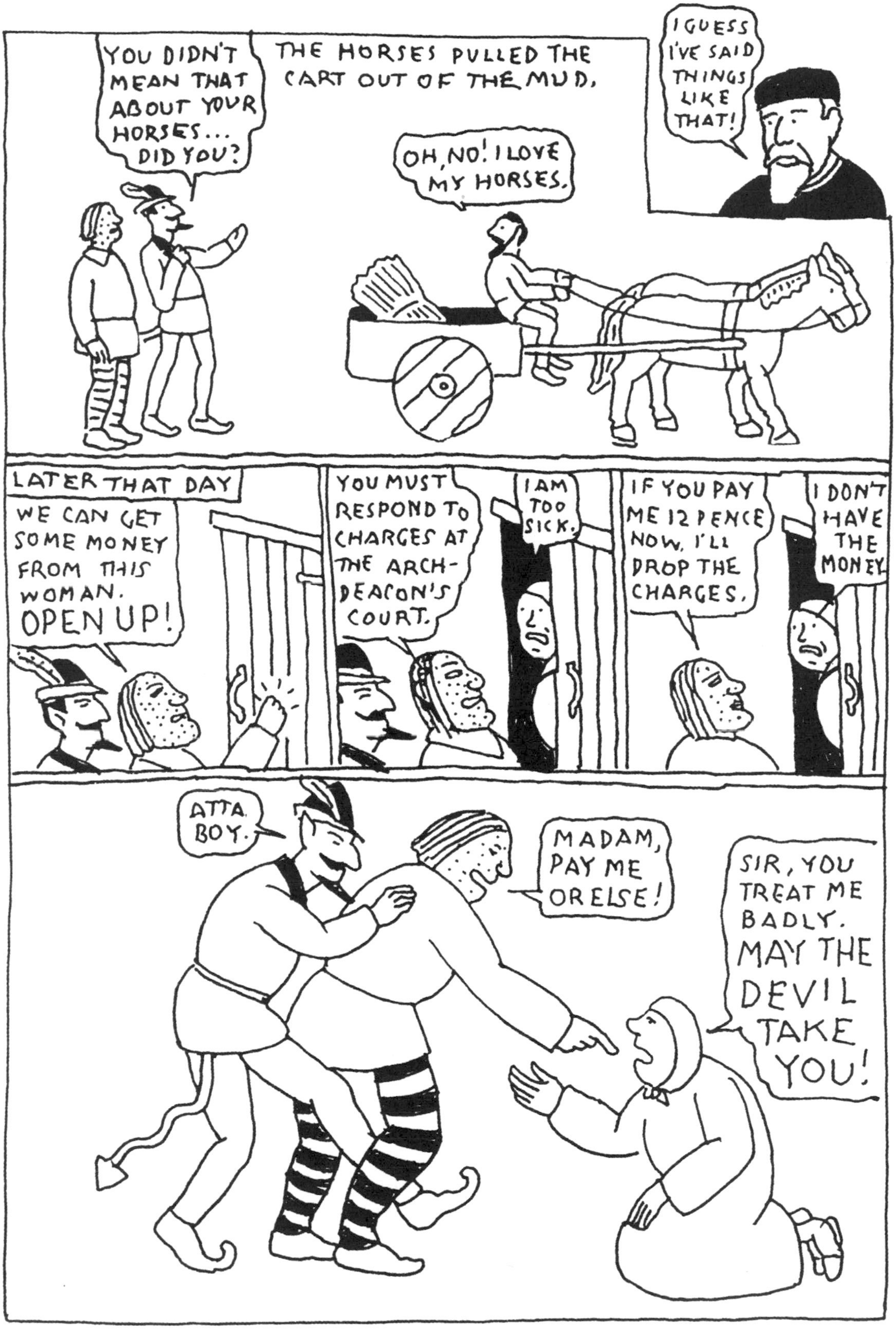
YOU DIDN'T MEAN THAT ABOUT YOUR HORSES... DID YOU?
THE HORSES PULLED THE CART OUT OF THE MUD.
I GUESS I'VE SAID THINGS LIKE THAT!
OH, NO! I LOVE MY HORSES.
LATER THAT DAY
WE CAN GET SOME MONEY FROM THIS WOMAN. OPEN UP!
YOU MUST RESPOND TO CHARGES AT THE ARCH-DEACON'S COURT.
I AM TOO SICK.
IF YOU PAY ME 12 PENCE NOW, I'LL DROP THE CHARGES.
I DON'T HAVE THE MONEY.
ATTA BOY.
MADAM, PAY ME OR ELSE!
SIR, YOU TREAT ME BADLY. MAY THE DEVIL TAKE YOU!

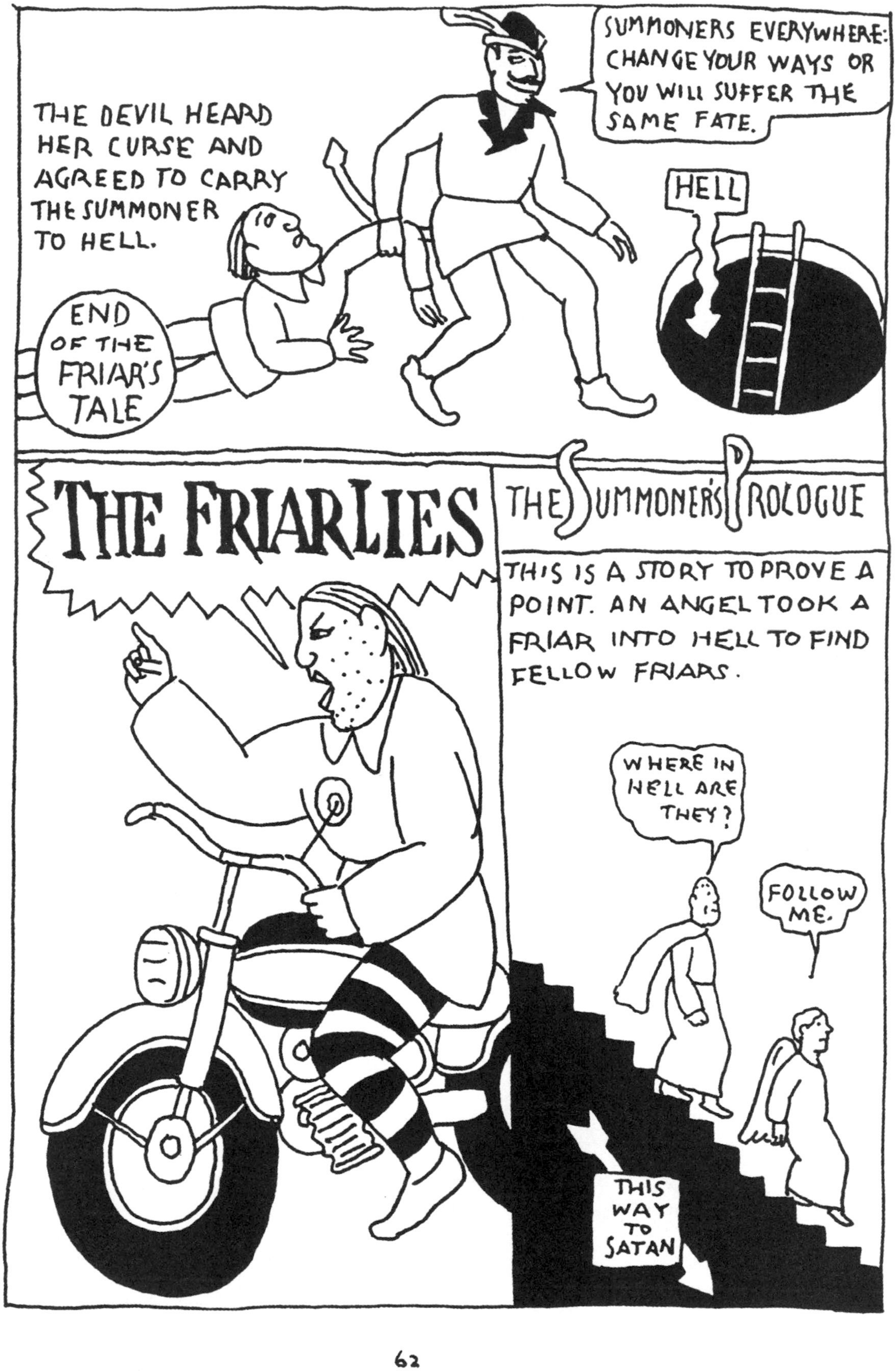
THE DEVIL HEARD HER CURSE AND AGREED TO CARRY THE SUMMONER TO HELL.
SUMMONERS EVERYWHERE: CHANGE YOUR WAYS OR YOU WILL SUFFER THE SAME FATE.
HELL
END OF THE FRIAR'S TALE
THE FRIAR LIES
THE SUMMONER'S PROLOGUE
THIS IS A STORY TO PROVE A POINT. AN ANGEL TOOK A FRIAR INTO HELL TO FIND FELLOW FRIARS.
WHERE IN HELL ARE THEY?
FOLLOW ME.
THIS WAY TO SATAN

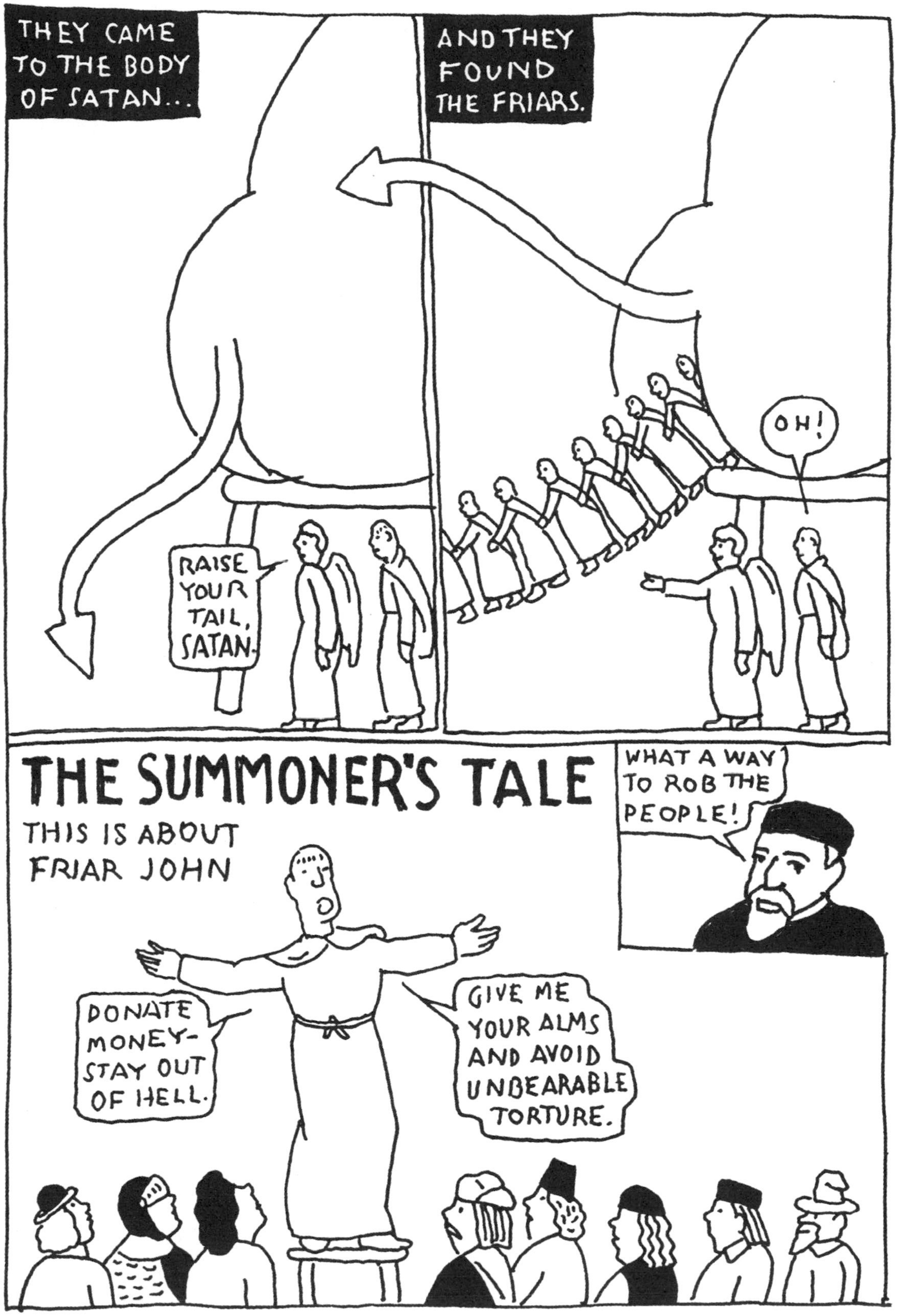
THEY CAME TO THE BODY OF SATAN...
RAISE YOUR TAIL, SATAN.
AND THEY FOUND THE FRIARS.
OH!
THE SUMMONER'S TALE
THIS IS ABOUT FRIAR JOHN
WHAT A WAY TO ROB THE PEOPLE!
DONATE MONEY-STAY OUT OF HELL.
GIVE ME YOUR ALMS AND AVOID UNBEARABLE TORTURE.

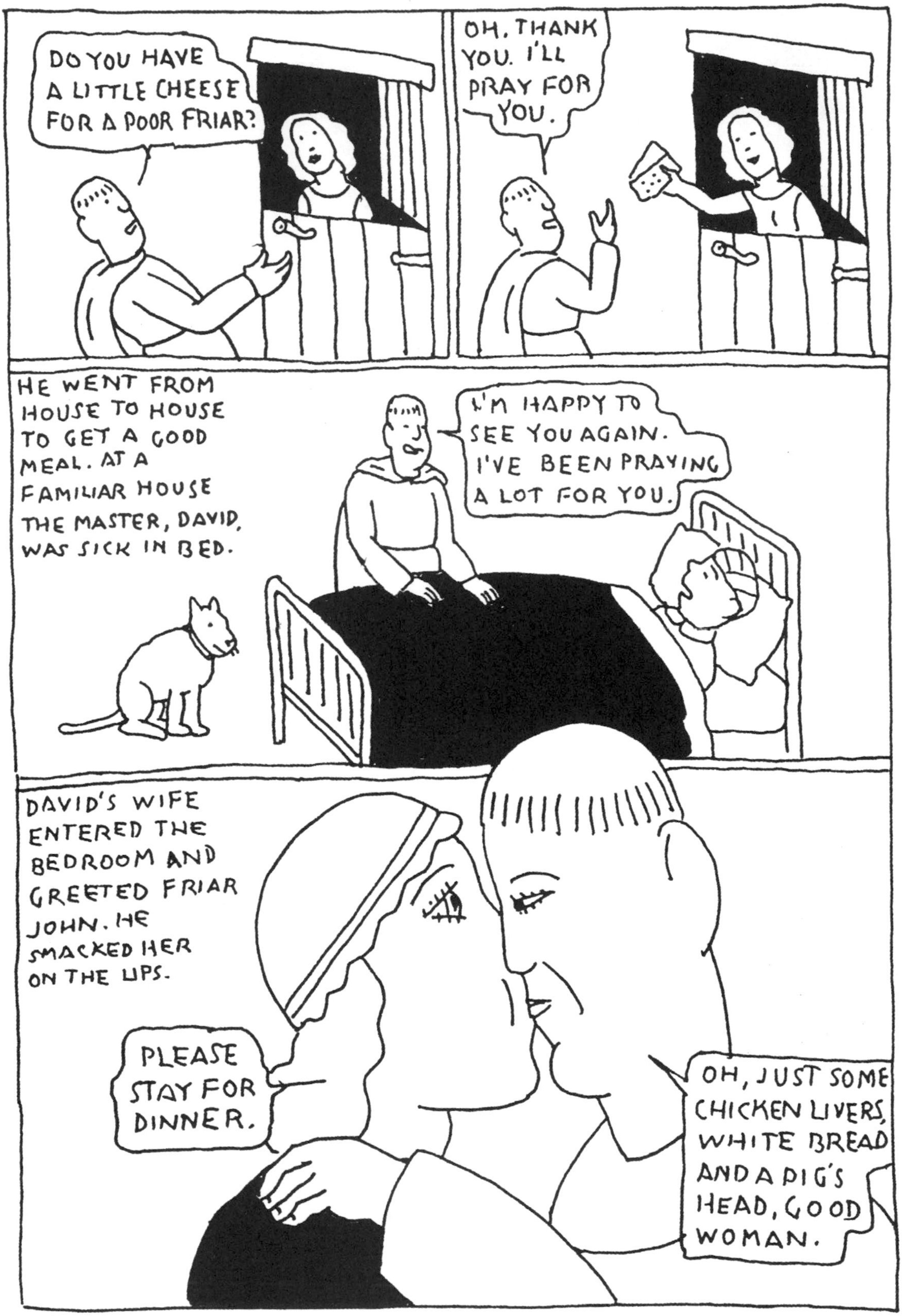
DO YOU HAVE A LITTLE CHEESE FOR A POOR FRIAR?
OH, THANK YOU. I'LL PRAY FOR YOU.
HE WENT FROM HOUSE TO HOUSE TO GET A GOOD MEAL. AT A FAMILIAR HOUSE THE MASTER, DAVID, WAS SICK IN BED.
I'M HAPPY TO SEE YOU AGAIN. I'VE BEEN PRAYING A LOT FOR YOU.
DAVID'S WIFE ENTERED THE BEDROOM AND GREETED FRIAR JOHN. HE SMACKED HER ON THE LIPS.
PLEASE STAY FOR DINNER.
OH, JUST SOME CHICKEN LIVERS, WHITE BREAD AND A PIG'S HEAD, GOOD WOMAN.

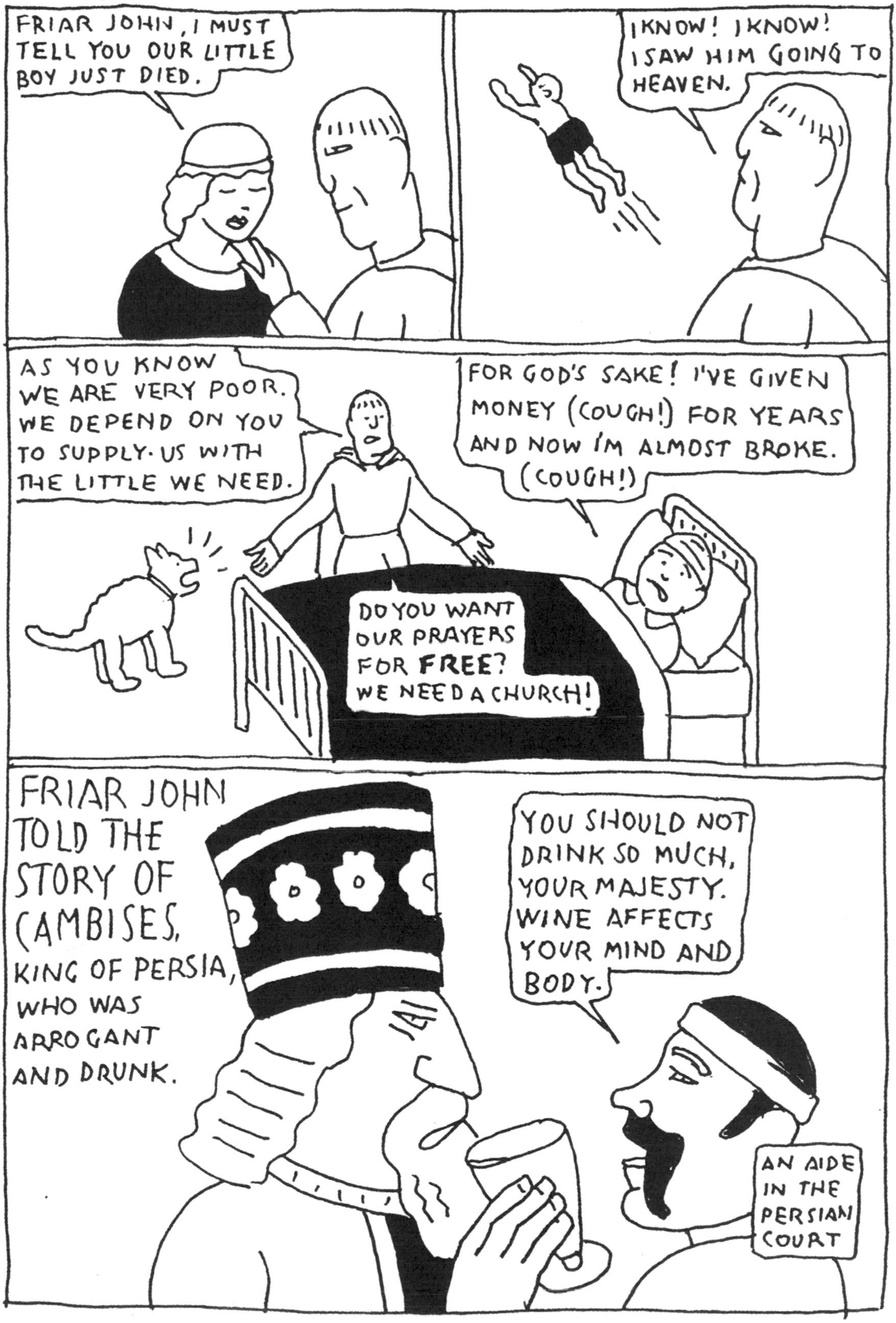
FRIAR JOHN, I MUST TELL YOU OUR LITTLE BOY JUST DIED.
I KNOW! I KNOW! I SAW HIM GOING TO HEAVEN.
AS YOU KNOW WE ARE VERY POOR. WE DEPEND ON YOU TO SUPPLY US WITH THE LITTLE WE NEED.
FOR GOD'S SAKE! I'VE GIVEN MONEY (COUGH!) FOR YEARS AND NOW I'M ALMOST BROKE. (COUGH!)
DO YOU WANT OUR PRAYERS FOR FREE? WE NEED A CHURCH!
FRIAR JOHN TOLD THE STORY OF CAMBISES, KING OF PERSIA, WHO WAS ARROGANT AND DRUNK.
YOU SHOULD NOT DRINK SO MUCH, YOUR MAJESTY. WINE AFFECTS YOUR MIND AND BODY.
AN AIDE IN THE PERSIAN COURT

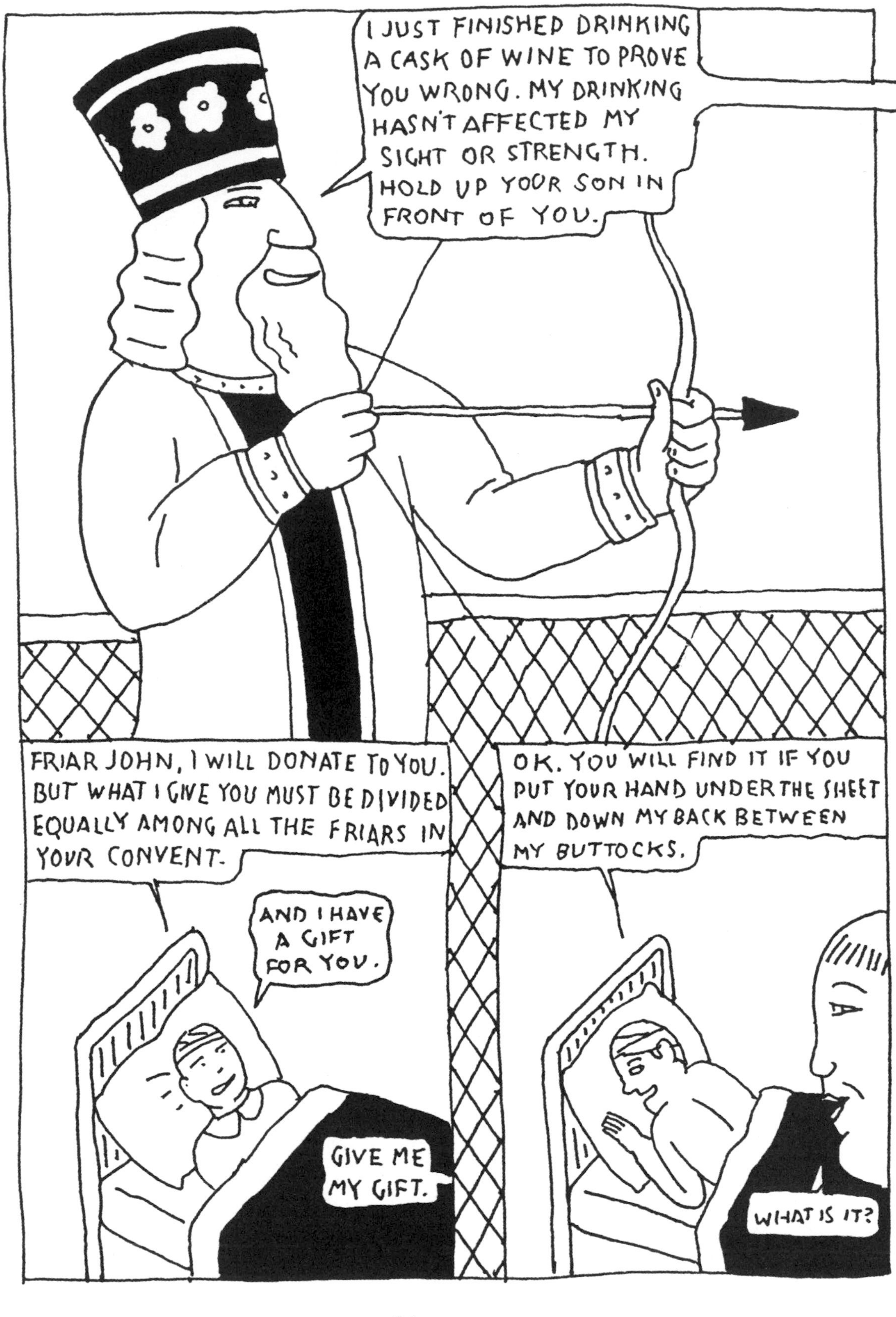
I JUST FINISHED DRINKING A CASK OF WINE TO PROVE YOU WRONG. MY DRINKING HASN'T AFFECTED MY SIGHT OR STRENGTH. HOLD UP YOUR SON IN FRONT OF YOU.
FRIAR JOHN, I WILL DONATE TO YOU. BUT WHAT I GIVE YOU MUST BE DIVIDED EQUALLY AMONG ALL THE FRIARS IN YOUR CONVENT.
AND I HAVE A GIFT FOR YOU.
GIVE ME MY GIFT.
OK. YOU WILL FIND IT IF YOU PUT YOUR HAND UNDER THE SHEET AND DOWN MY BACK BETWEEN MY BUTTOCKS.
WHAT IS IT?

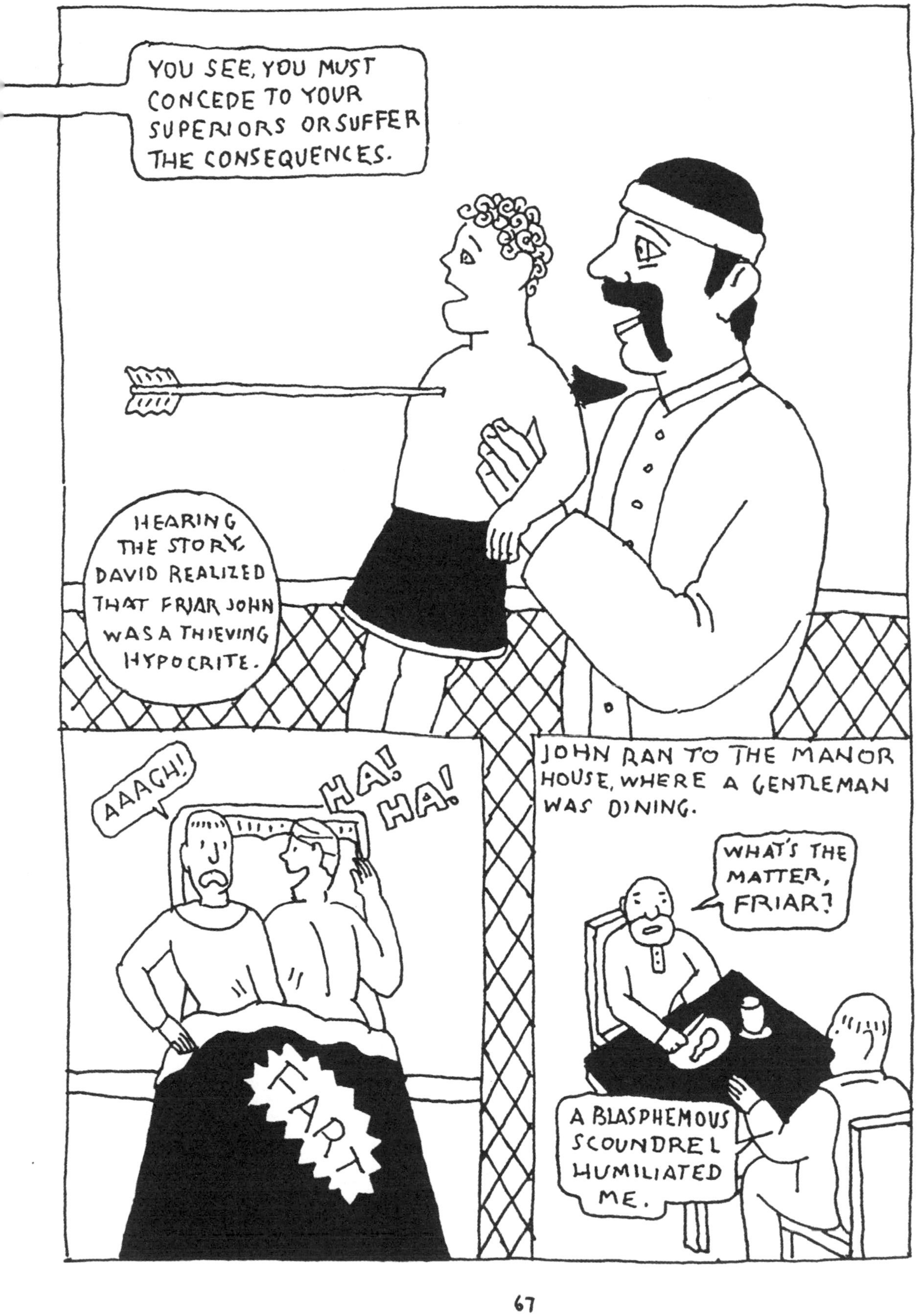
YOU SEE, YOU MUST CONCEDE TO YOUR SUPERIORS OR SUFFER THE CONSEQUENCES.
HEARING THE STORY, DAVID REALIZED THAT FRIAR JOHN WAS A THIEVING HYPOCRITE.
AAAGH!
HA! HA!
FART
JOHN RAN TO THE MANOR HOUSE, WHERE A GENTLEMAN WAS DINING.
WHAT'S THE MATTER, FRIAR?
A BLASPHEMOUS SCOUNDREL HUMILIATED ME.

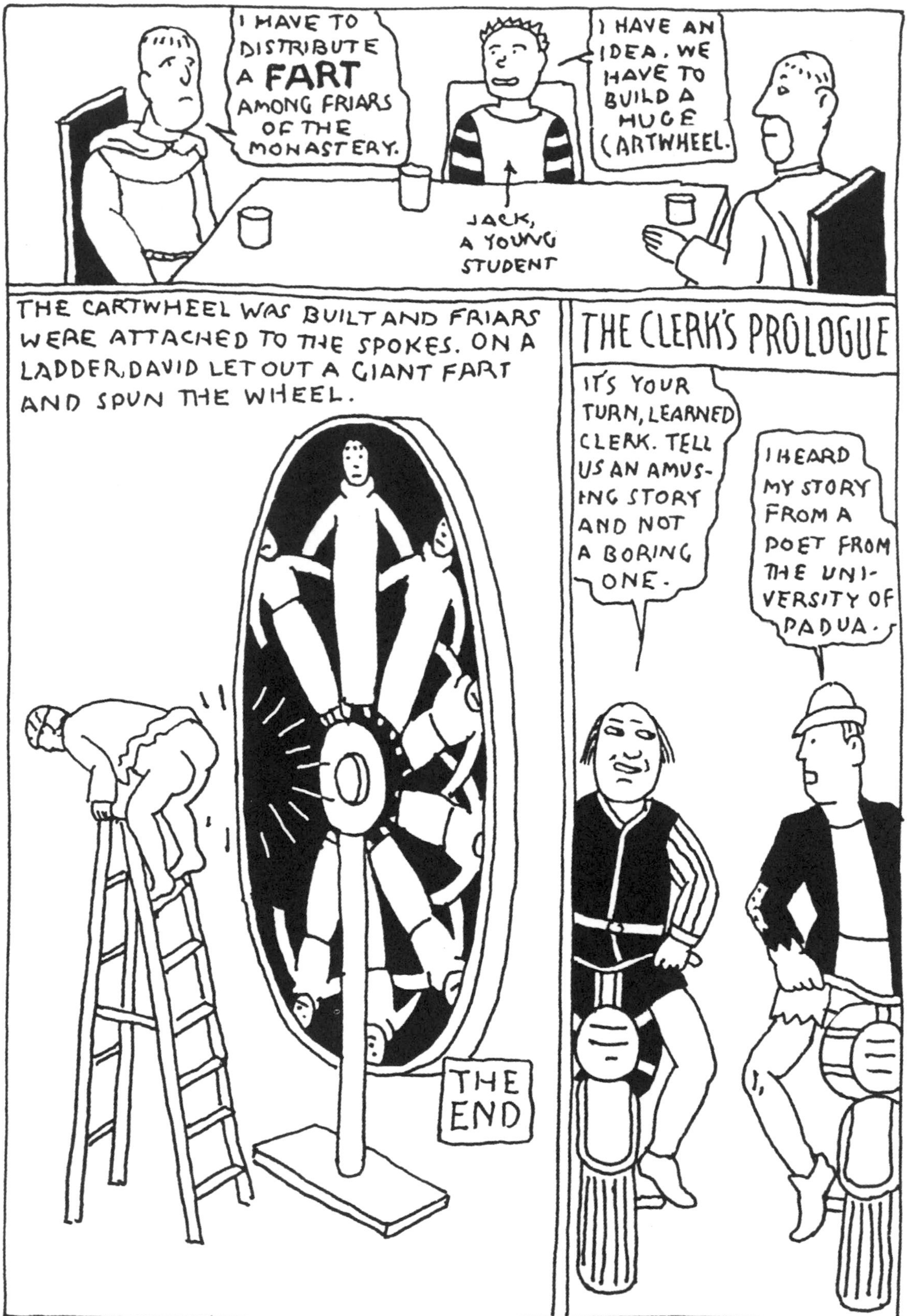
I HAVE TO DISTRIBUTE A FART AMONG FRIARS OF THE MONASTERY.
I HAVE AN IDEA. WE HAVE TO BUILD A HUGE CARTWHEEL.
JACK, A YOUNG STUDENT
THE CARTWHEEL WAS BUILT AND FRIARS WERE ATTACHED TO THE SPOKES. ON A LADDER, DAVID LET OUT A GIANT FART AND SPUN THE WHEEL.
THE END
THE CLERK'S PROLOGUE
IT'S YOUR TURN, LEARNED CLERK. TELL US AN AMUSING STORY AND NOT A BORING ONE.
I HEARD MY STORY FROM A POET FROM THE UNIVERSITY OF PADUA.

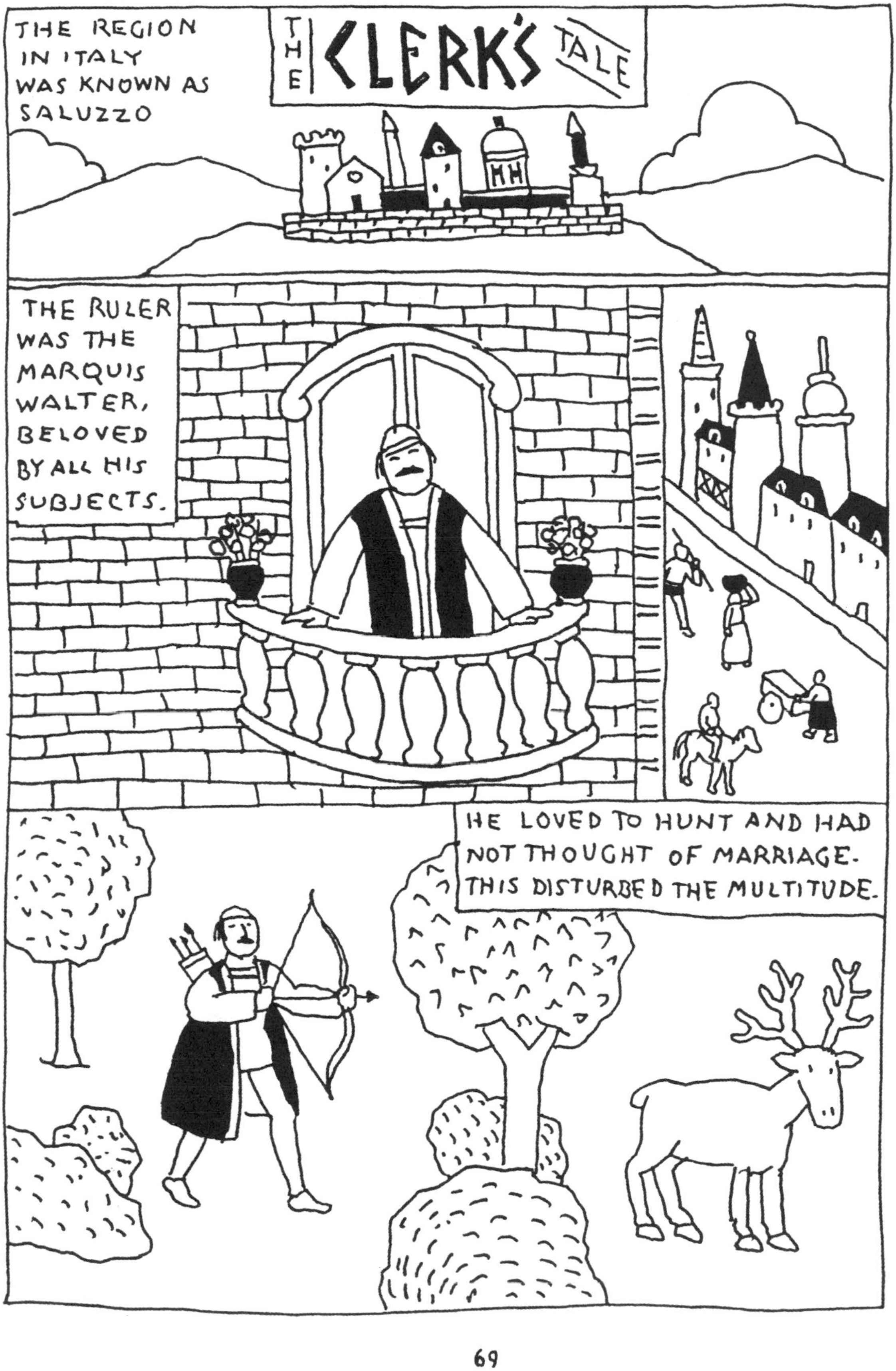
THE REGION IN ITALY WAS KNOWN AS SALUZZO
THE CLERK'S TALE
THE RULER WAS THE MARQUIS WALTER, BELOVED BY ALL HIS SUBJECTS.
HE LOVED TO HUNT AND HAD NOT THOUGHT OF MARRIAGE. THIS DISTURBED THE MULTITUDE.

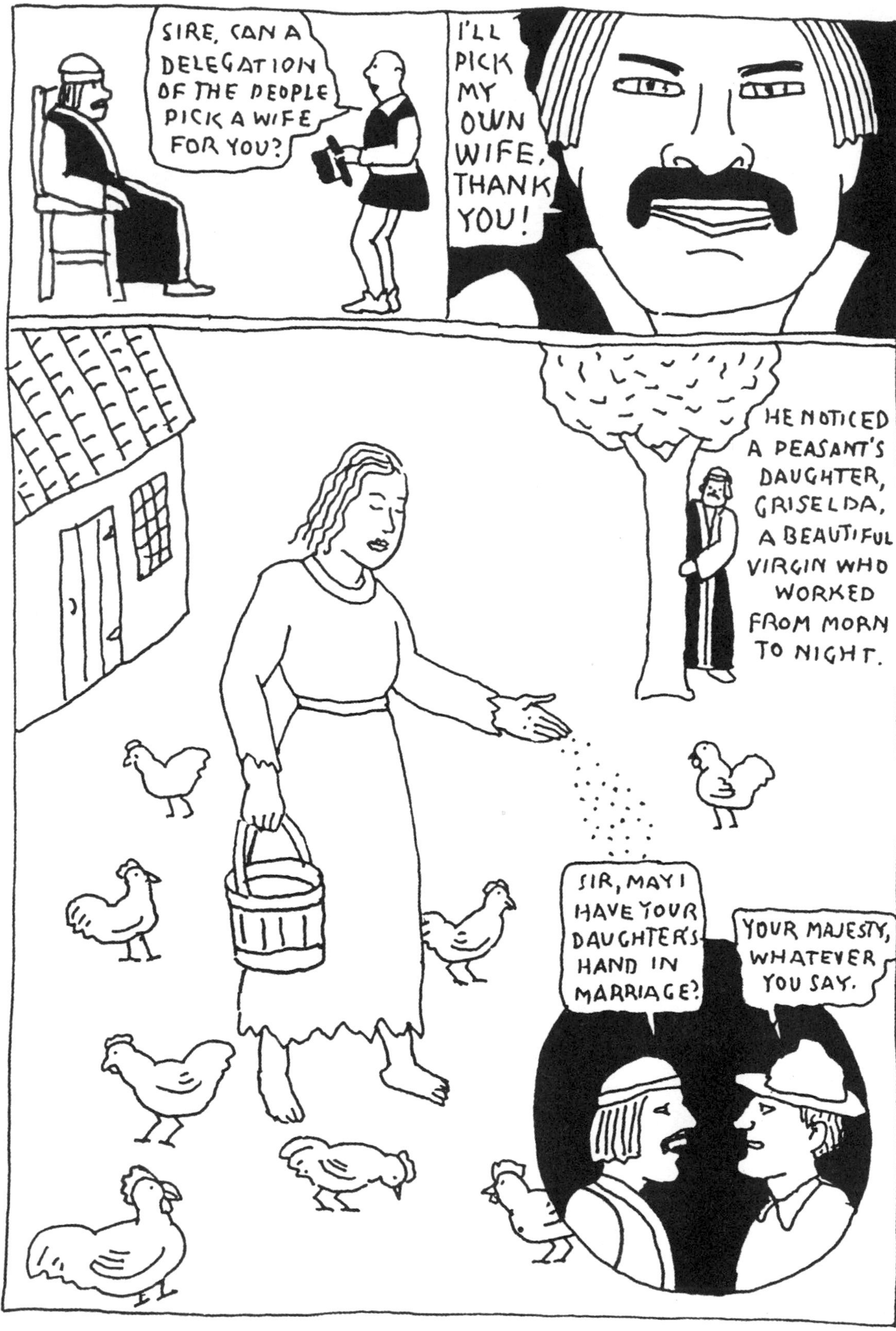
SIRE, CAN A DELEGATION OF THE PEOPLE PICK A WIFE FOR YOU?
I'LL PICK MY OWN WIFE, THANK YOU!
HE NOTICED A PEASANT'S DAUGHTER, GRISELDA, A BEAUTIFUL VIRGIN WHO WORKED FROM MORN TO NIGHT.
SIR, MAY I HAVE YOUR DAUGHTER'S HAND IN MARRIAGE?
YOUR MAJESTY, WHATEVER YOU SAY.

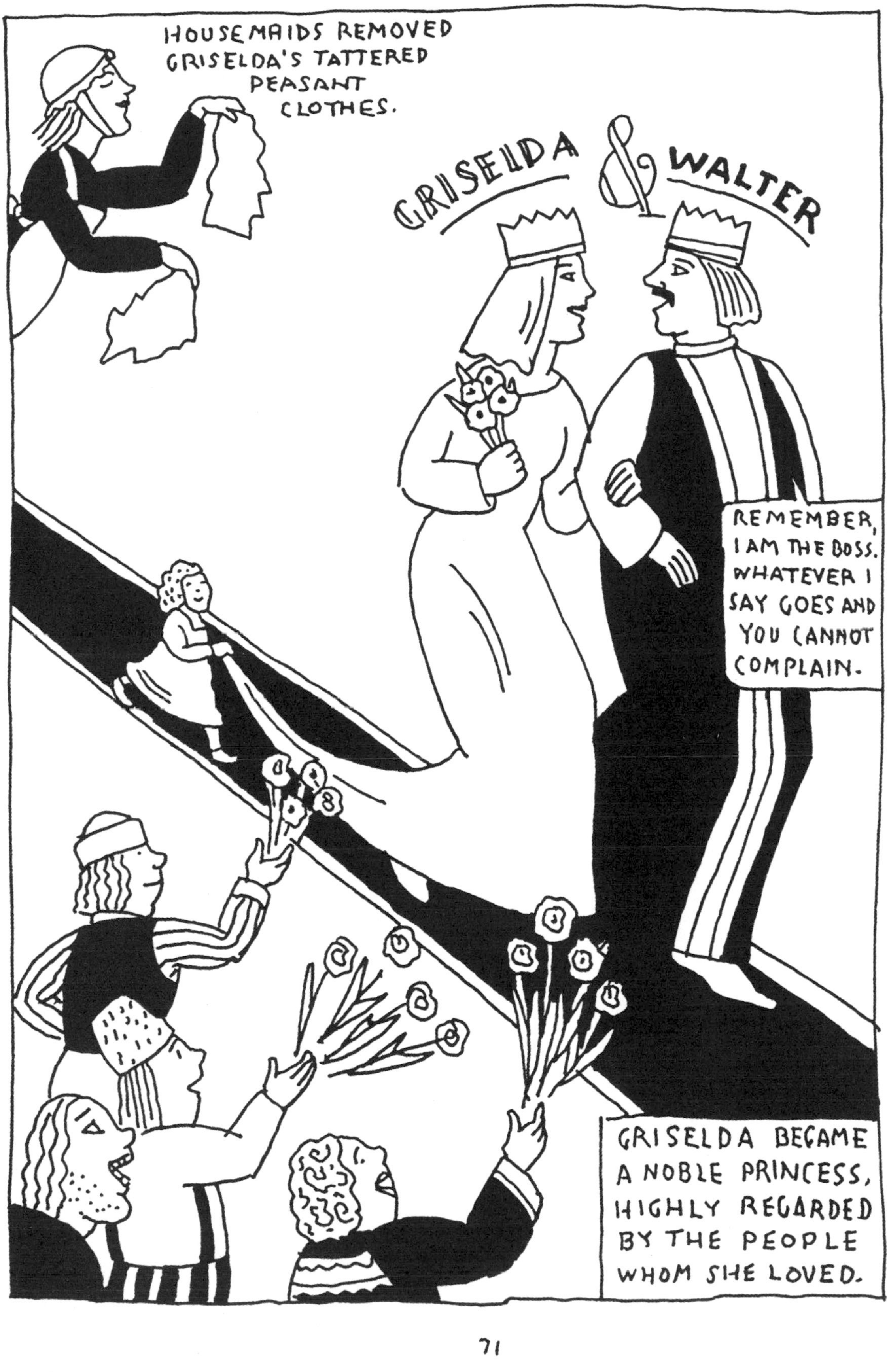
HOUSEMAIDS REMOVED GRISELDA'S TATTERED PEASANT CLOTHES.
GRISELDA & WALTER
REMEMBER, I AM THE BOSS. WHATEVER I SAY GOES AND YOU CANNOT COMPLAIN.
GRISELDA BECAME A NOBLE PRINCESS, HIGHLY REGARDED BY THE PEOPLE WHOM SHE LOVED.

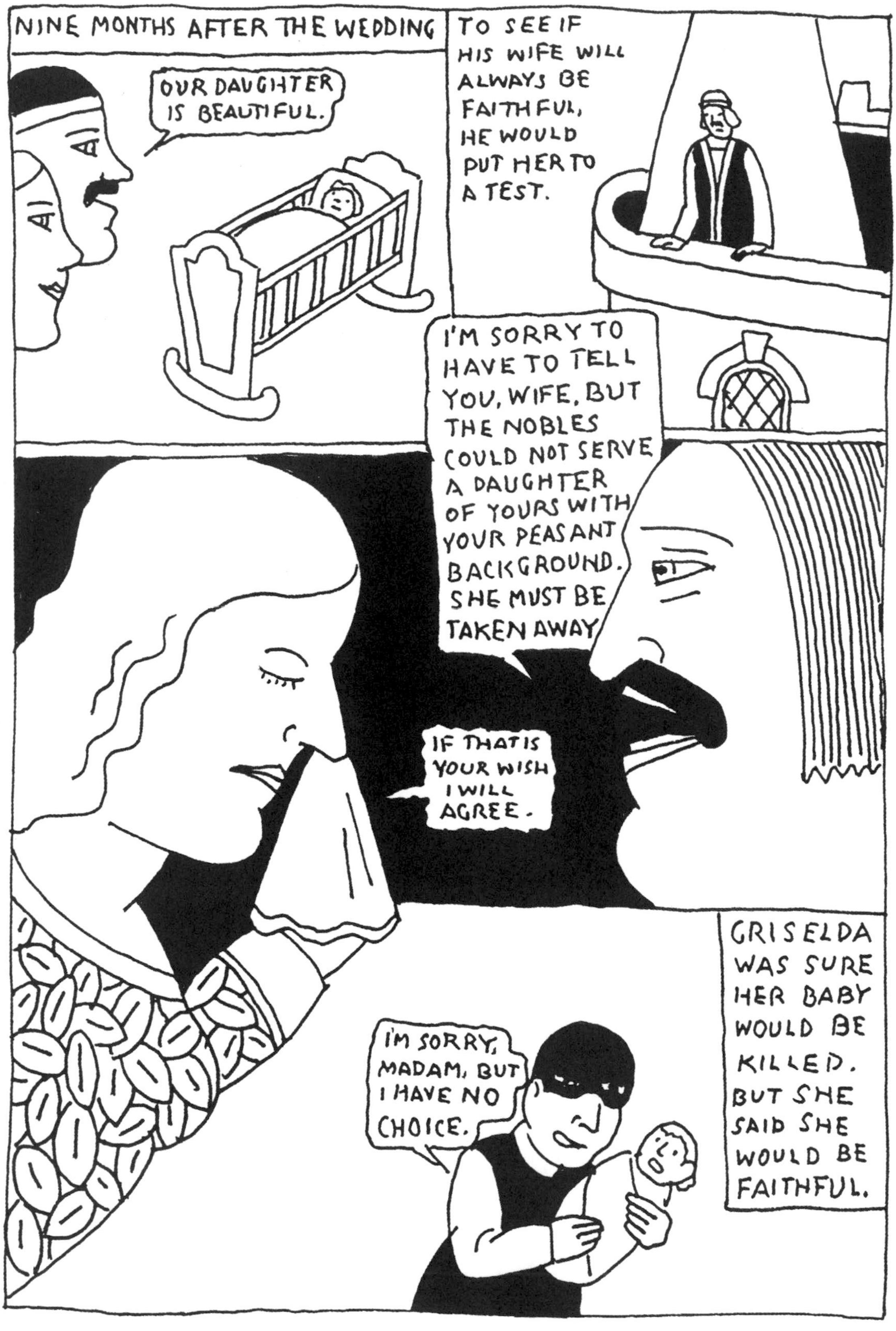
NINE MONTHS AFTER THE WEDDING
OUR DAUGHTER IS BEAUTIFUL.
TO SEE IF HIS WIFE WILL ALWAYS BE FAITHFUL, HE WOULD PUT HER TO A TEST.
I'M SORRY TO HAVE TO TELL YOU, WIFE, BUT THE NOBLES COULD NOT SERVE A DAUGHTER OF YOURS WITH YOUR PEASANT BACKGROUND. SHE MUST BE TAKEN AWAY
IF THAT IS YOUR WISH I WILL AGREE.
I'M SORRY, MADAM, BUT I HAVE NO CHOICE.
GRISELDA WAS SURE HER BABY WOULD BE KILLED. BUT SHE SAID SHE WOULD BE FAITHFUL.

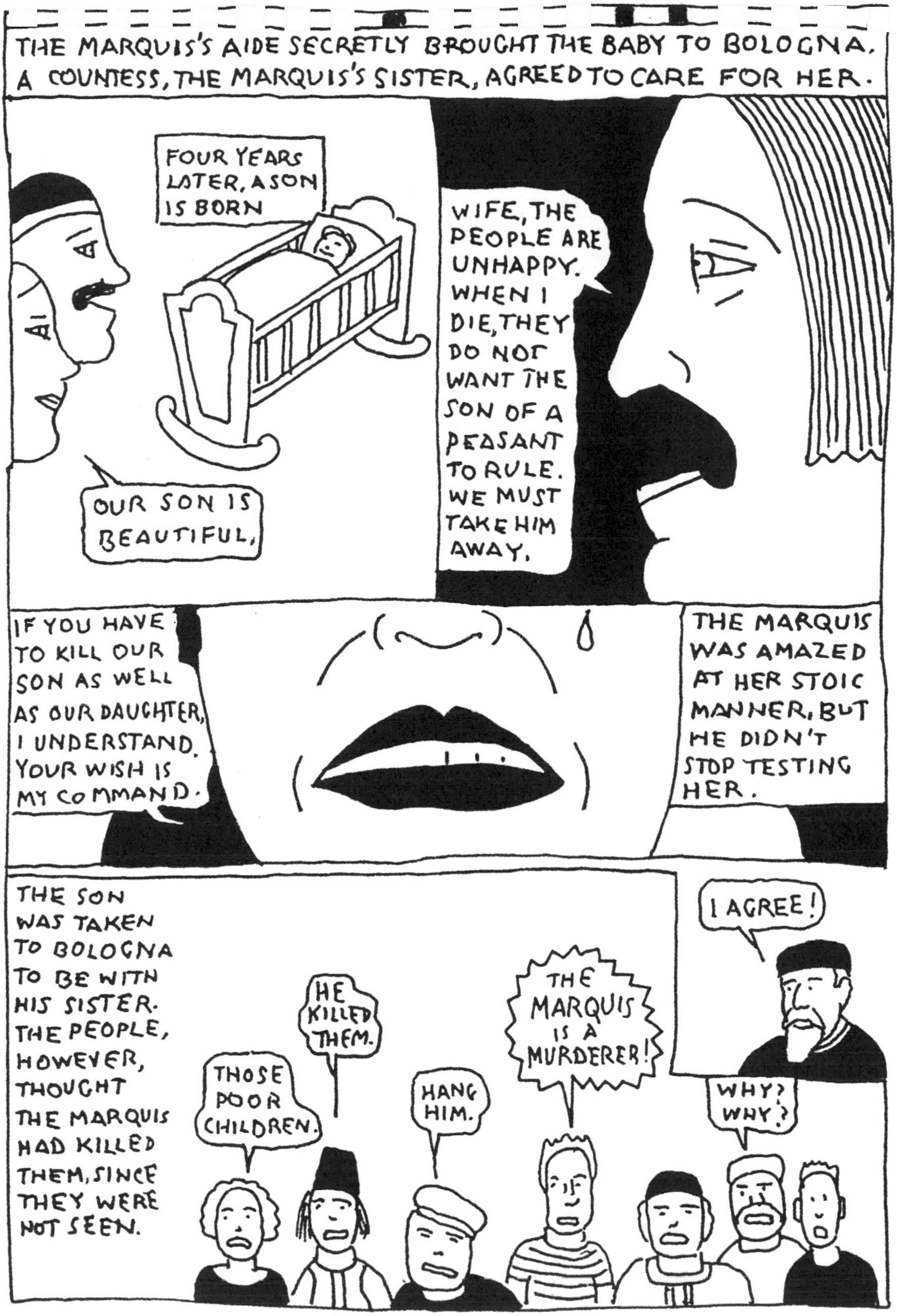
THE MARQUIS'S AIDE SECRETLY BROUGHT THE BABY TO BOLOGNA. A COUNTESS, THE MARQUIS'S SISTER, AGREED TO CARE FOR HER.
FOUR YEARS LATER, A SON IS BORN
OUR SON IS BEAUTIFUL.
WIFE, THE PEOPLE ARE UNHAPPY. WHEN I DIE, THEY DO NOT WANT THE SON OF A PEASANT TO RULE. WE MUST TAKE HIM AWAY.
IF YOU HAVE TO KILL OUR SON AS WELL AS OUR DAUGHTER, I UNDERSTAND. YOUR WISH IS MY COMMAND.
THE MARQUIS WAS AMAZED AT HER STOIC MANNER, BUT HE DIDN'T STOP TESTING HER.
THE SON WAS TAKEN TO BOLOGNA TO BE WITH HIS SISTER. THE PEOPLE, HOWEVER, THOUGHT THE MARQUIS HAD KILLED THEM, SINCE THEY WERE NOT SEEN.
THOSE POOR CHILDREN.
HE KILLED THEM.
HANG HIM.
THE MARQUIS IS A MURDERER!
I AGREE!
WHY? WHY?

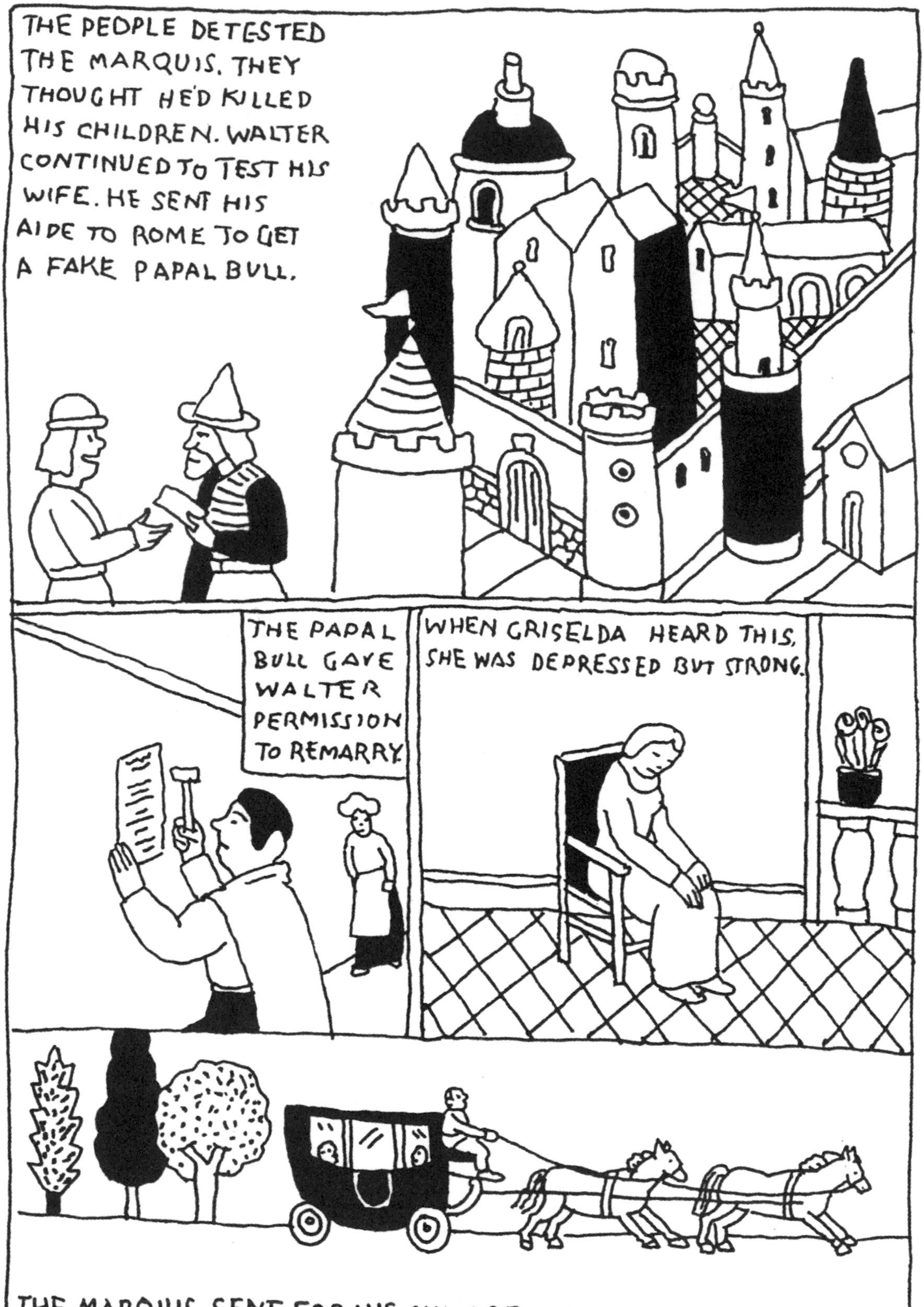
THE PEOPLE DETESTED THE MARQUIS. THEY THOUGHT HE'D KILLED HIS CHILDREN. WALTER CONTINUED TO TEST HIS WIFE. HE SENT HIS AIDE TO ROME TO GET A FAKE PAPAL BULL.
THE PAPAL BULL GAVE WALTER PERMISSION TO REMARRY.
WHEN GRISELDA HEARD THIS, SHE WAS DEPRESSED BUT STRONG.
THE MARQUIS SENT FOR HIS CHILDREN TO COME TO SALUZZO.

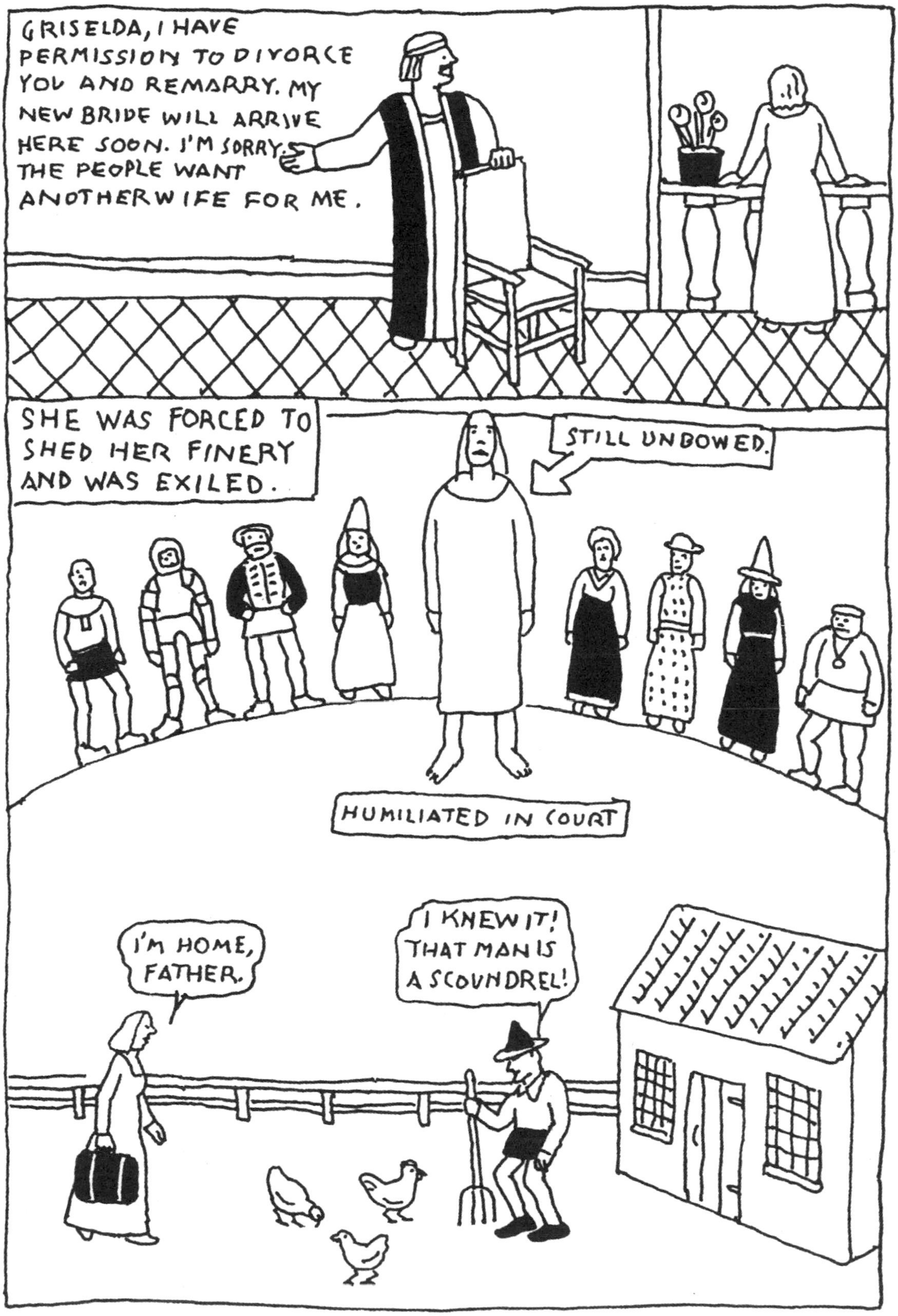
GRISELDA, I HAVE PERMISSION TO DIVORCE YOU AND REMARRY. MY NEW BRIDE WILL ARRIVE HERE SOON. I'M SORRY. THE PEOPLE WANT ANOTHER WIFE FOR ME.
SHE WAS FORCED TO SHED HER FINERY AND WAS EXILED.
STILL UNBOWED.
HUMILIATED IN COURT
I'M HOME, FATHER.
I KNEW IT! THAT MAN IS A SCOUNDREL!

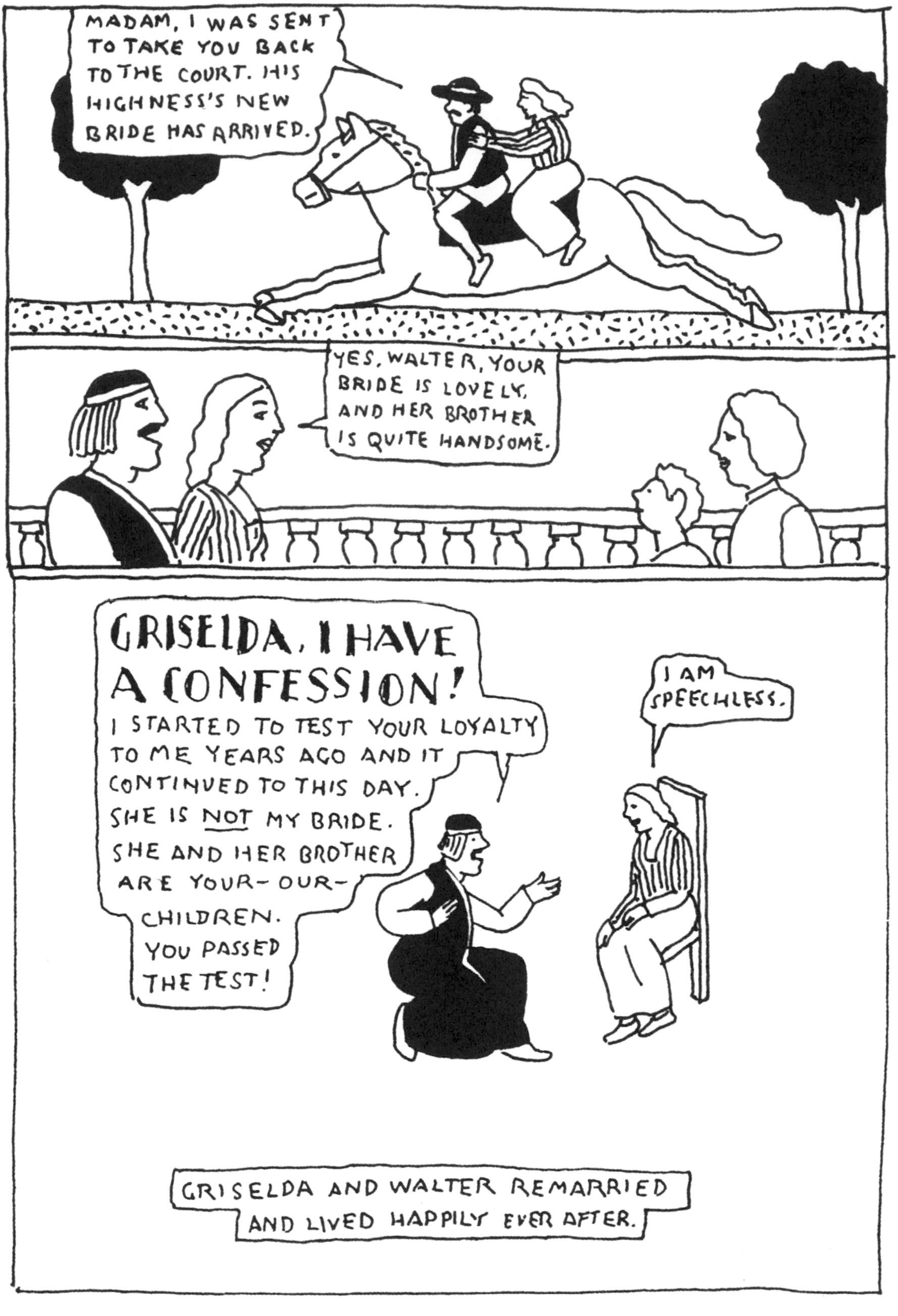
MADAM, I WAS SENT TO TAKE YOU BACK TO THE COURT. HIS HIGHNESS'S NEW BRIDE HAS ARRIVED.
YES, WALTER, YOUR BRIDE IS LOVELY, AND HER BROTHER IS QUITE HANDSOME.
GRISELDA, I HAVE A CONFESSION! I STARTED TO TEST YOUR LOYALTY TO ME YEARS AGO AND IT CONTINUED TO THIS DAY. SHE IS NOT MY BRIDE. SHE AND HER BROTHER ARE YOUR- OUR- CHILDREN. YOU PASSED THE TEST!
I AM SPEECHLESS.
GRISELDA AND WALTER REMARRIED AND LIVED HAPPILY EVER AFTER.

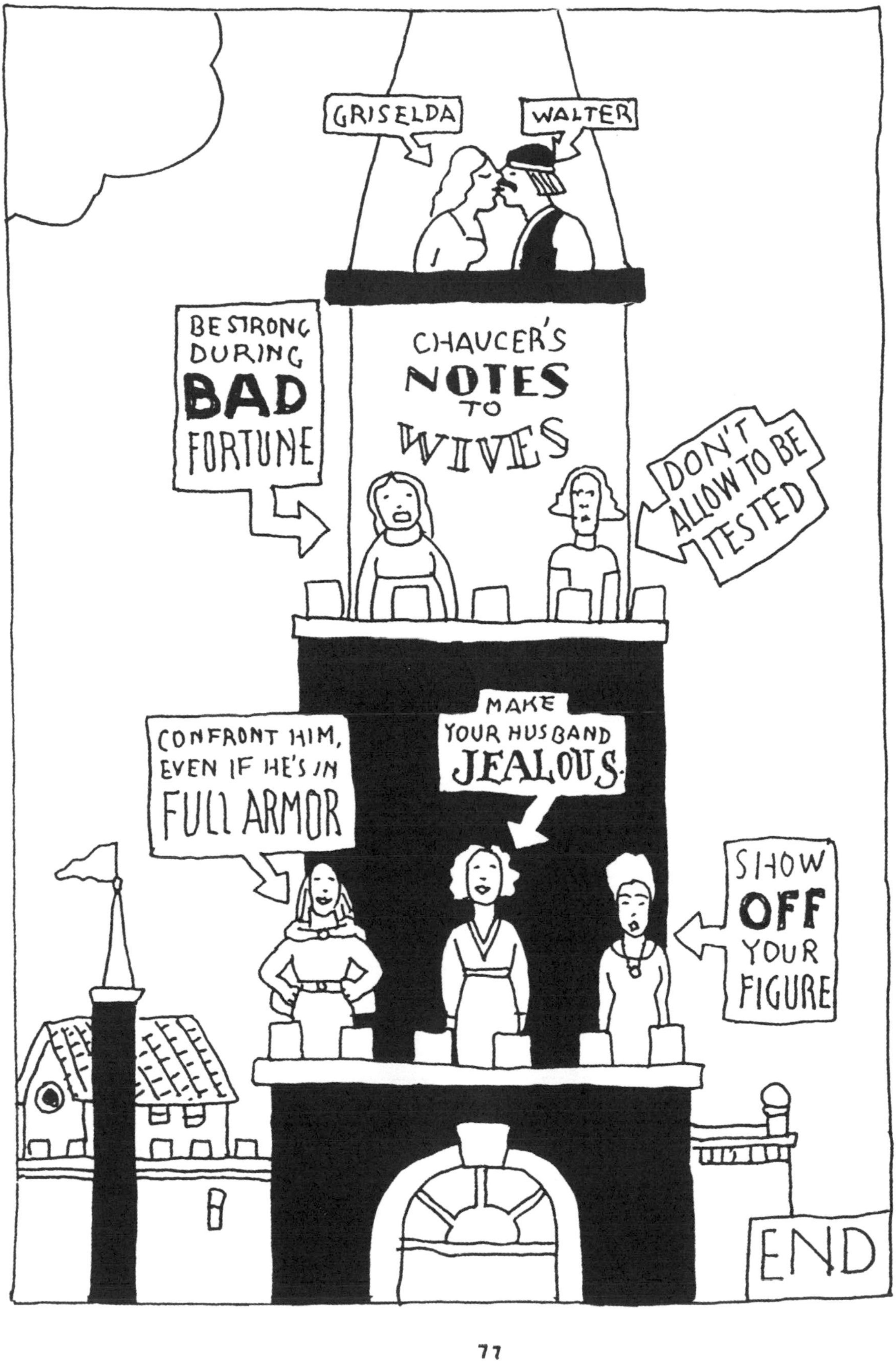
GRISELDA
WALTER
BE STRONG DURING BAD FORTUNE
CHAUCER'S NOTES TO WIVES
DON'T ALLOW TO BE TESTED
CONFRONT HIM, EVEN IF HE'S IN FULL ARMOR
MAKE YOUR HUSBAND JEALOUS.
SHOW OFF YOUR FIGURE
END

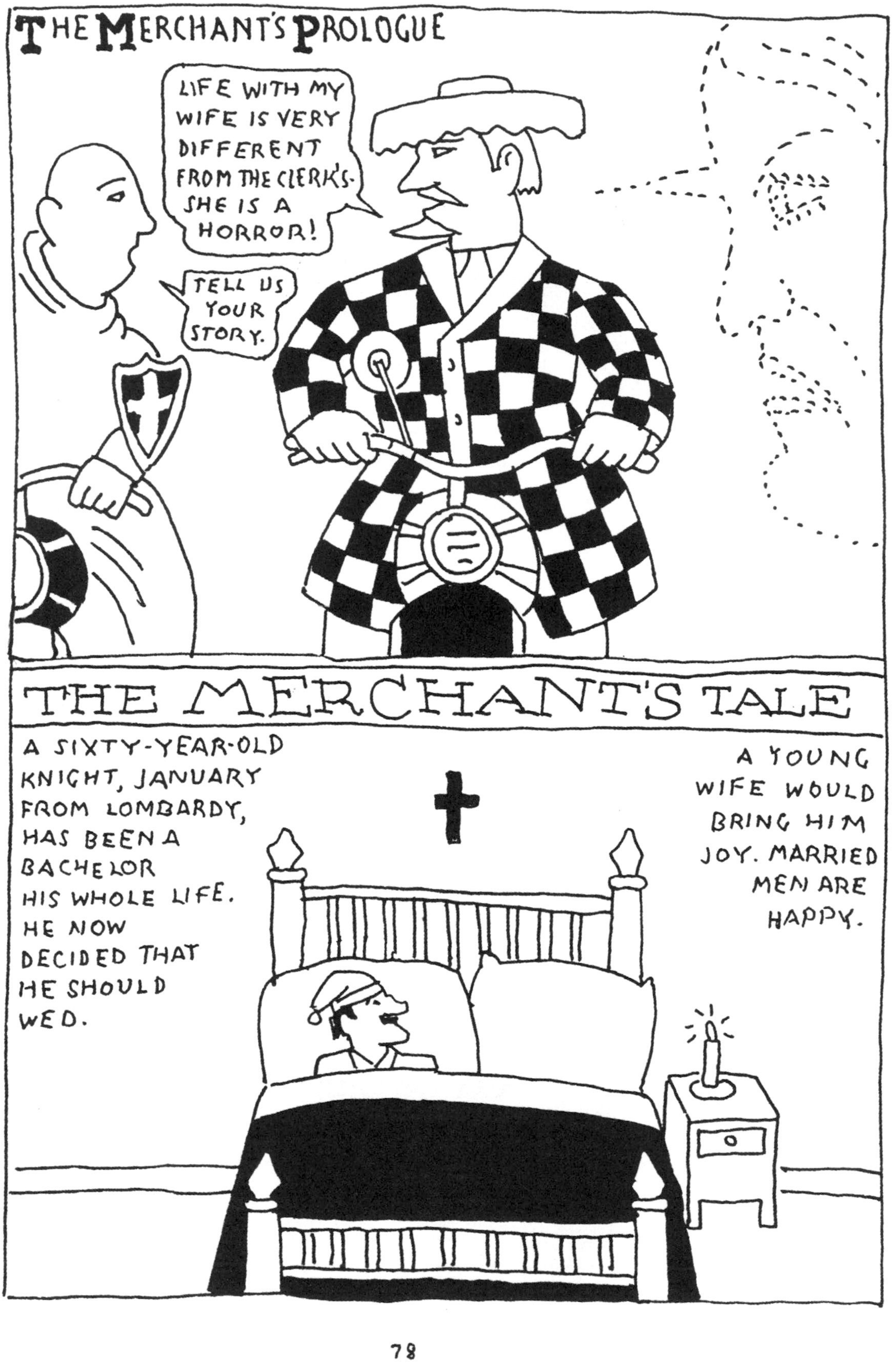
THE MERCHANT'S PROLOGUE
LIFE WITH MY WIFE IS VERY DIFFERENT FROM THE CLERK'S- SHE IS A HORROR!
TELL US YOUR STORY.
THE MERCHANT'S TALE
A SIXTY-YEAR-OLD KNIGHT, JANUARY FROM LOMBARDY, HAS BEEN A BACHELOR HIS WHOLE LIFE. HE NOW DECIDED THAT HE SHOULD WED.
A YOUNG WIFE WOULD BRING HIM JOY. MARRIED MEN ARE HAPPY.

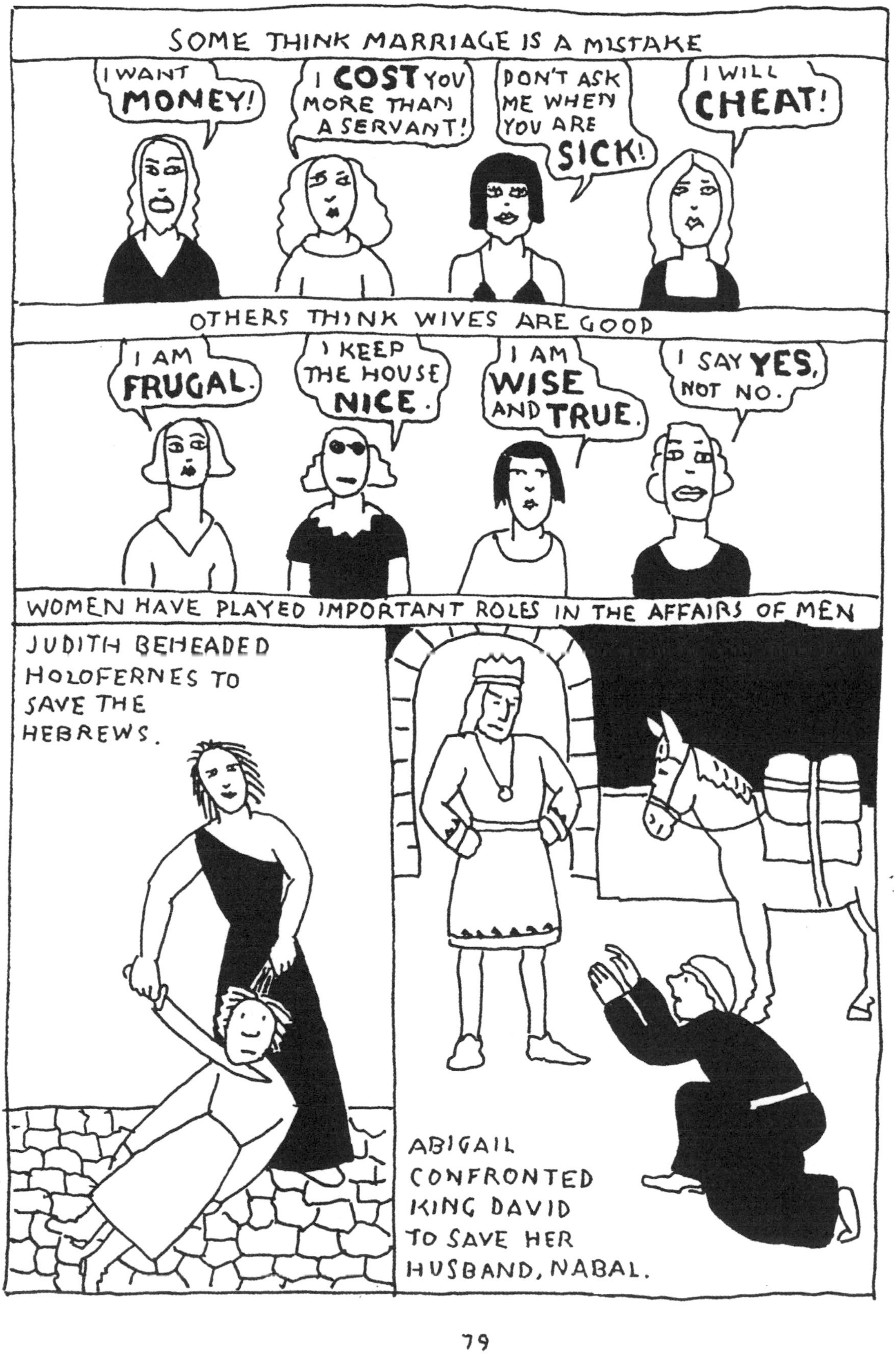
SOME THINK MARRIAGE IS A MISTAKE
I WANT MONEY!
I COST YOU MORE THAN A SERVANT!
DON'T ASK ME WHEN YOU ARE SICK!
I WILL CHEAT!
OTHERS THINK WIVES ARE GOOD
I AM FRUGAL.
I KEEP THE HOUSE NICE.
I AM WISE AND TRUE.
I SAY YES, NOT NO.
WOMEN HAVE PLAYED IMPORTANT ROLES IN THE AFFAIRS OF MEN
JUDITH BEHEADED HOLOFERNES TO SAVE THE HEBREWS.
ABIGAIL CONFRONTED KING DAVID TO SAVE HER HUSBAND, NABAL.

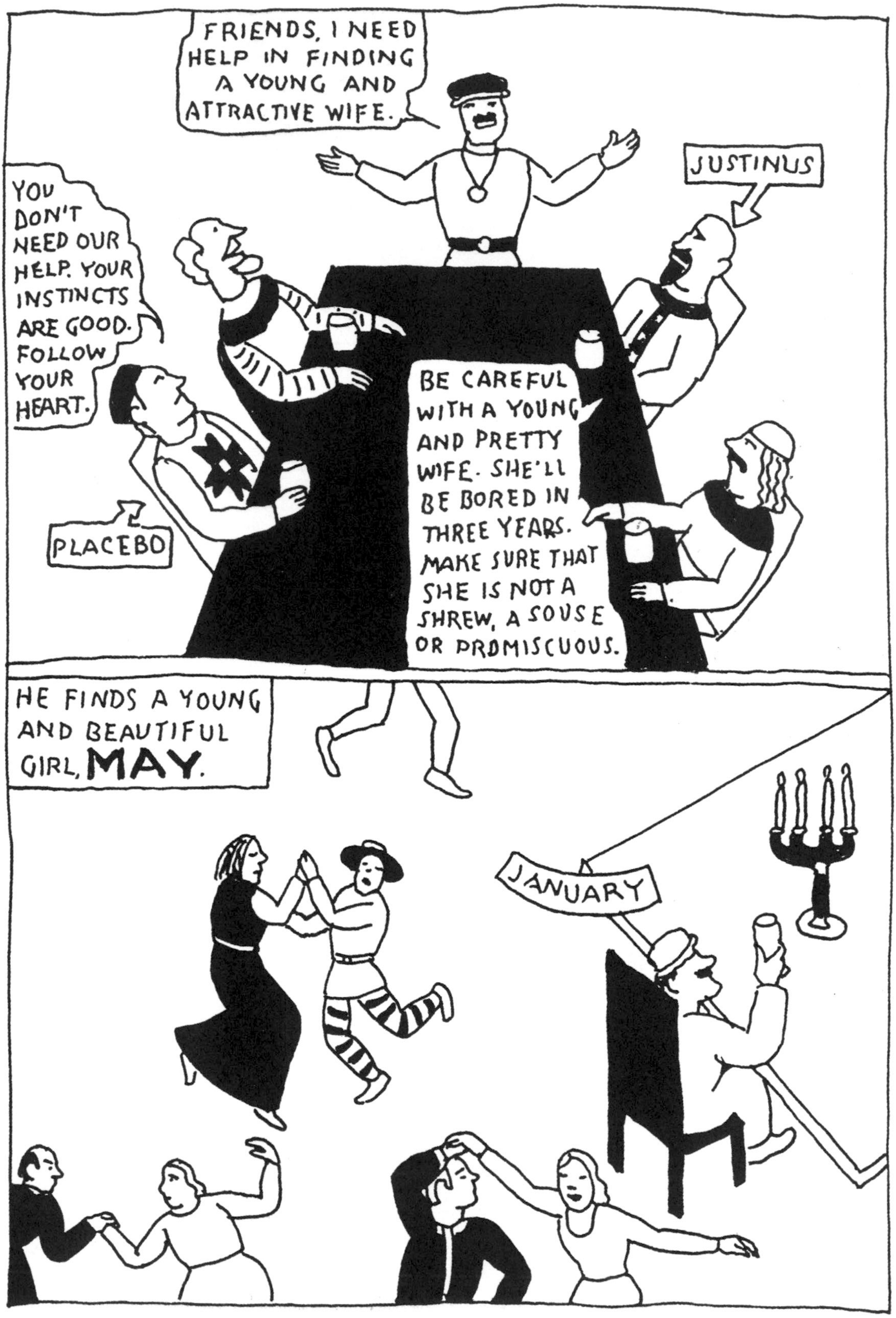
FRIENDS, I NEED HELP IN FINDING A YOUNG AND ATTRACTIVE WIFE.
JUSTINUS
YOU DON'T NEED OUR HELP. YOUR INSTINCTS ARE GOOD. FOLLOW YOUR HEART.
BE CAREFUL WITH A YOUNG AND PRETTY WIFE. SHE'LL BE BORED IN THREE YEARS. MAKE SURE THAT SHE IS NOT A SHREW, A SOUSE OR PROMISCUOUS.
PLACEBO
HE FINDS A YOUNG AND BEAUTIFUL GIRL, MAY.
JANUARY

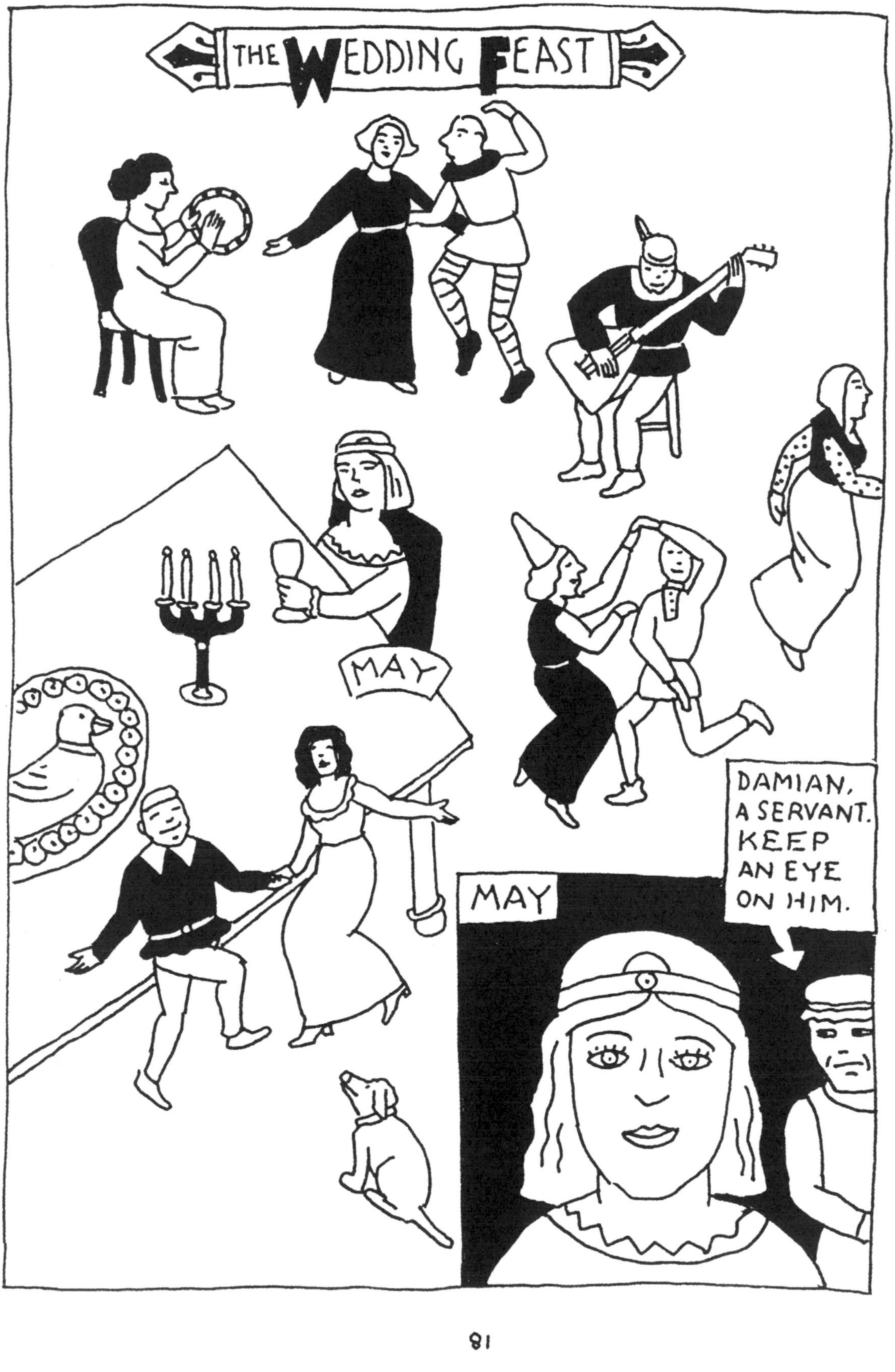
THE WEDDING FEAST
MAY
DAMIAN, A SERVANT. KEEP AN EYE ON HIM.
MAY

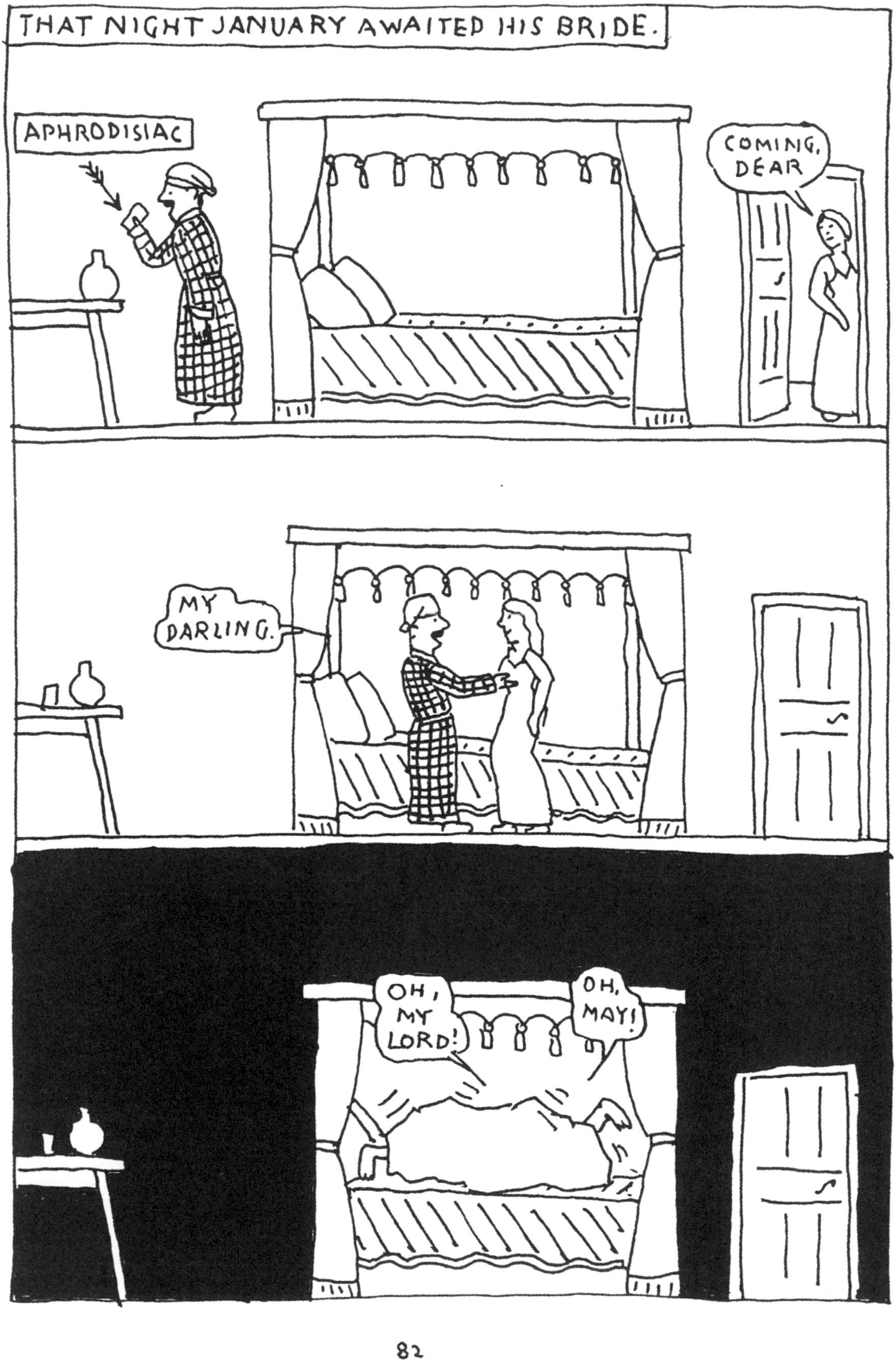
THAT NIGHT JANUARY AWAITED HIS BRIDE.
APHRODISIAC
COMING, DEAR
MY DARLING.
OH, MY LORD!
OH, MAY!

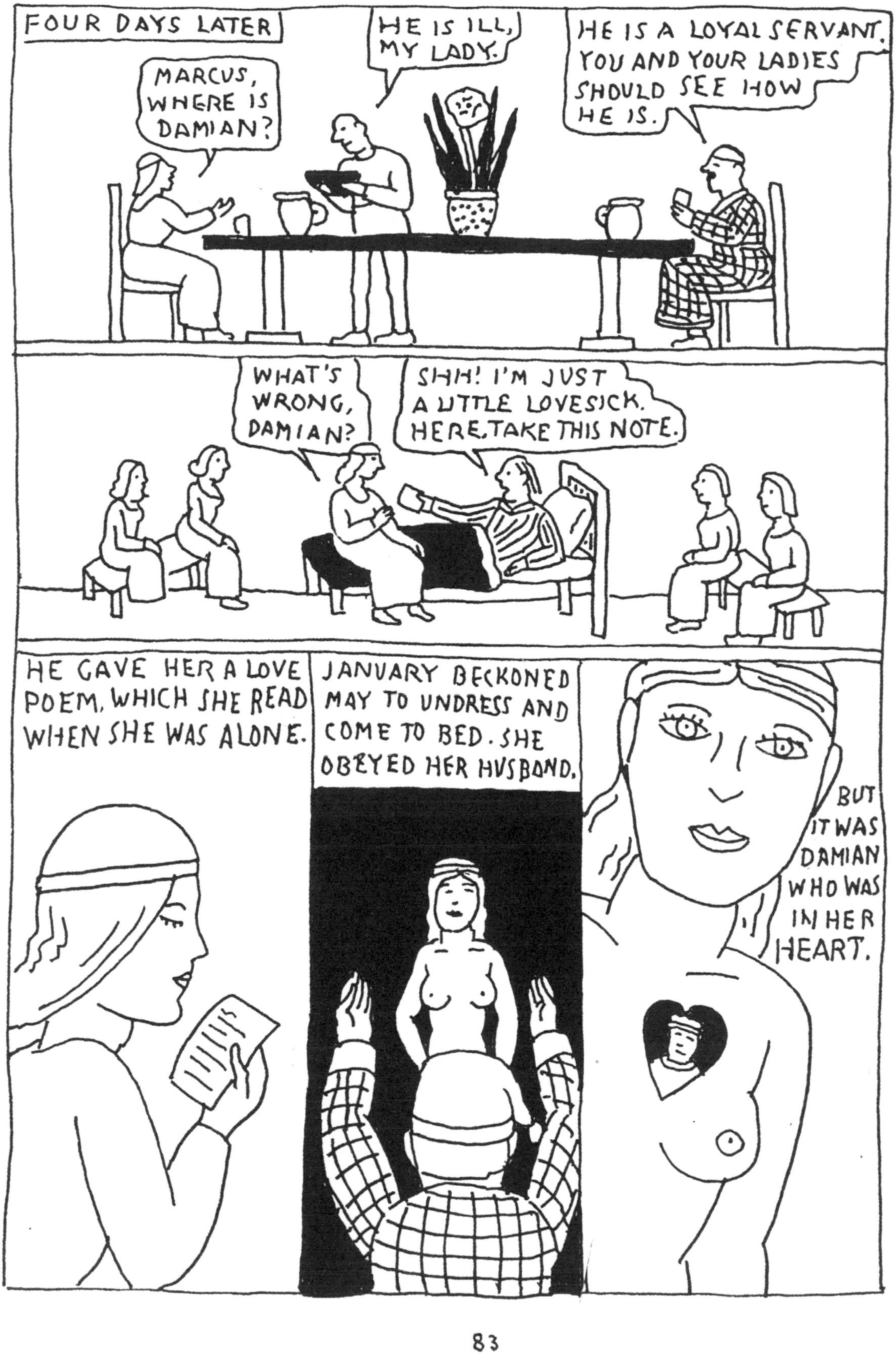
FOUR DAYS LATER
MARCUS, WHERE IS DAMIAN?
HE IS ILL, MY LADY.
HE IS A LOYAL SERVANT. YOU AND YOUR LADIES SHOULD SEE HOW HE IS.
WHAT'S WRONG, DAMIAN?
SHH! I'M JUST A LITTLE LOVESICK. HERE, TAKE THIS NOTE.
HE GAVE HER A LOVE POEM, WHICH SHE READ WHEN SHE WAS ALONE.
JANUARY BECKONED MAY TO UNDRESS AND COME TO BED. SHE OBEYED HER HUSBAND.
BUT IT WAS DAMIAN WHO WAS IN HER HEART.

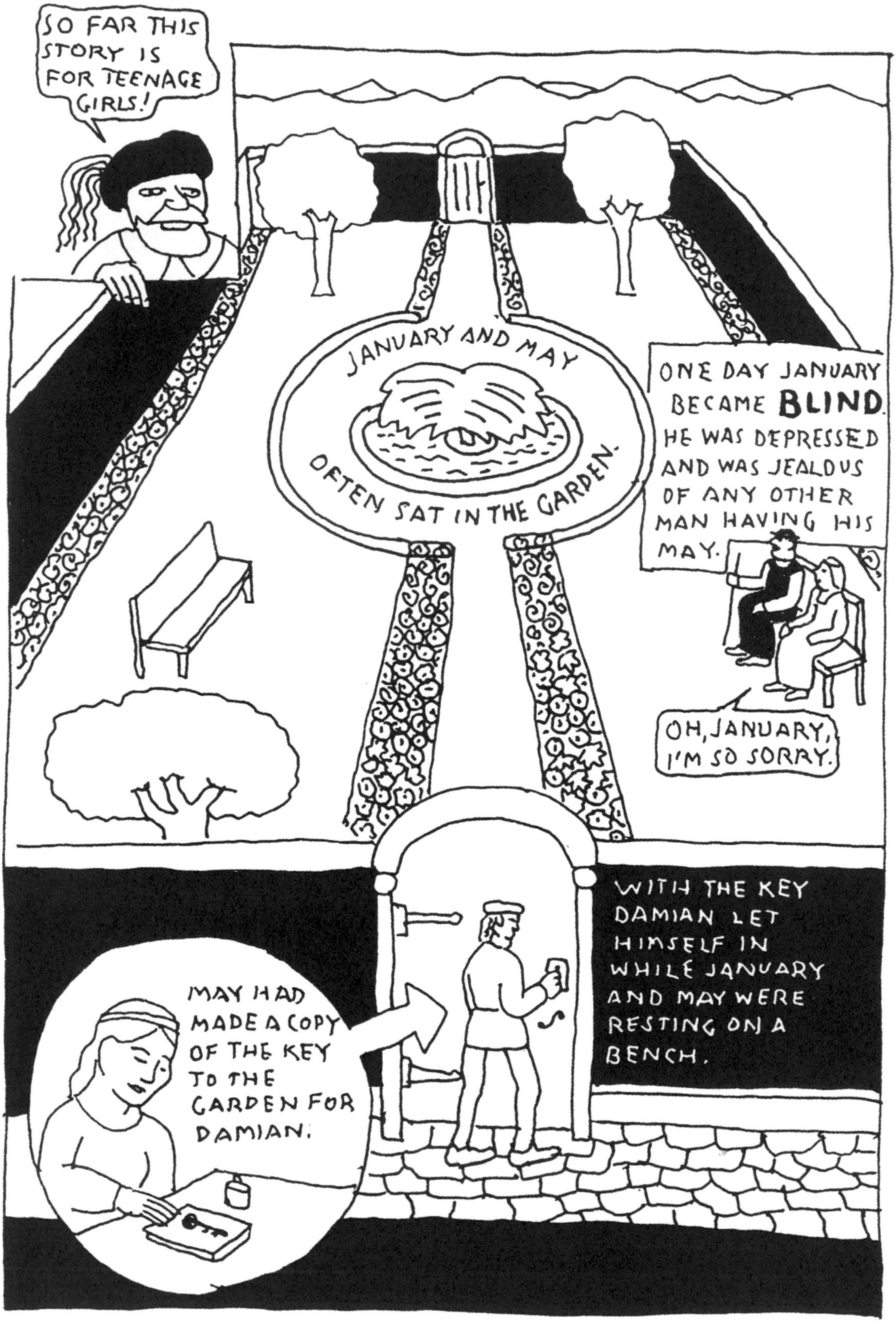
SO FAR THIS STORY IS FOR TEENAGE GIRLS!
JANUARY AND MAY OFTEN SAT IN THE GARDEN.
ONE DAY JANUARY BECAME BLIND. HE WAS DEPRESSED AND WAS JEALOUS OF ANY OTHER MAN HAVING HIS MAY.
OH, JANUARY, I'M SO SORRY.
MAY HAD MADE A COPY OF THE KEY TO THE GARDEN FOR DAMIAN.
WITH THE KEY DAMIAN LET HIMSELF IN WHILE JANUARY AND MAY WERE RESTING ON A BENCH.

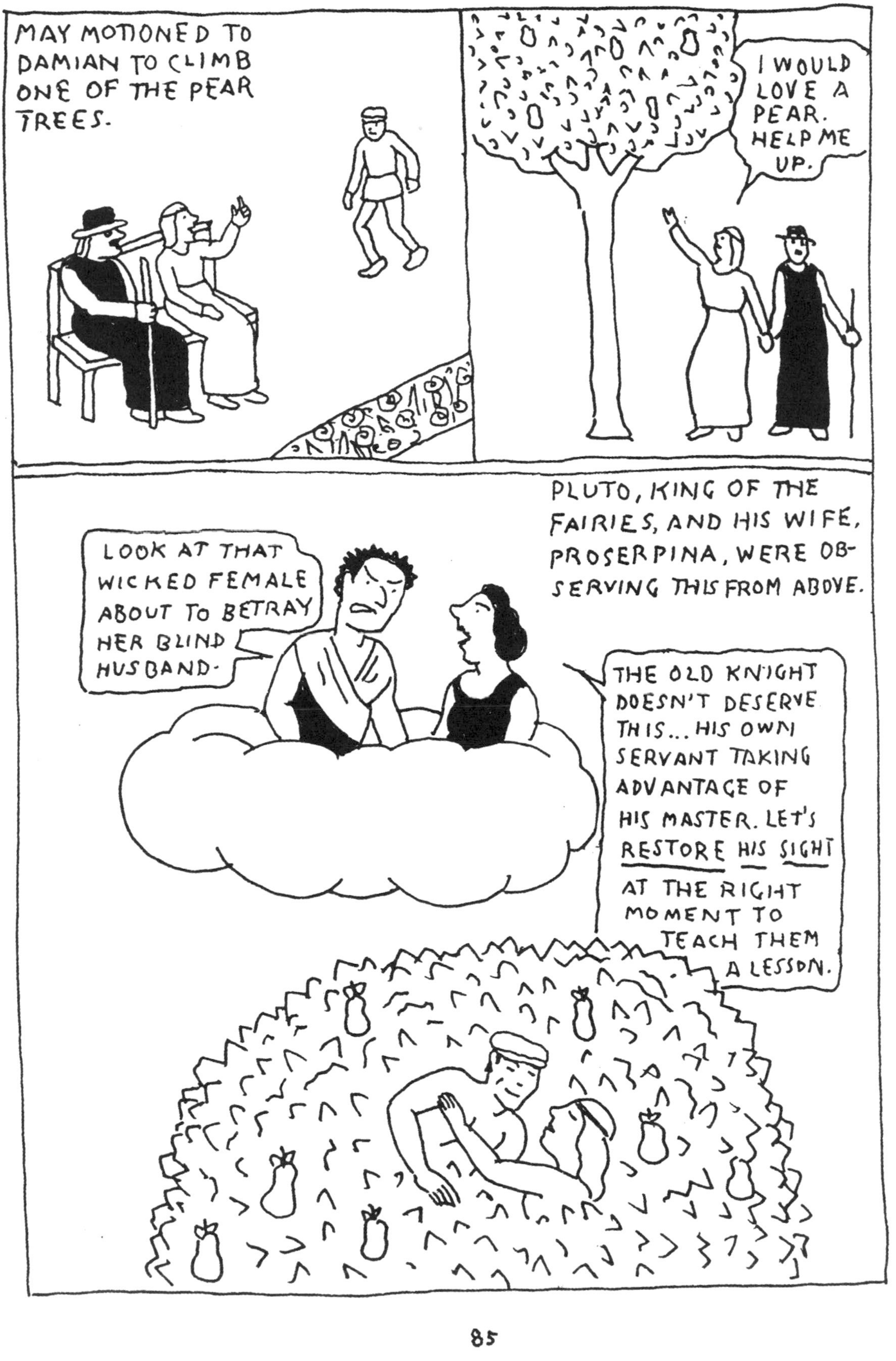
MAY MOTIONED TO DAMIAN TO CLIMB ONE OF THE PEAR TREES.
I WOULD LOVE A PEAR. HELP ME UP.
PLUTO, KING OF THE FAIRIES, AND HIS WIFE, PROSERPINA, WERE OBSERVING THIS FROM ABOVE.
LOOK AT THAT WICKED FEMALE ABOUT TO BETRAY HER BLIND HUSBAND.
THE OLD KNIGHT DOESN'T DESERVE THIS... HIS OWN SERVANT TAKING ADVANTAGE OF HIS MASTER. LET'S RESTORE HIS SIGHT AT THE RIGHT MOMENT TO TEACH THEM A LESSON.

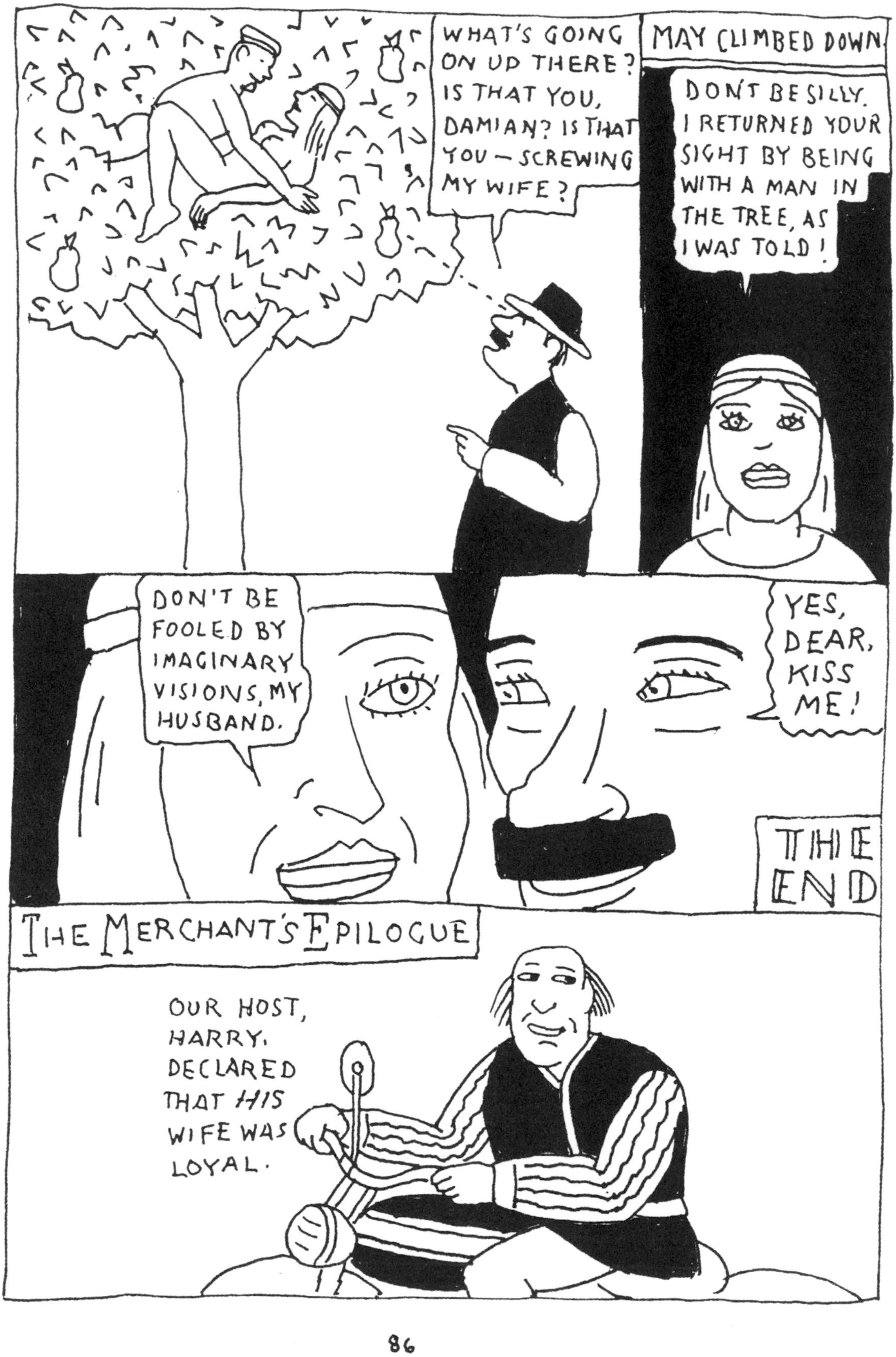
WHAT'S GOING ON UP THERE? IS THAT YOU, DAMIAN? IS THAT YOU — SCREWING MY WIFE?
MAY CLIMBED DOWN
DON'T BE SILLY. I RETURNED YOUR SIGHT BY BEING WITH A MAN IN THE TREE, AS I WAS TOLD!
DON'T BE FOOLED BY IMAGINARY VISIONS, MY HUSBAND.
YES, DEAR, KISS ME!
THE END
THE MERCHANT'S EPILOGUE
OUR HOST, HARRY, DECLARED THAT *HIS* WIFE WAS LOYAL.

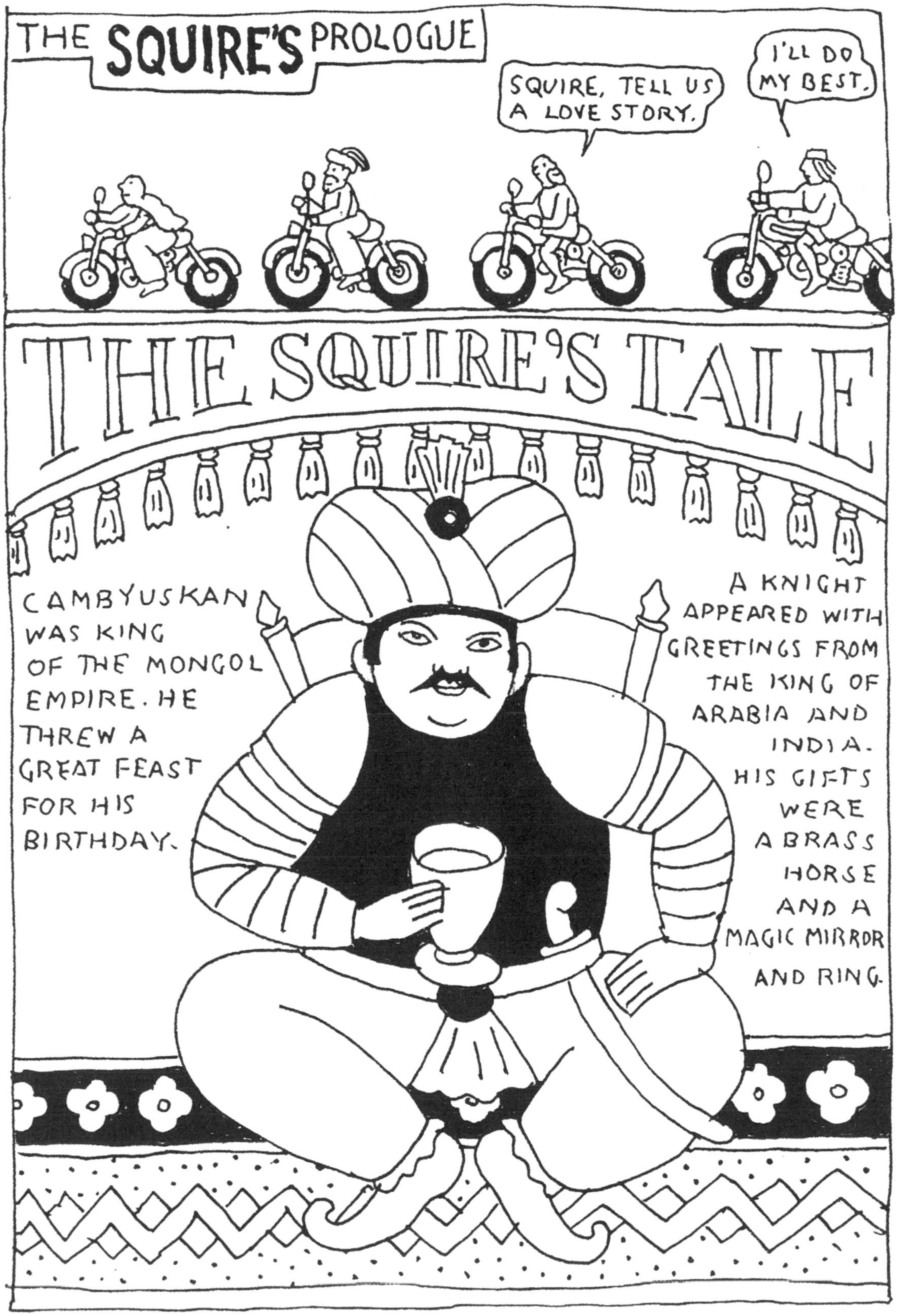
THE SQUIRE'S PROLOGUE
SQUIRE, TELL US A LOVE STORY.
I'LL DO MY BEST.
THE SQUIRE'S TALE
CAMBYUSKAN WAS KING OF THE MONGOL EMPIRE. HE THREW A GREAT FEAST FOR HIS BIRTHDAY.
A KNIGHT APPEARED WITH GREETINGS FROM THE KING OF ARABIA AND INDIA. HIS GIFTS WERE A BRASS HORSE AND A MAGIC MIRROR AND RING.

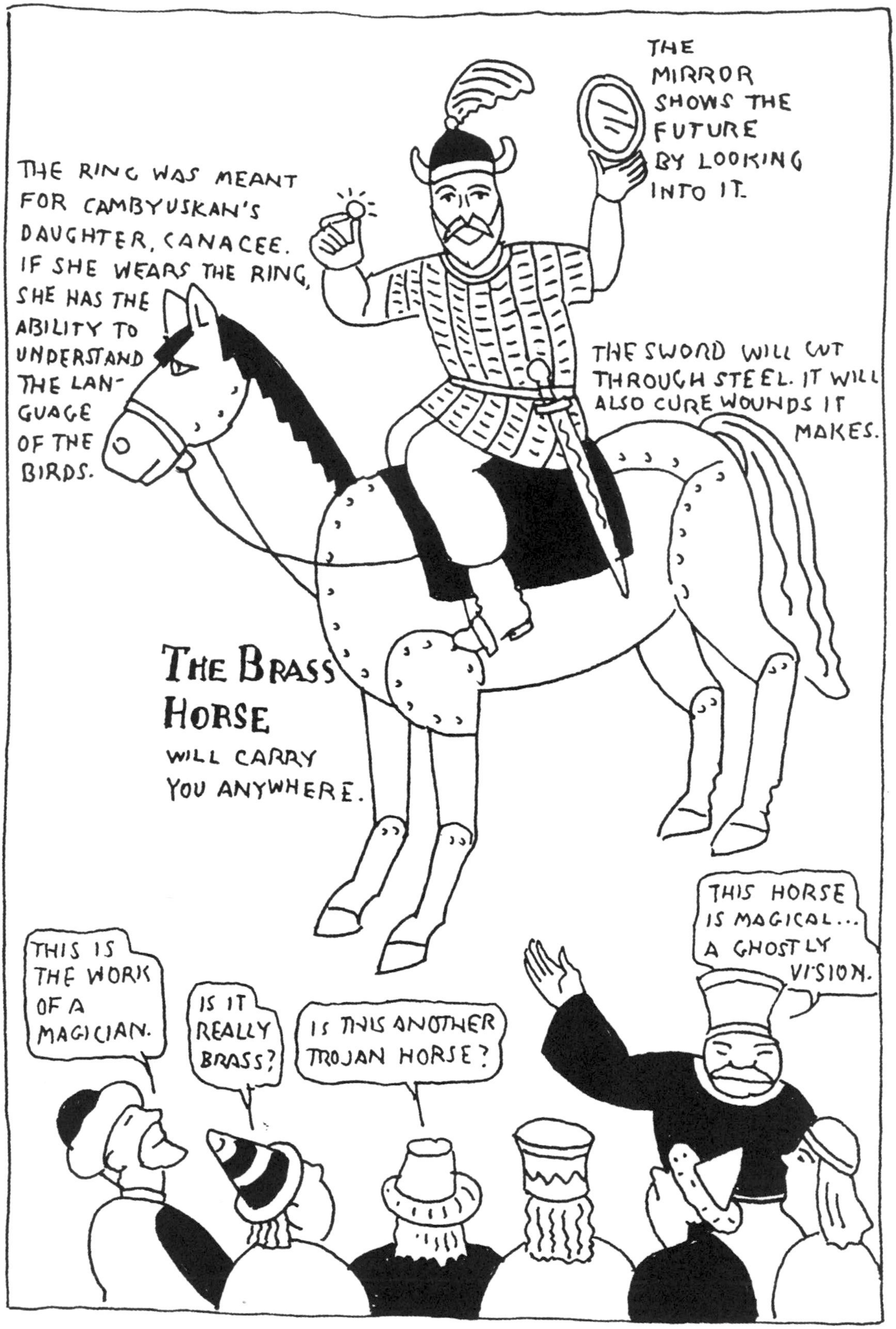
THE RING WAS MEANT FOR CAMBYUSKAN'S DAUGHTER, CANACEE. IF SHE WEARS THE RING, SHE HAS THE ABILITY TO UNDERSTAND THE LANGUAGE OF THE BIRDS.
THE MIRROR SHOWS THE FUTURE BY LOOKING INTO IT.
THE SWORD WILL CUT THROUGH STEEL. IT WILL ALSO CURE WOUNDS IT MAKES.
THE BRASS HORSE
WILL CARRY YOU ANYWHERE.
THIS IS THE WORK OF A MAGICIAN.
IS IT REALLY BRASS?
IS THIS ANOTHER TROJAN HORSE?
THIS HORSE IS MAGICAL... A GHOSTLY VISION.

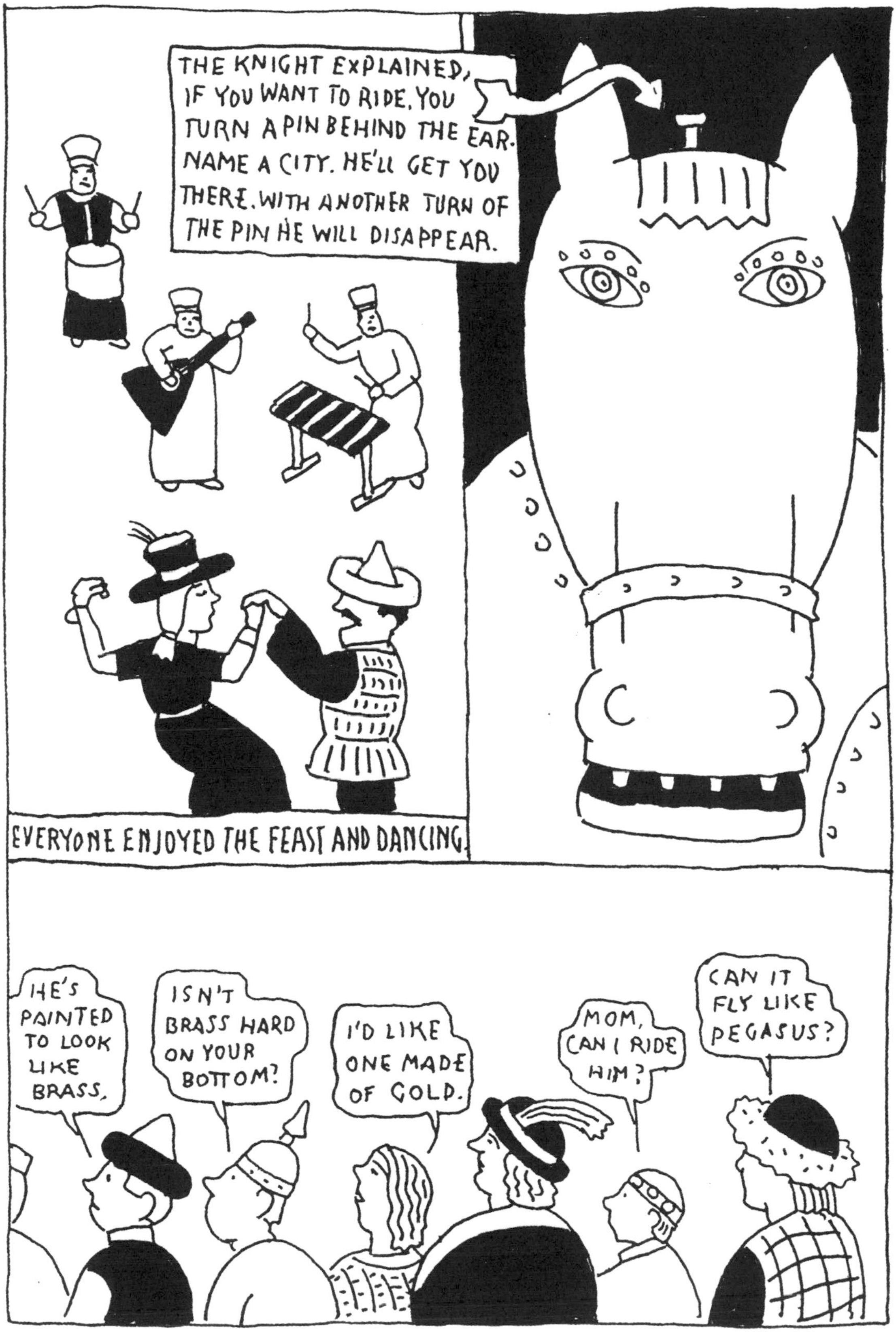
THE KNIGHT EXPLAINED, IF YOU WANT TO RIDE, YOU TURN A PIN BEHIND THE EAR. NAME A CITY. HE'LL GET YOU THERE. WITH ANOTHER TURN OF THE PIN HE WILL DISAPPEAR.
EVERYONE ENJOYED THE FEAST AND DANCING.
HE'S PAINTED TO LOOK LIKE BRASS.
ISN'T BRASS HARD ON YOUR BOTTOM?
I'D LIKE ONE MADE OF GOLD.
MOM, CAN I RIDE HIM?
CAN IT FLY LIKE PEGASUS?

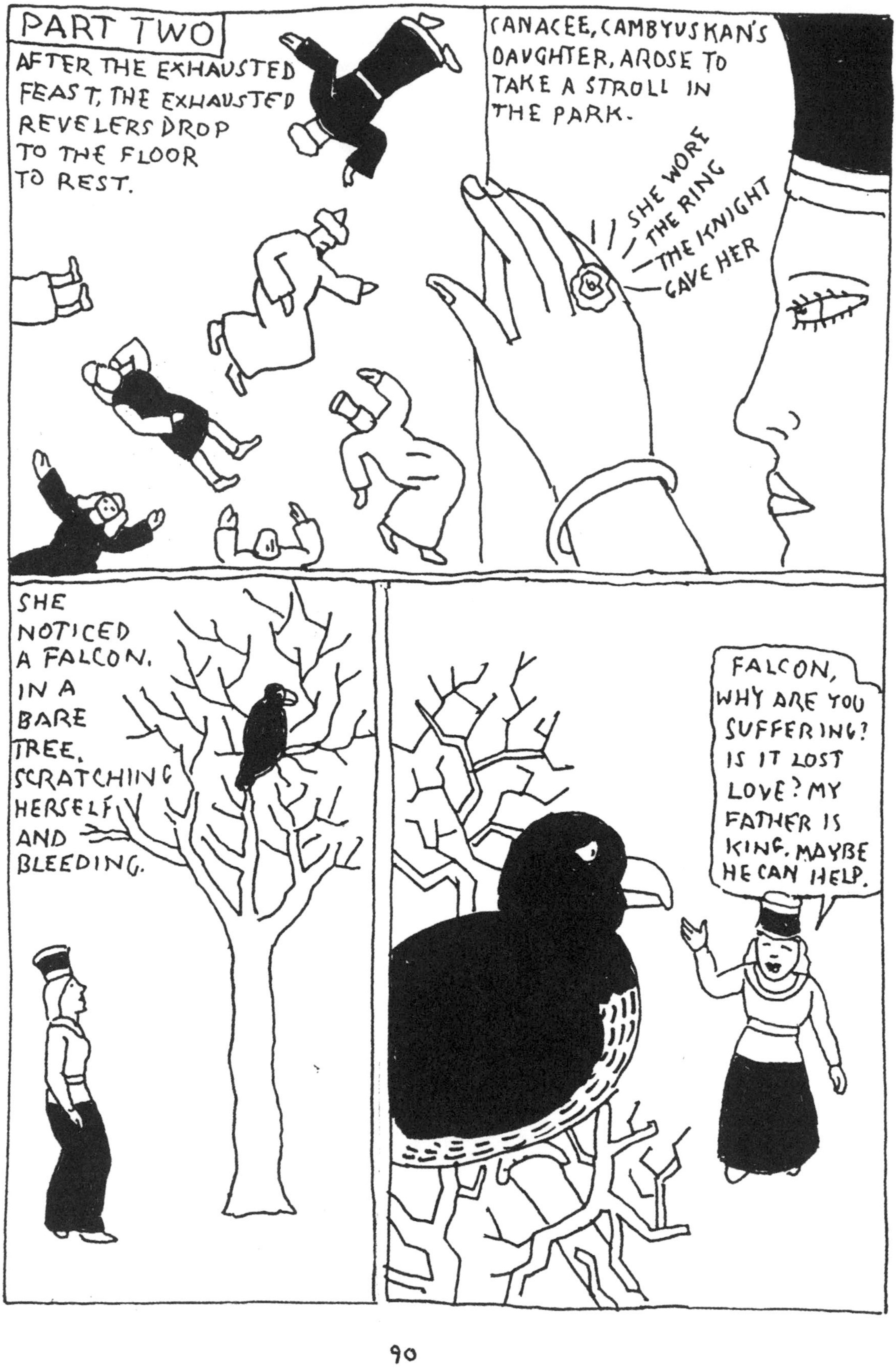
PART TWO
AFTER THE EXHAUSTED FEAST, THE EXHAUSTED REVELERS DROP TO THE FLOOR TO REST.
CANACEE, CAMBYUSKAN'S DAUGHTER, AROSE TO TAKE A STROLL IN THE PARK.
SHE WORE THE RING THE KNIGHT GAVE HER
SHE NOTICED A FALCON. IN A BARE TREE. SCRATCHING HERSELF AND BLEEDING.
FALCON, WHY ARE YOU SUFFERING? IS IT LOST LOVE? MY FATHER IS KING. MAYBE HE CAN HELP.

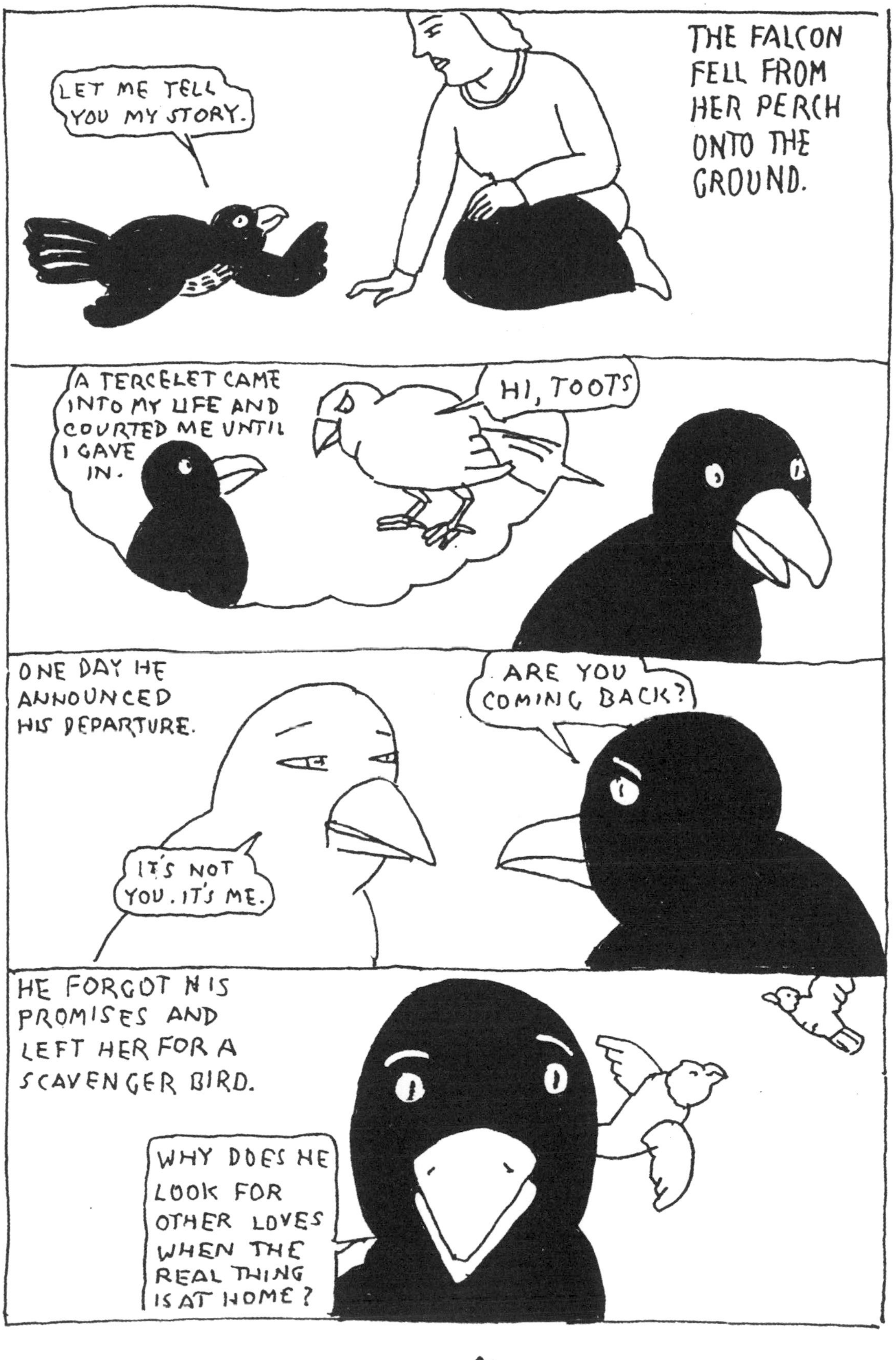
LET ME TELL YOU MY STORY.
THE FALCON FELL FROM HER PERCH ONTO THE GROUND.
A TERCELET CAME INTO MY LIFE AND COURTED ME UNTIL I GAVE IN.
HI, TOOTS
ONE DAY HE ANNOUNCED HIS DEPARTURE.
ARE YOU COMING BACK?
IT'S NOT YOU. IT'S ME.
HE FORGOT HIS PROMISES AND LEFT HER FOR A SCAVENGER BIRD.
WHY DOES HE LOOK FOR OTHER LOVES WHEN THE REAL THING IS AT HOME?

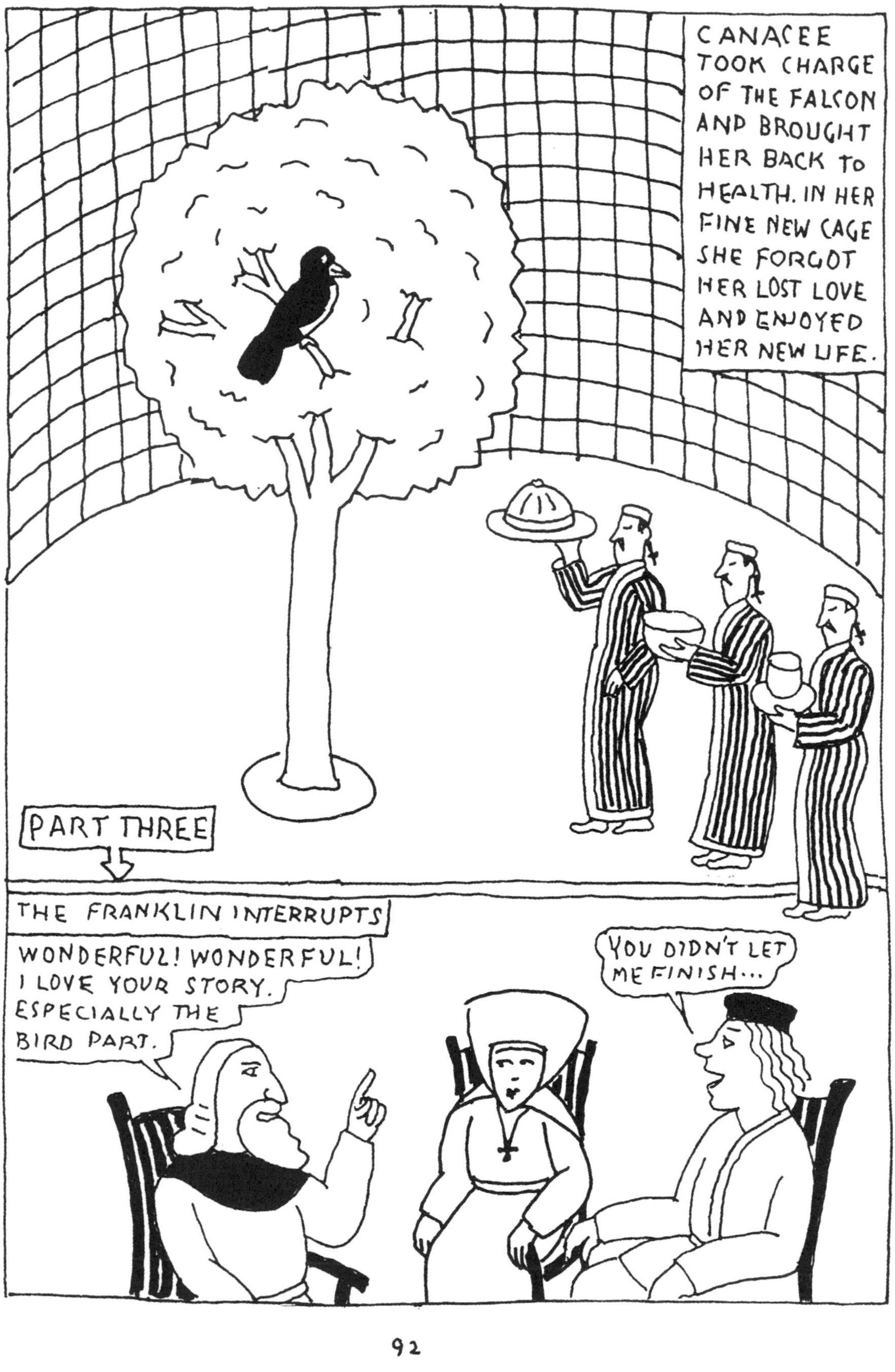
CANACEE TOOK CHARGE OF THE FALCON AND BROUGHT HER BACK TO HEALTH. IN HER FINE NEW CAGE SHE FORGOT HER LOST LOVE AND ENJOYED HER NEW LIFE.
PART THREE
THE FRANKLIN INTERRUPTS
WONDERFUL! WONDERFUL! I LOVE YOUR STORY. ESPECIALLY THE BIRD PART.
YOU DIDN'T LET ME FINISH...

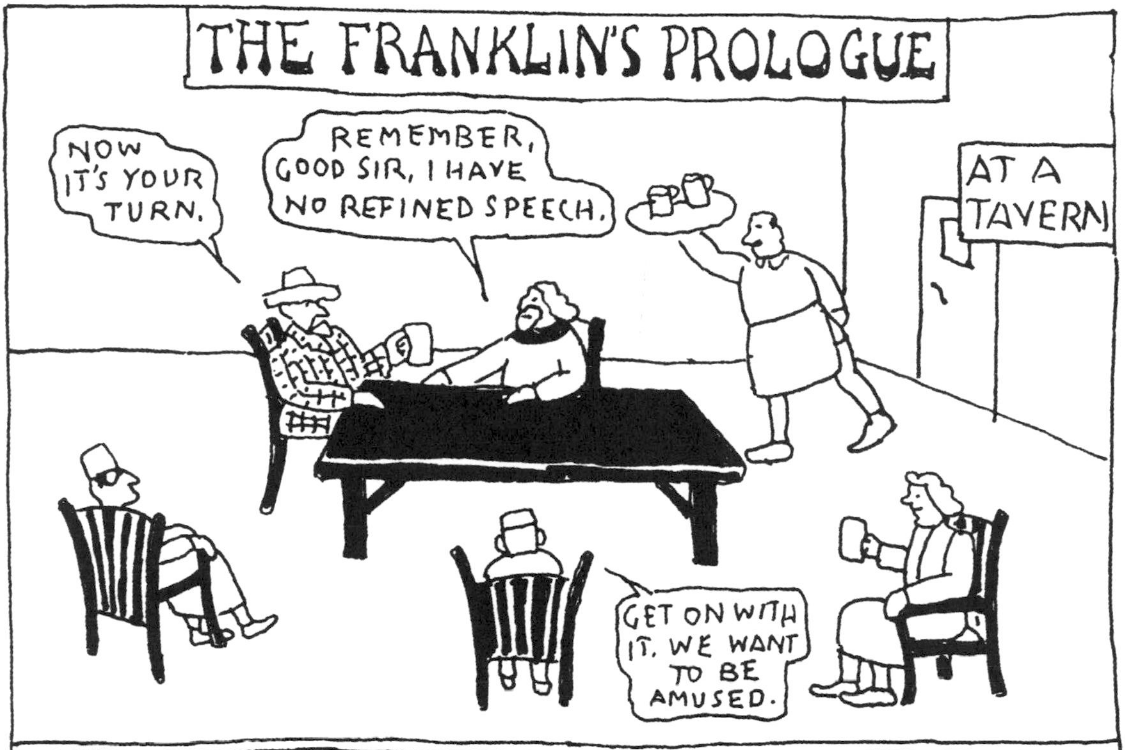
THE FRANKLIN'S PROLOGUE
NOW IT'S YOUR TURN.
REMEMBER, GOOD SIR, I HAVE NO REFINED SPEECH.
AT A TAVERN
GET ON WITH IT. WE WANT TO BE AMUSED.

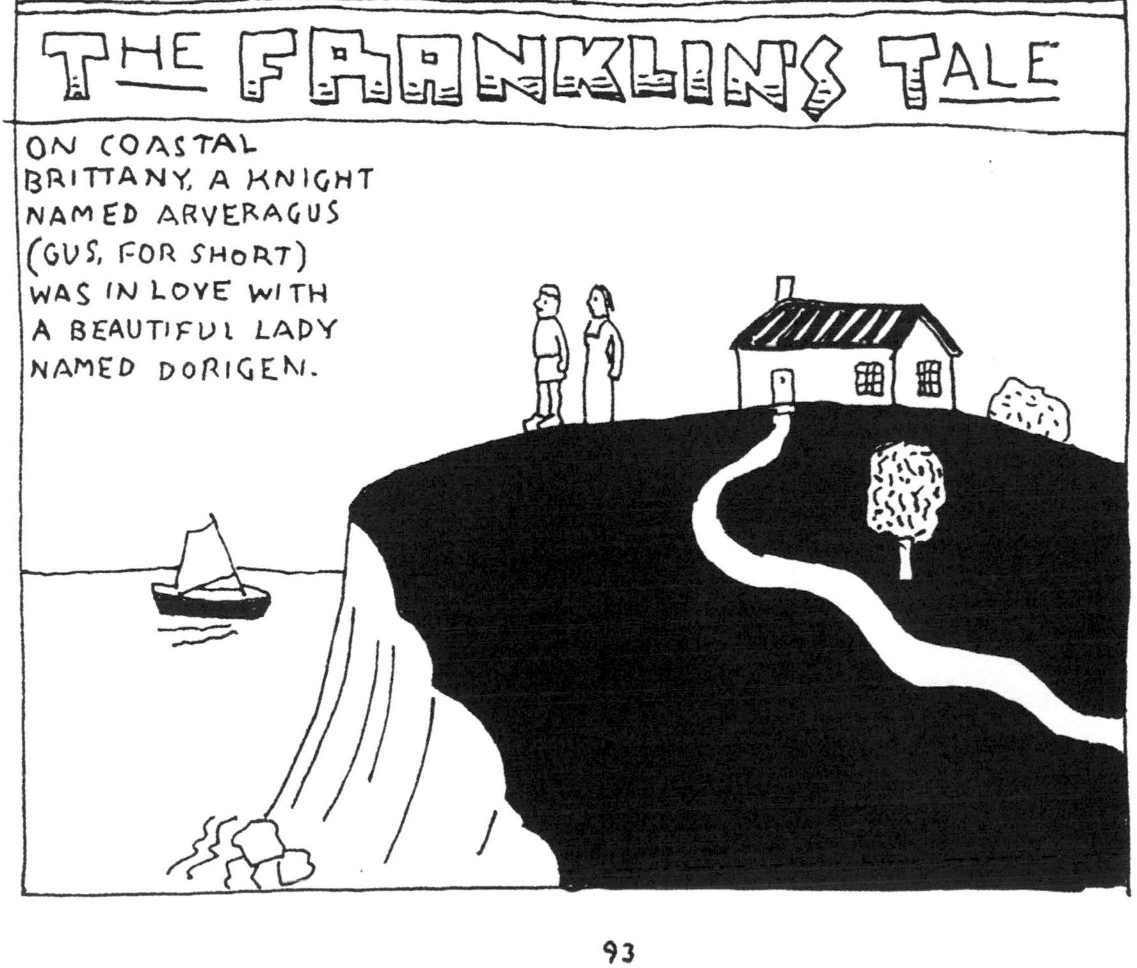
THE FRANKLIN'S TALE
ON COASTAL BRITTANY, A KNIGHT NAMED ARVERAGUS (GUS, FOR SHORT) WAS IN LOVE WITH A BEAUTIFUL LADY NAMED DORIGEN.

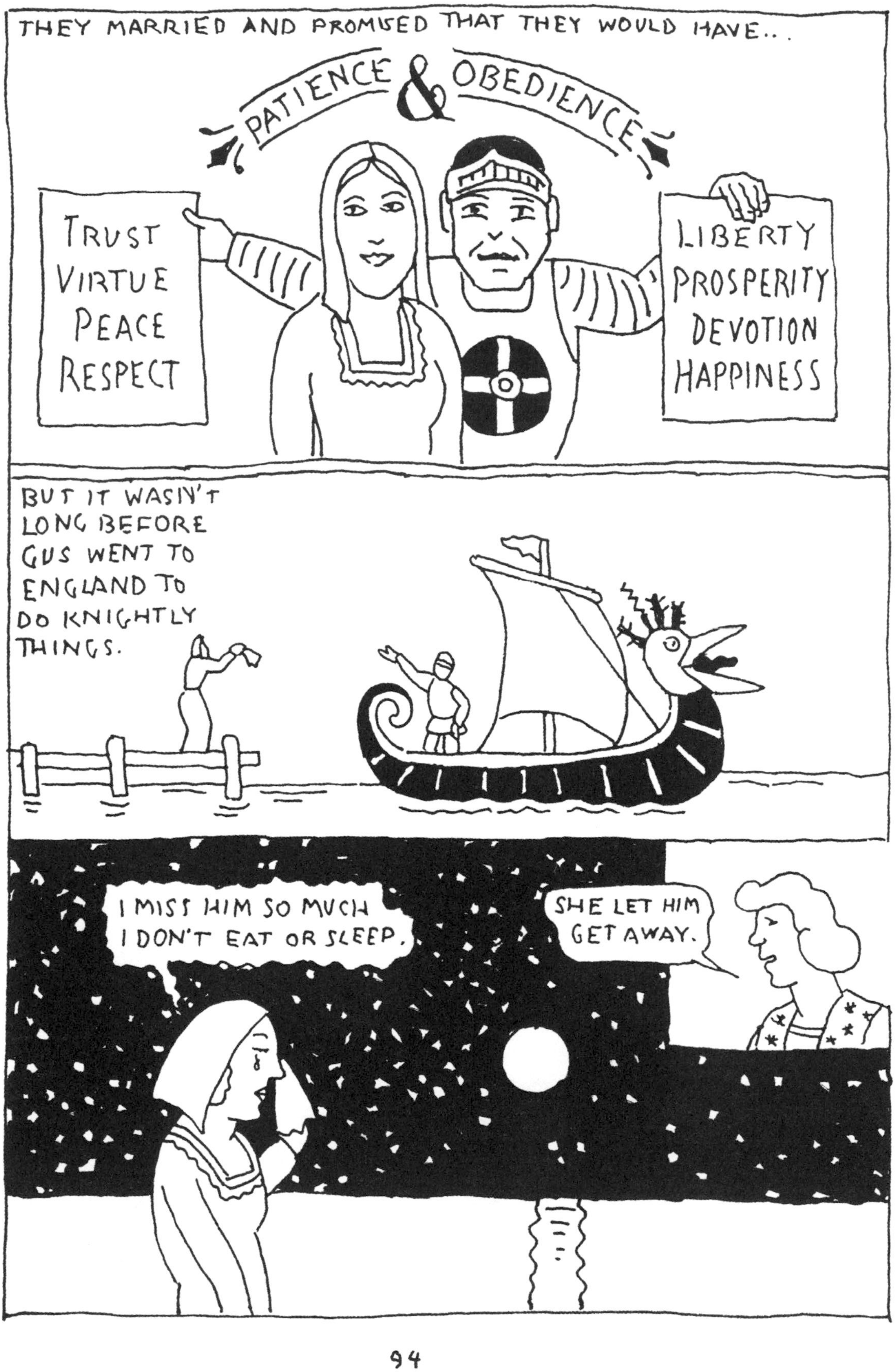
THEY MARRIED AND PROMISED THAT THEY WOULD HAVE...
PATIENCE & OBEDIENCE
TRUST
VIRTUE
PEACE
RESPECT
LIBERTY
PROSPERITY
DEVOTION
HAPPINESS
BUT IT WASN'T LONG BEFORE GUS WENT TO ENGLAND TO DO KNIGHTLY THINGS.
I MISS HIM SO MUCH I DON'T EAT OR SLEEP.
SHE LET HIM GET AWAY.

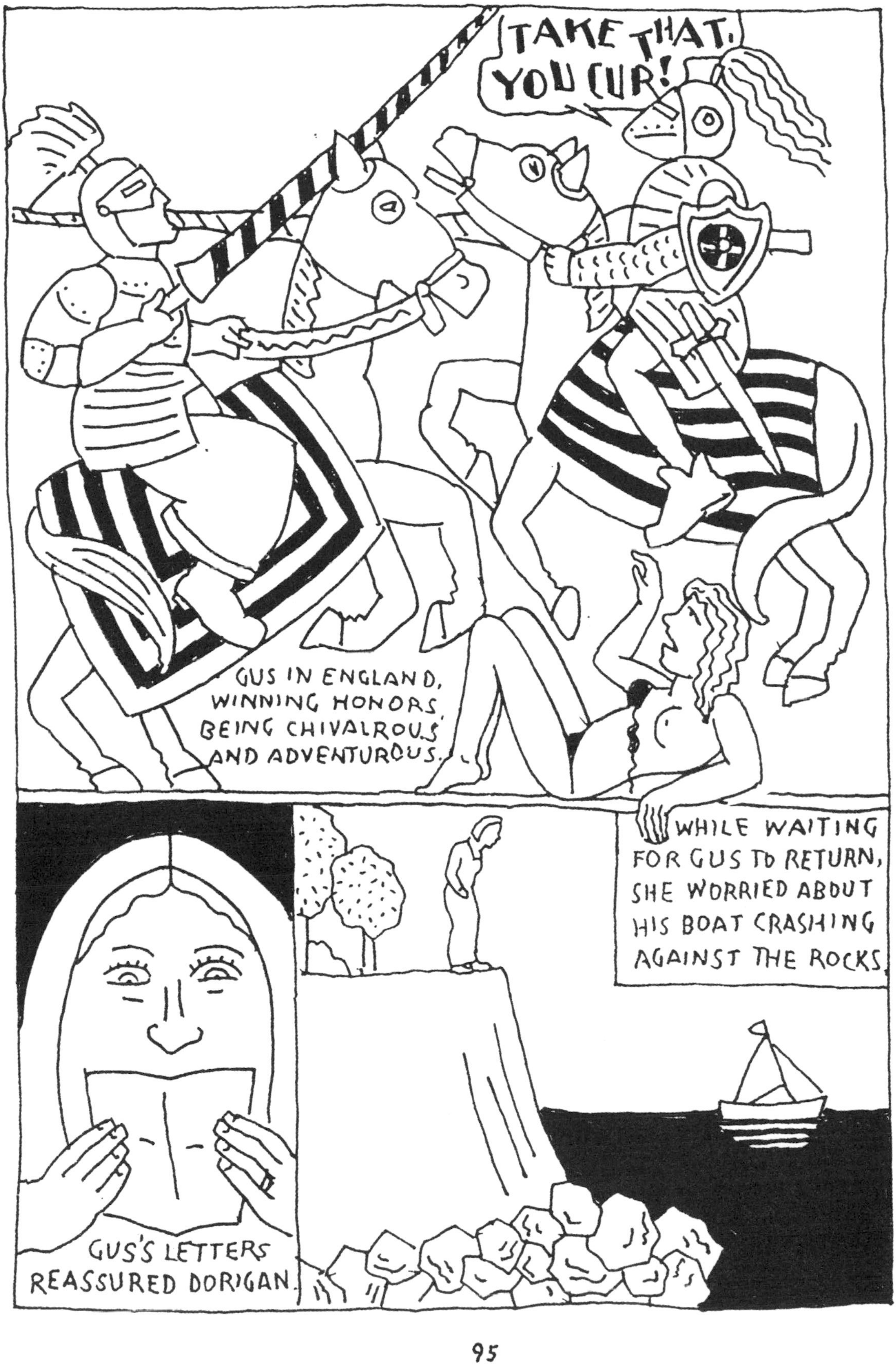
TAKE THAT, YOU CUR!
GUS IN ENGLAND, WINNING HONORS, BEING CHIVALROUS AND ADVENTUROUS.
GUS'S LETTERS REASSURED DORIGAN.
WHILE WAITING FOR GUS TO RETURN, SHE WORRIED ABOUT HIS BOAT CRASHING AGAINST THE ROCKS.

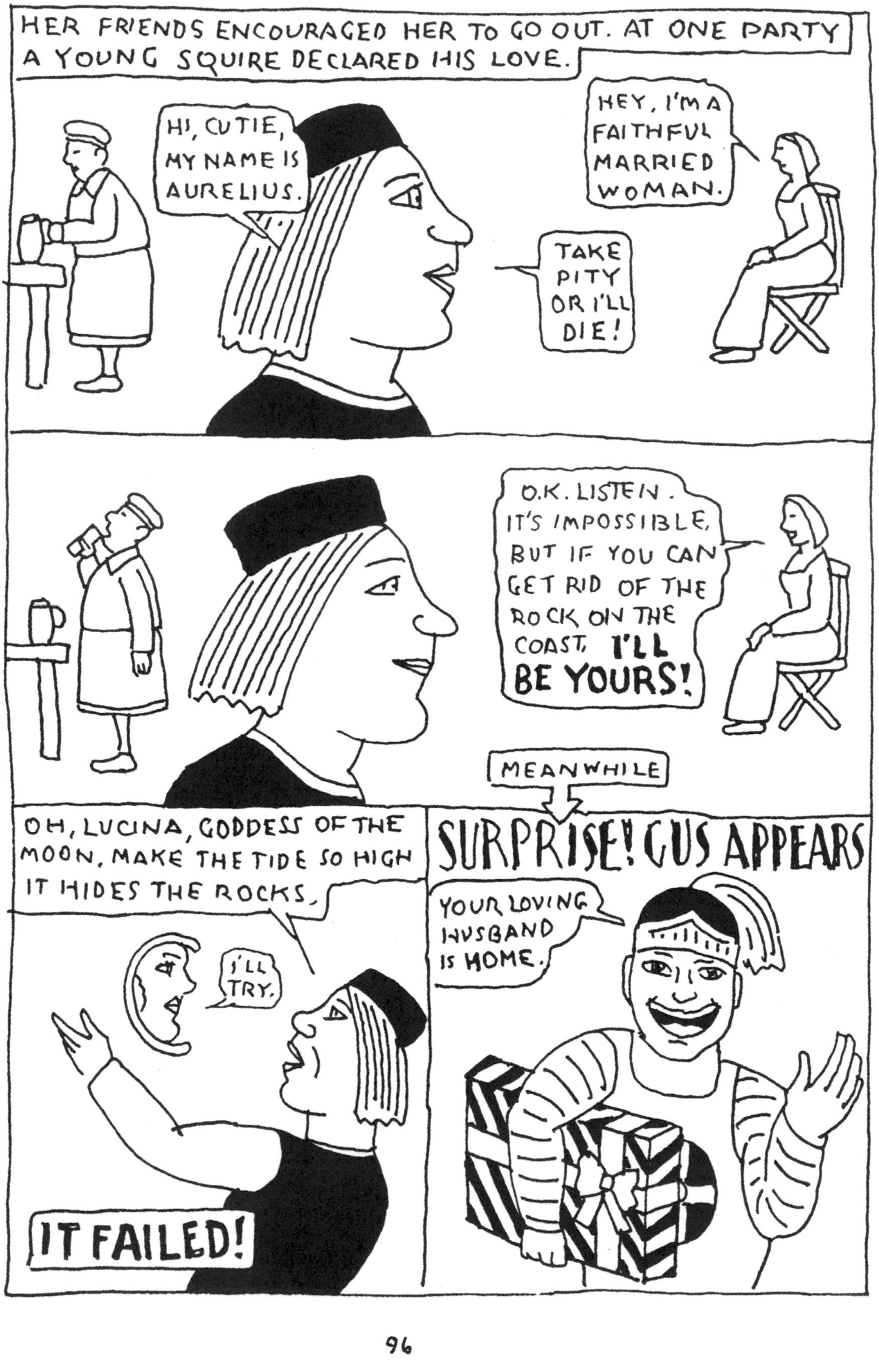
HER FRIENDS ENCOURAGED HER TO GO OUT. AT ONE PARTY A YOUNG SQUIRE DECLARED HIS LOVE.
HI, CUTIE, MY NAME IS AURELIUS.
HEY, I'M A FAITHFUL MARRIED WOMAN.
TAKE PITY OR I'LL DIE!
O.K. LISTEN. IT'S IMPOSSIBLE, BUT IF YOU CAN GET RID OF THE ROCK ON THE COAST, I'LL BE YOURS!
OH, LUCINA, GODDESS OF THE MOON, MAKE THE TIDE SO HIGH IT HIDES THE ROCKS.
I'LL TRY.
IT FAILED!
MEANWHILE
SURPRISE! GUS APPEARS
YOUR LOVING HUSBAND IS HOME.

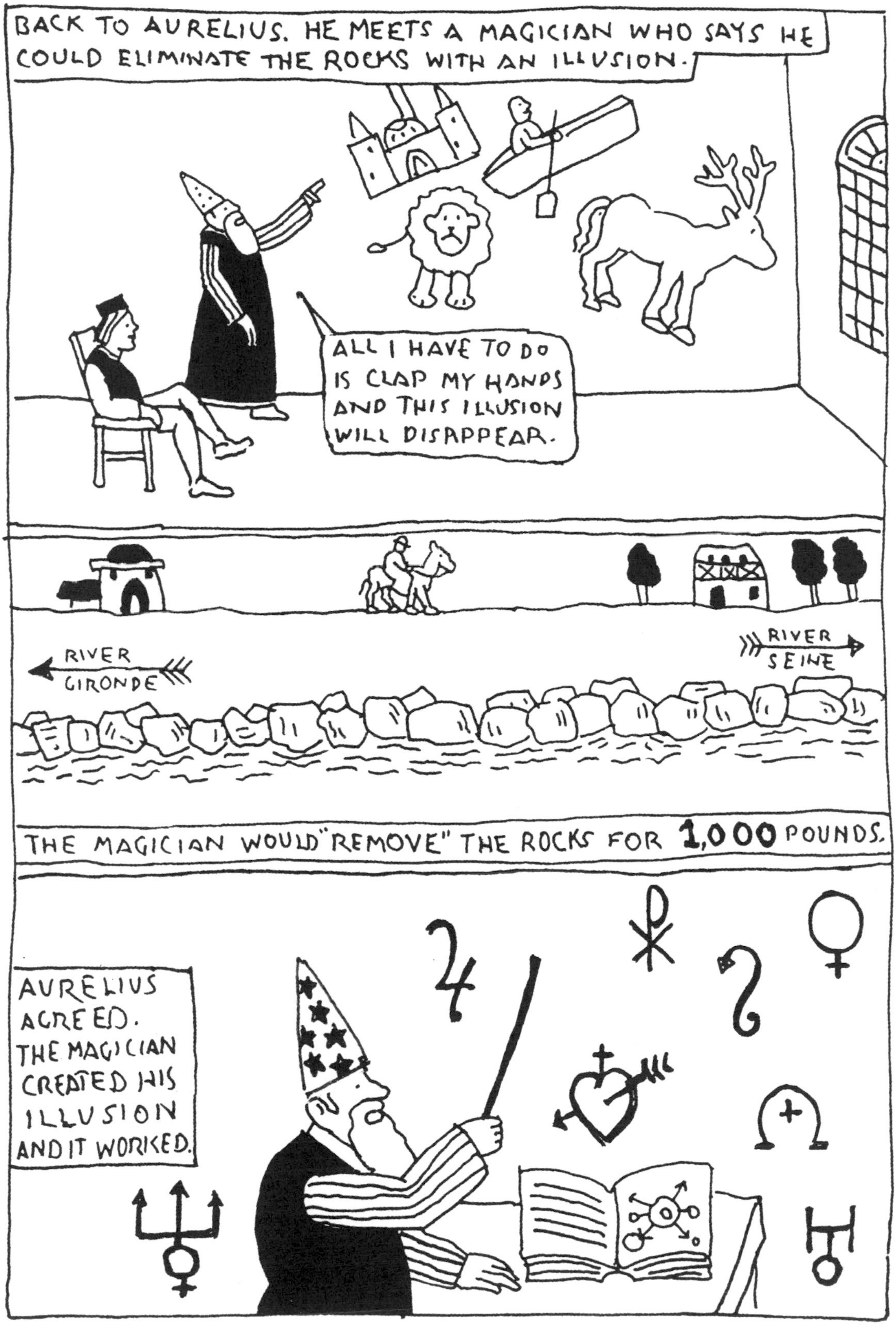
BACK TO AURELIUS. HE MEETS A MAGICIAN WHO SAYS HE COULD ELIMINATE THE ROCKS WITH AN ILLUSION.
ALL I HAVE TO DO IS CLAP MY HANDS AND THIS ILLUSION WILL DISAPPEAR.
RIVER GIRONDE
RIVER SEINE
THE MAGICIAN WOULD "REMOVE" THE ROCKS FOR 1,000 POUNDS.
AURELIUS AGREED. THE MAGICIAN CREATED HIS ILLUSION AND IT WORKED.

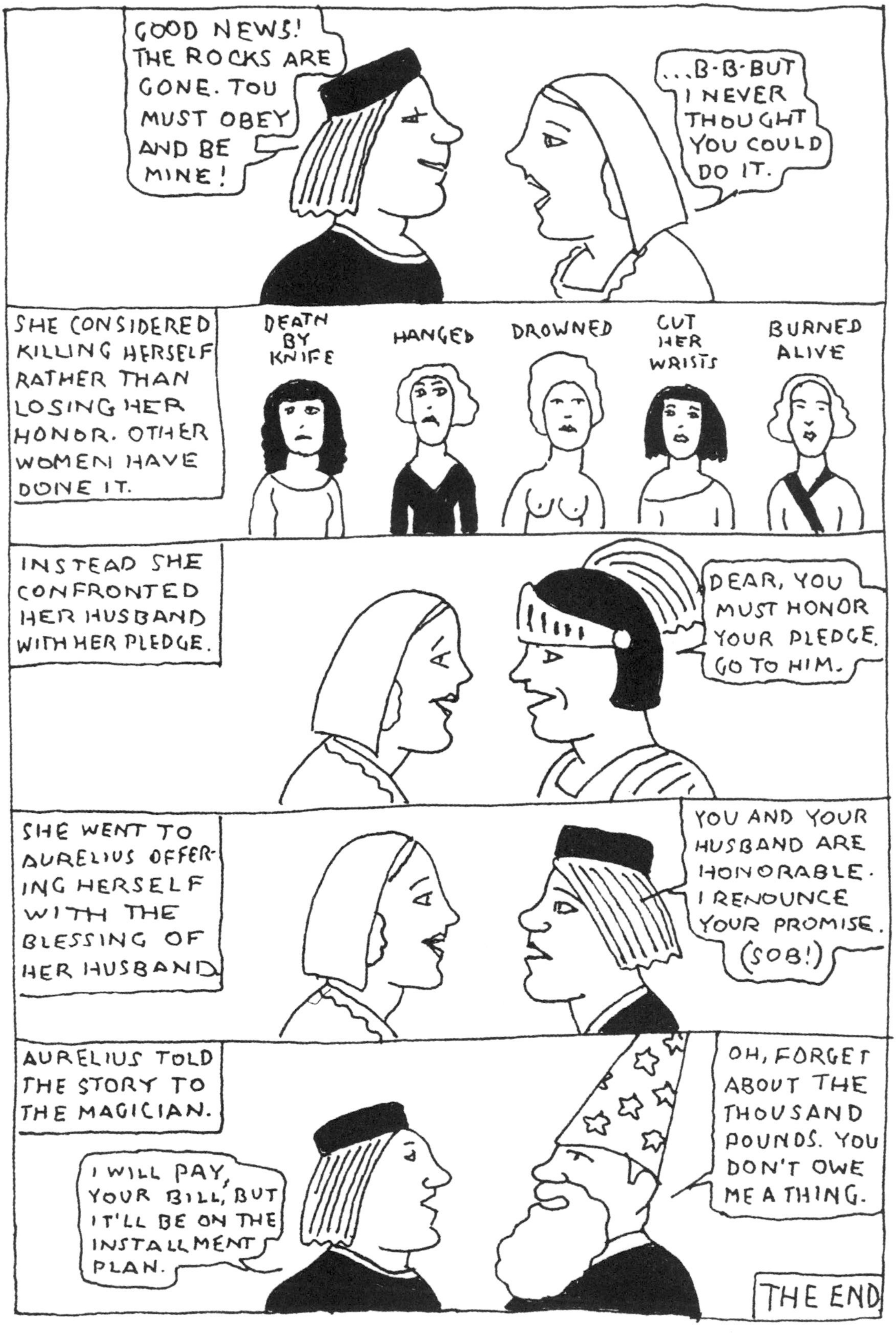
GOOD NEWS! THE ROCKS ARE GONE. TOU MUST OBEY AND BE MINE!
...B-B-BUT I NEVER THOUGHT YOU COULD DO IT.
SHE CONSIDERED KILLING HERSELF RATHER THAN LOSING HER HONOR. OTHER WOMEN HAVE DONE IT.
DEATH BY KNIFE
HANGED
DROWNED
CUT HER WRISTS
BURNED ALIVE
INSTEAD SHE CONFRONTED HER HUSBAND WITH HER PLEDGE.
DEAR, YOU MUST HONOR YOUR PLEDGE. GO TO HIM.
SHE WENT TO AURELIUS OFFER-ING HERSELF WITH THE BLESSING OF HER HUSBAND.
YOU AND YOUR HUSBAND ARE HONORABLE. I RENOUNCE YOUR PROMISE. (SOB!)
AURELIUS TOLD THE STORY TO THE MAGICIAN.
I WILL PAY, YOUR BILL, BUT IT'LL BE ON THE INSTALLMENT PLAN.
OH, FORGET ABOUT THE THOUSAND POUNDS. YOU DON'T OWE ME A THING.
THE END

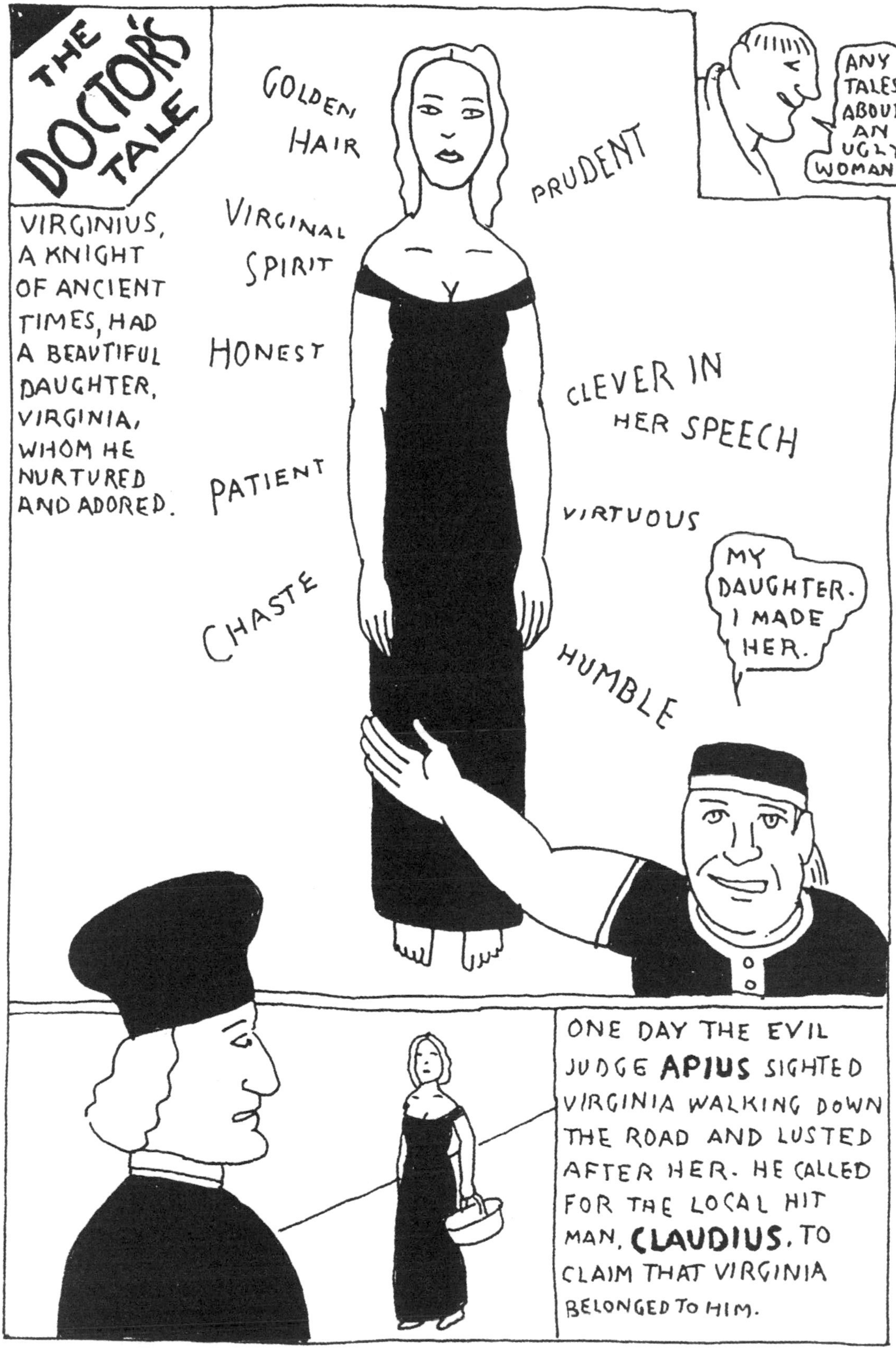

THE DOCTOR'S TALE
VIRGINIUS, A KNIGHT OF ANCIENT TIMES, HAD A BEAUTIFUL DAUGHTER, VIRGINIA, WHOM HE NURTURED AND ADORED.
GOLDEN HAIR
VIRGINAL SPIRIT
HONEST
PATIENT
CHASTE
PRUDENT
CLEVER IN HER SPEECH
VIRTUOUS
HUMBLE
ANY TALES ABOUT AN UGLY WOMAN?
MY DAUGHTER. I MADE HER.
ONE DAY THE EVIL JUDGE APIUS SIGHTED VIRGINIA WALKING DOWN THE ROAD AND LUSTED AFTER HER. HE CALLED FOR THE LOCAL HIT MAN, CLAUDIUS, TO CLAIM THAT VIRGINIA BELONGED TO HIM.

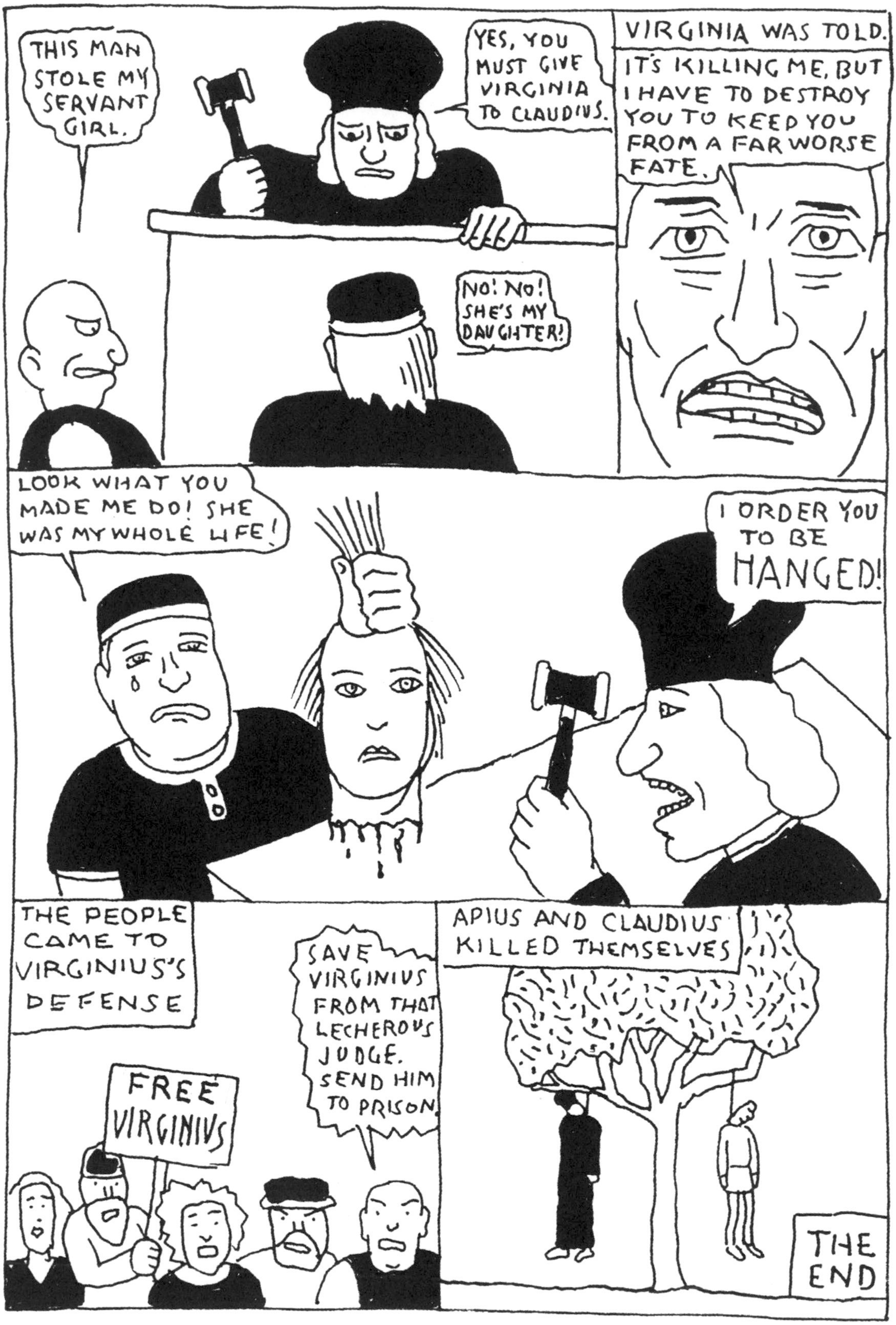
THIS MAN STOLE MY SERVANT GIRL.
YES, YOU MUST GIVE VIRGINIA TO CLAUDIUS.
NO! NO! SHE'S MY DAUGHTER!
VIRGINIA WAS TOLD.
IT'S KILLING ME, BUT I HAVE TO DESTROY YOU TO KEEP YOU FROM A FAR WORSE FATE.
LOOK WHAT YOU MADE ME DO! SHE WAS MY WHOLE LIFE!
I ORDER YOU TO BE HANGED!
THE PEOPLE CAME TO VIRGINIUS'S DEFENSE
SAVE VIRGINIUS FROM THAT LECHEROUS JUDGE. SEND HIM TO PRISON.
FREE VIRGINIUS
APIUS AND CLAUDIUS KILLED THEMSELVES
THE END

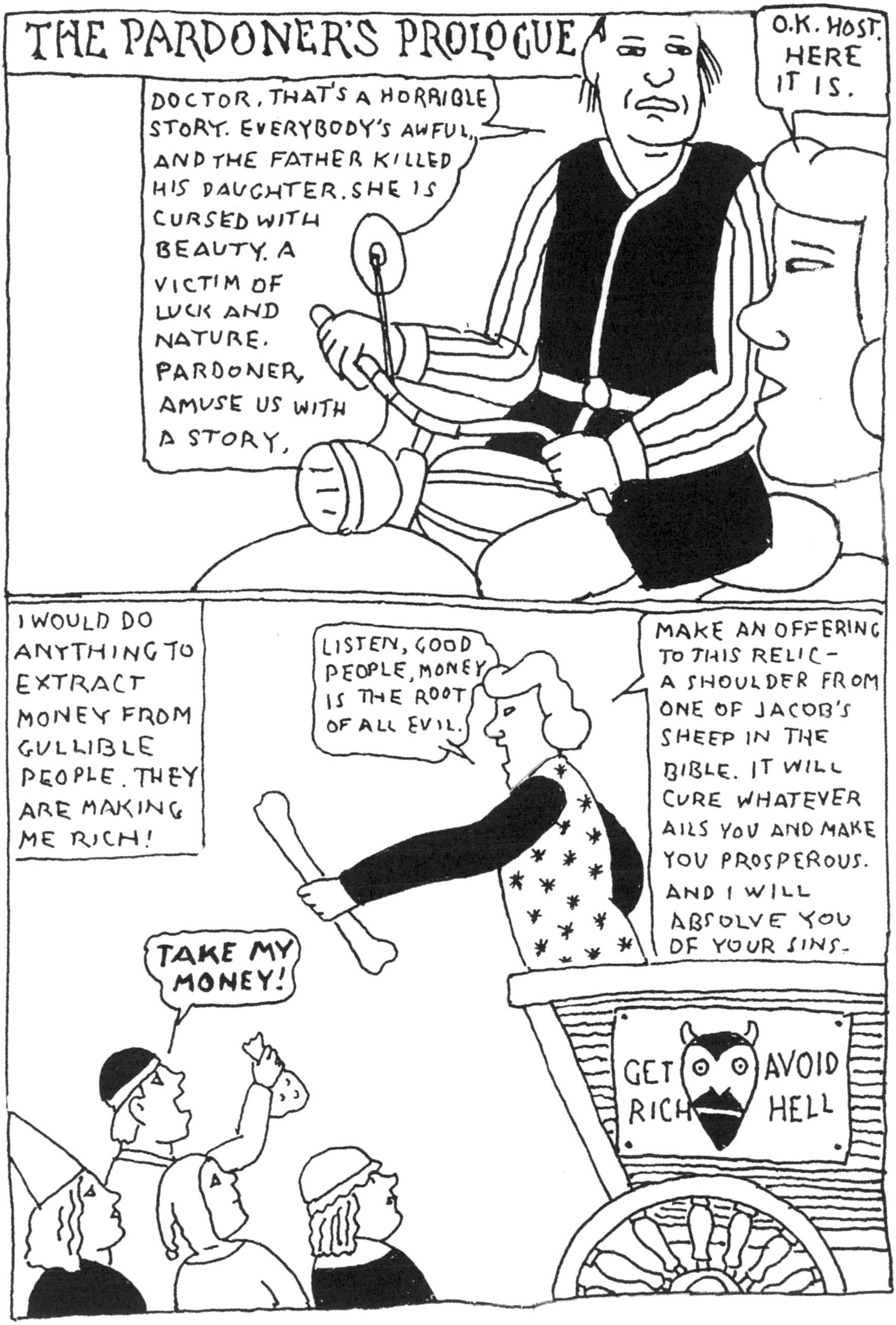
THE PARDONER'S PROLOGUE
DOCTOR, THAT'S A HORRIBLE STORY. EVERYBODY'S AWFUL, AND THE FATHER KILLED HIS DAUGHTER. SHE IS CURSED WITH BEAUTY. A VICTIM OF LUCK AND NATURE. PARDONER, AMUSE US WITH A STORY.
O.K. HOST. HERE IT IS.
I WOULD DO ANYTHING TO EXTRACT MONEY FROM GULLIBLE PEOPLE. THEY ARE MAKING ME RICH!
LISTEN, GOOD PEOPLE, MONEY IS THE ROOT OF ALL EVIL.
MAKE AN OFFERING TO THIS RELIC - A SHOULDER FROM ONE OF JACOB'S SHEEP IN THE BIBLE. IT WILL CURE WHATEVER AILS YOU AND MAKE YOU PROSPEROUS. AND I WILL ABSOLVE YOU OF YOUR SINS.
TAKE MY MONEY!
GET RICH
AVOID HELL

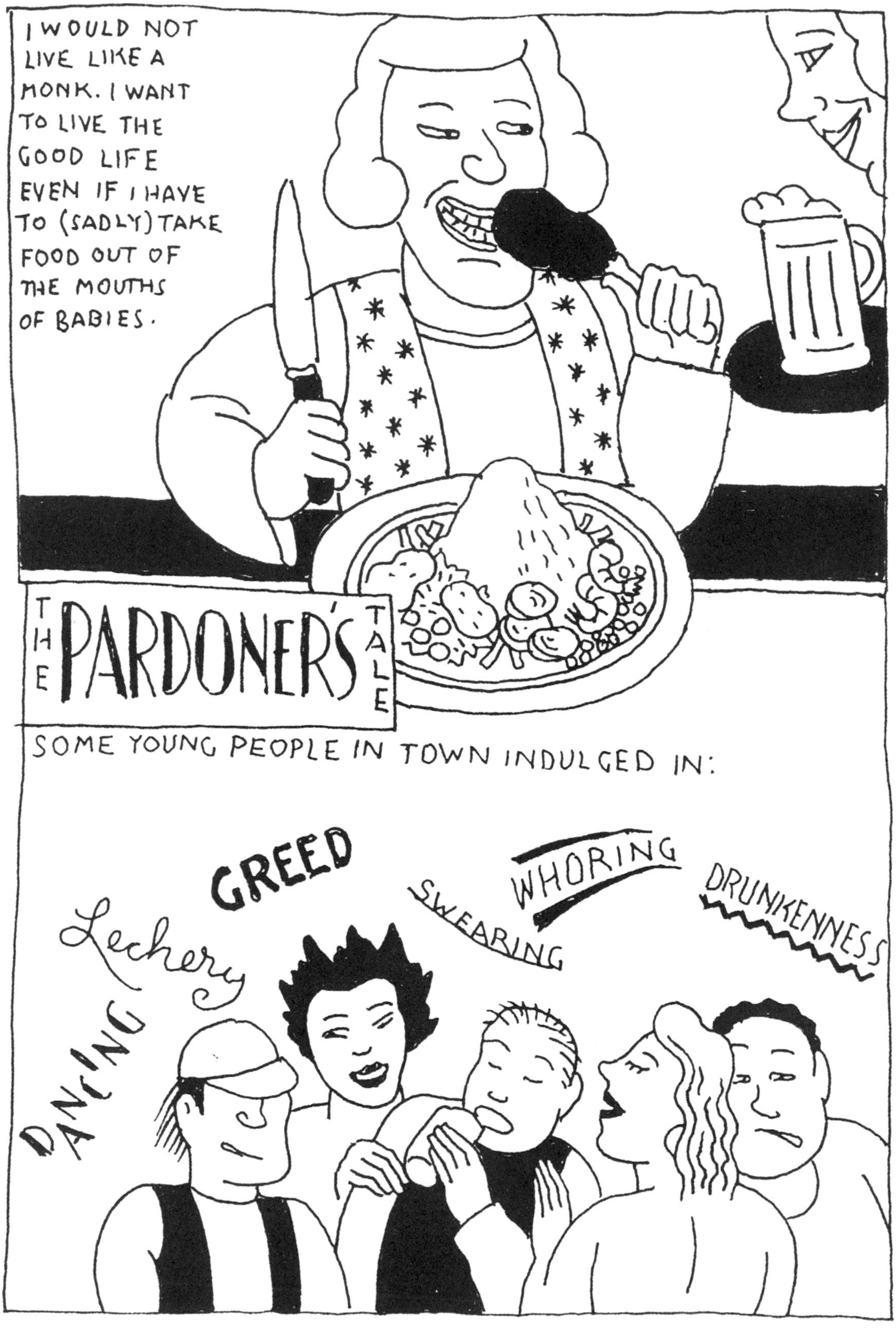
I WOULD NOT LIVE LIKE A MONK. I WANT TO LIVE THE GOOD LIFE EVEN IF I HAVE TO (SADLY) TAKE FOOD OUT OF THE MOUTHS OF BABIES.
THE PARDONER'S TALE
SOME YOUNG PEOPLE IN TOWN INDULGED IN:
DANCING
Lechery
GREED
SWEARING
WHORING
DRUNKENNESS

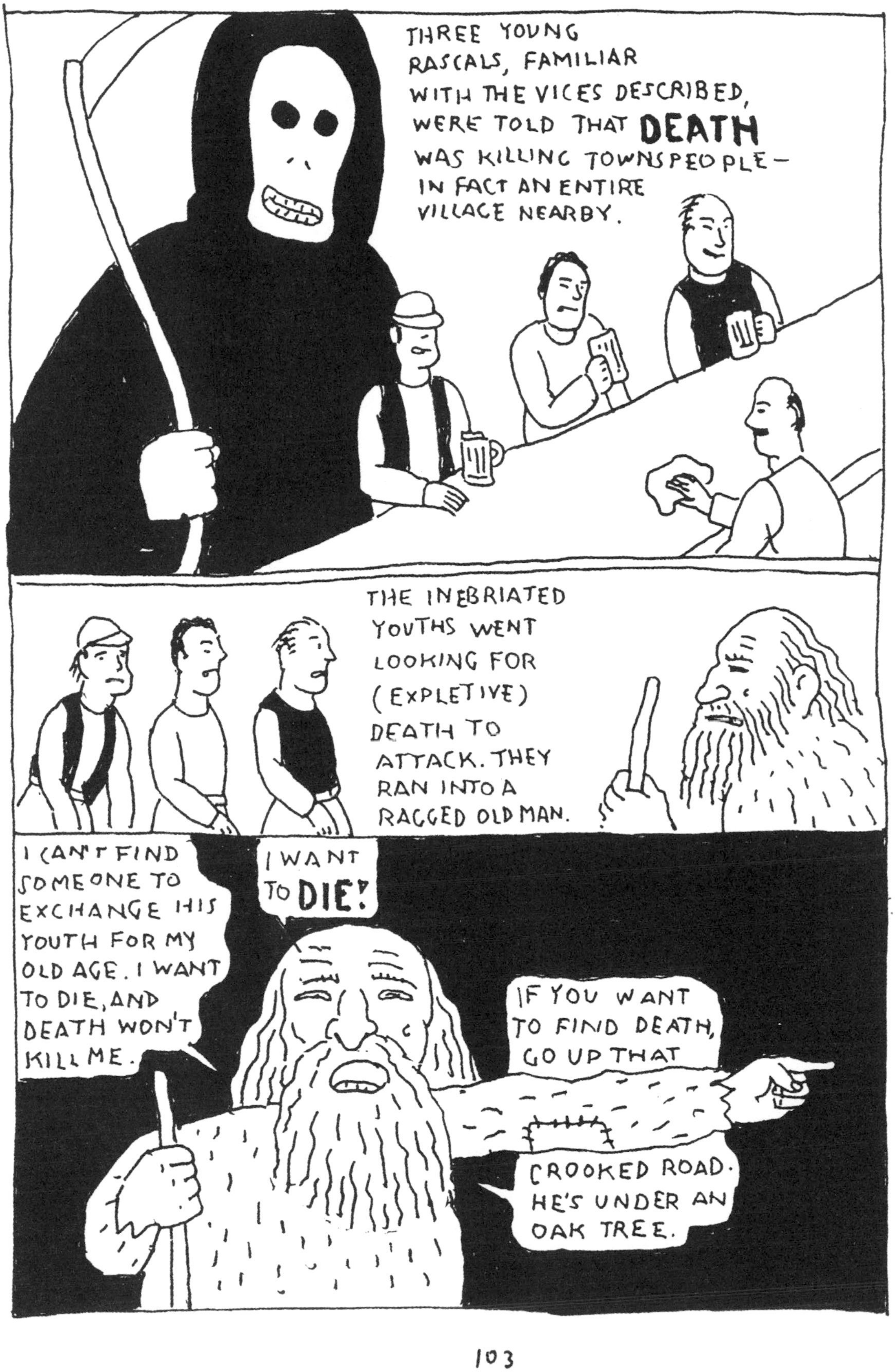
THREE YOUNG RASCALS, FAMILIAR WITH THE VICES DESCRIBED, WERE TOLD THAT DEATH WAS KILLING TOWNSPEOPLE— IN FACT AN ENTIRE VILLAGE NEARBY.
THE INEBRIATED YOUTHS WENT LOOKING FOR (EXPLETIVE) DEATH TO ATTACK. THEY RAN INTO A RAGGED OLD MAN.
I CAN'T FIND SOMEONE TO EXCHANGE HIS YOUTH FOR MY OLD AGE. I WANT TO DIE, AND DEATH WON'T KILL ME.
I WANT TO DIE!
IF YOU WANT TO FIND DEATH, GO UP THAT
CROOKED ROAD. HE'S UNDER AN OAK TREE.

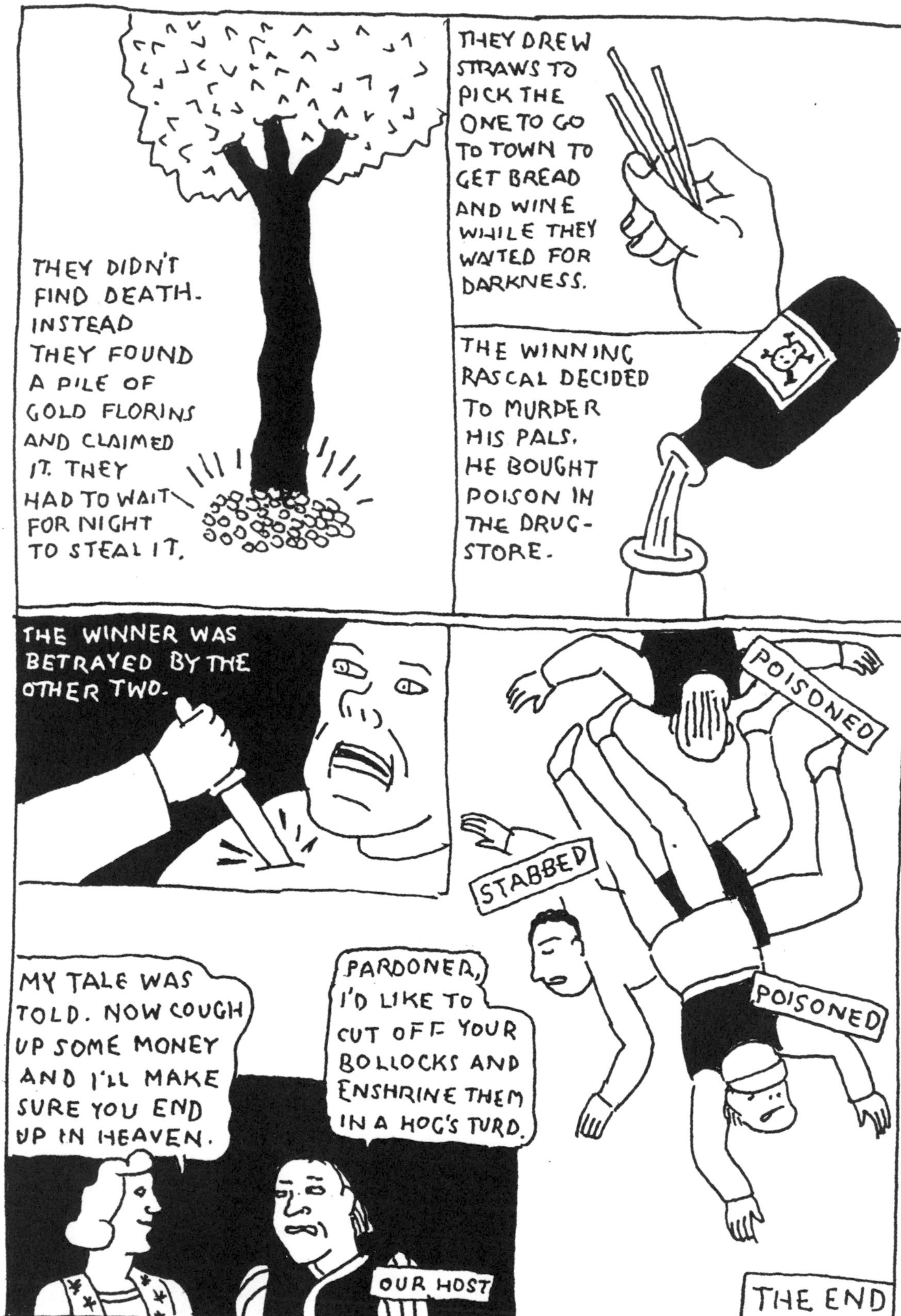
THEY DIDN'T FIND DEATH. INSTEAD THEY FOUND A PILE OF GOLD FLORINS AND CLAIMED IT. THEY HAD TO WAIT FOR NIGHT TO STEAL IT.
THEY DREW STRAWS TO PICK THE ONE TO GO TO TOWN TO GET BREAD AND WINE WHILE THEY WAITED FOR DARKNESS.
THE WINNING RASCAL DECIDED TO MURDER HIS PALS. HE BOUGHT POISON IN THE DRUG-STORE.
THE WINNER WAS BETRAYED BY THE OTHER TWO.
POISONED
STABBED
POISONED
MY TALE WAS TOLD. NOW COUGH UP SOME MONEY AND I'LL MAKE SURE YOU END UP IN HEAVEN.
PARDONER, I'D LIKE TO CUT OFF YOUR BOLLOCKS AND ENSHRINE THEM IN A HOG'S TURD.
OUR HOST
THE END

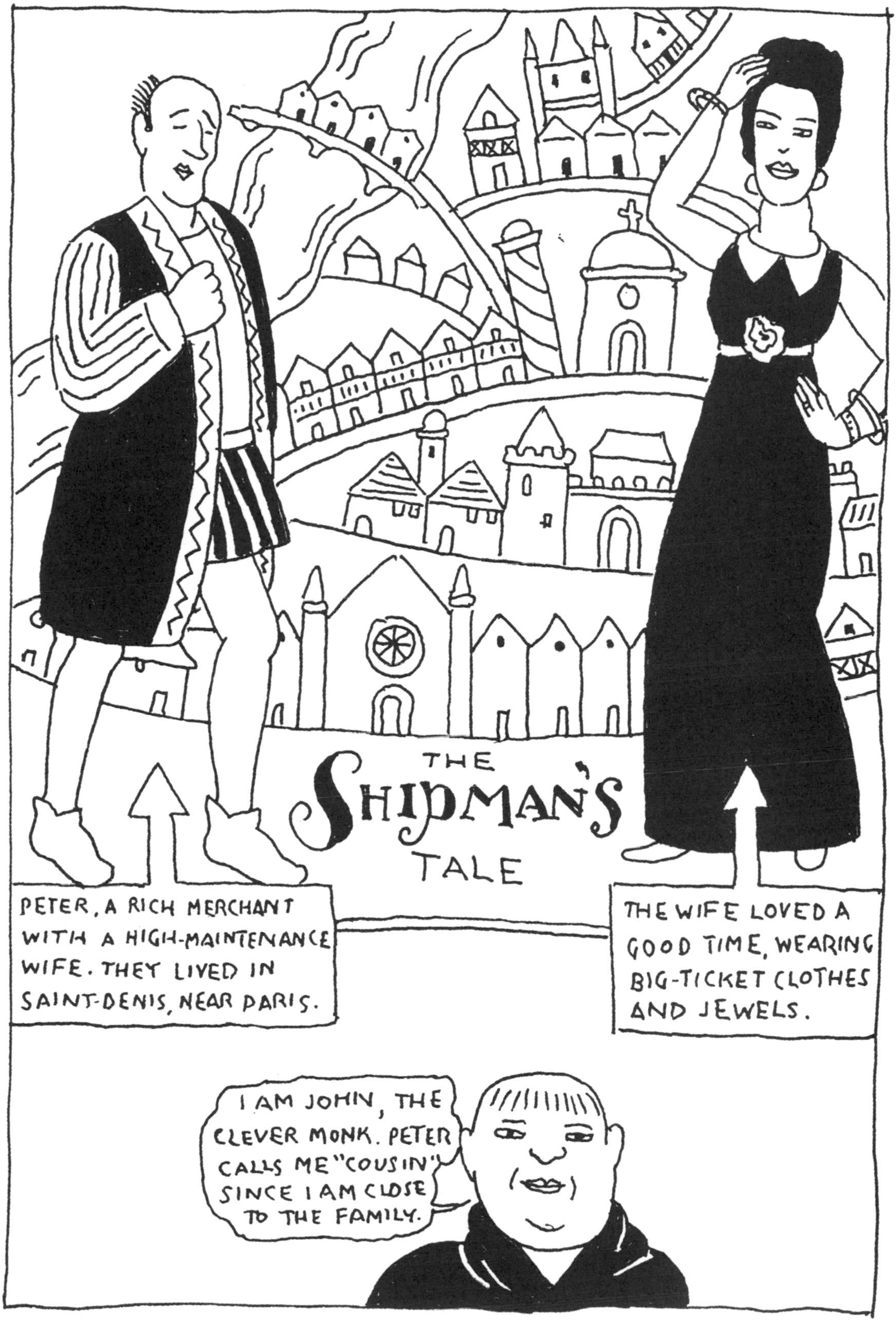
THE SHIPMAN'S TALE
PETER, A RICH MERCHANT WITH A HIGH-MAINTENANCE WIFE. THEY LIVED IN SAINT-DENIS, NEAR PARIS.
THE WIFE LOVED A GOOD TIME, WEARING BIG-TICKET CLOTHES AND JEWELS.
I AM JOHN, THE CLEVER MONK. PETER CALLS ME "COUSIN" SINCE I AM CLOSE TO THE FAMILY.

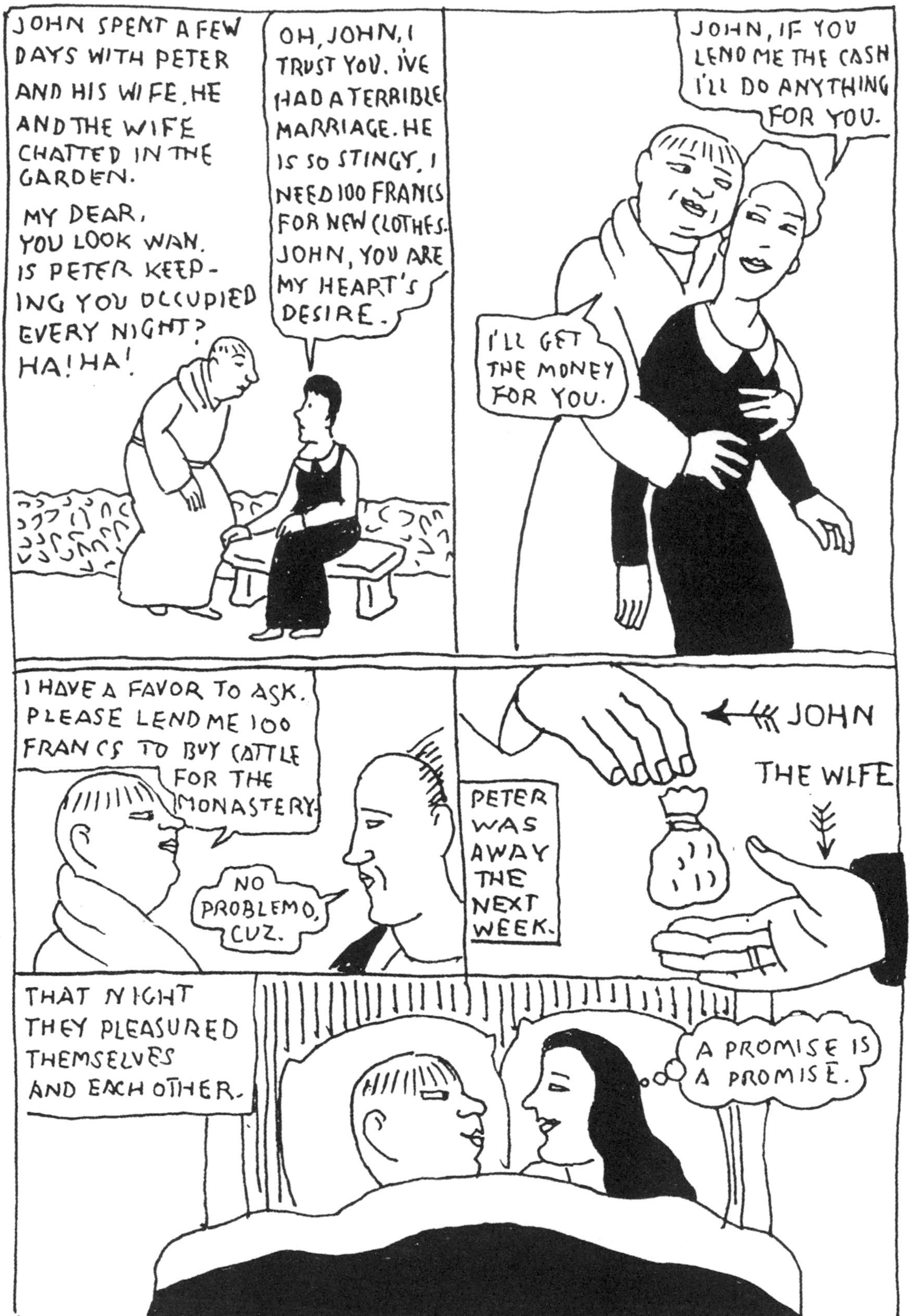
JOHN SPENT A FEW DAYS WITH PETER AND HIS WIFE. HE AND THE WIFE CHATTED IN THE GARDEN.
MY DEAR, YOU LOOK WAN. IS PETER KEEP-ING YOU OCCUPIED EVERY NIGHT? HA! HA!
OH, JOHN, I TRUST YOU. I'VE HAD A TERRIBLE MARRIAGE. HE IS SO STINGY. I NEED 100 FRANCS FOR NEW CLOTHES. JOHN, YOU ARE MY HEART'S DESIRE.
JOHN, IF YOU LEND ME THE CASH I'LL DO ANYTHING FOR YOU.
I'LL GET THE MONEY FOR YOU.
I HAVE A FAVOR TO ASK. PLEASE LEND ME 100 FRANCS TO BUY CATTLE FOR THE MONASTERY.
NO PROBLEMO, CUZ.
PETER WAS AWAY THE NEXT WEEK.
JOHN
THE WIFE
THAT NIGHT THEY PLEASURED THEMSELVES AND EACH OTHER.
A PROMISE IS A PROMISE.

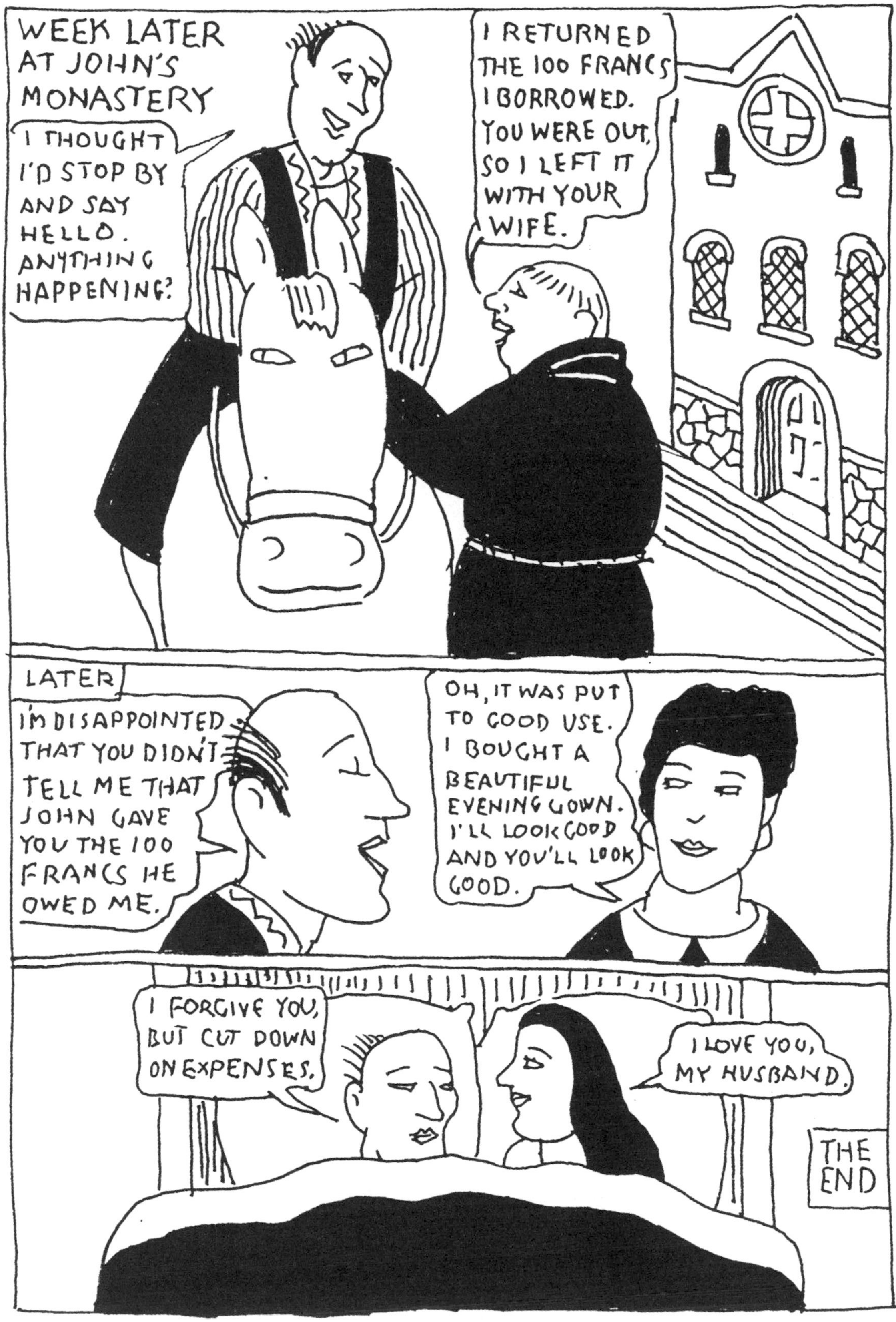
WEEK LATER AT JOHN'S MONASTERY
I THOUGHT I'D STOP BY AND SAY HELLO. ANYTHING HAPPENING?
I RETURNED THE 100 FRANCS I BORROWED. YOU WERE OUT, SO I LEFT IT WITH YOUR WIFE.
LATER
I'M DISAPPOINTED THAT YOU DIDN'T TELL ME THAT JOHN GAVE YOU THE 100 FRANCS HE OWED ME.
OH, IT WAS PUT TO GOOD USE. I BOUGHT A BEAUTIFUL EVENING GOWN. I'LL LOOK GOOD AND YOU'LL LOOK GOOD.
I FORGIVE YOU, BUT CUT DOWN ON EXPENSES.
I LOVE YOU, MY HUSBAND.
THE END

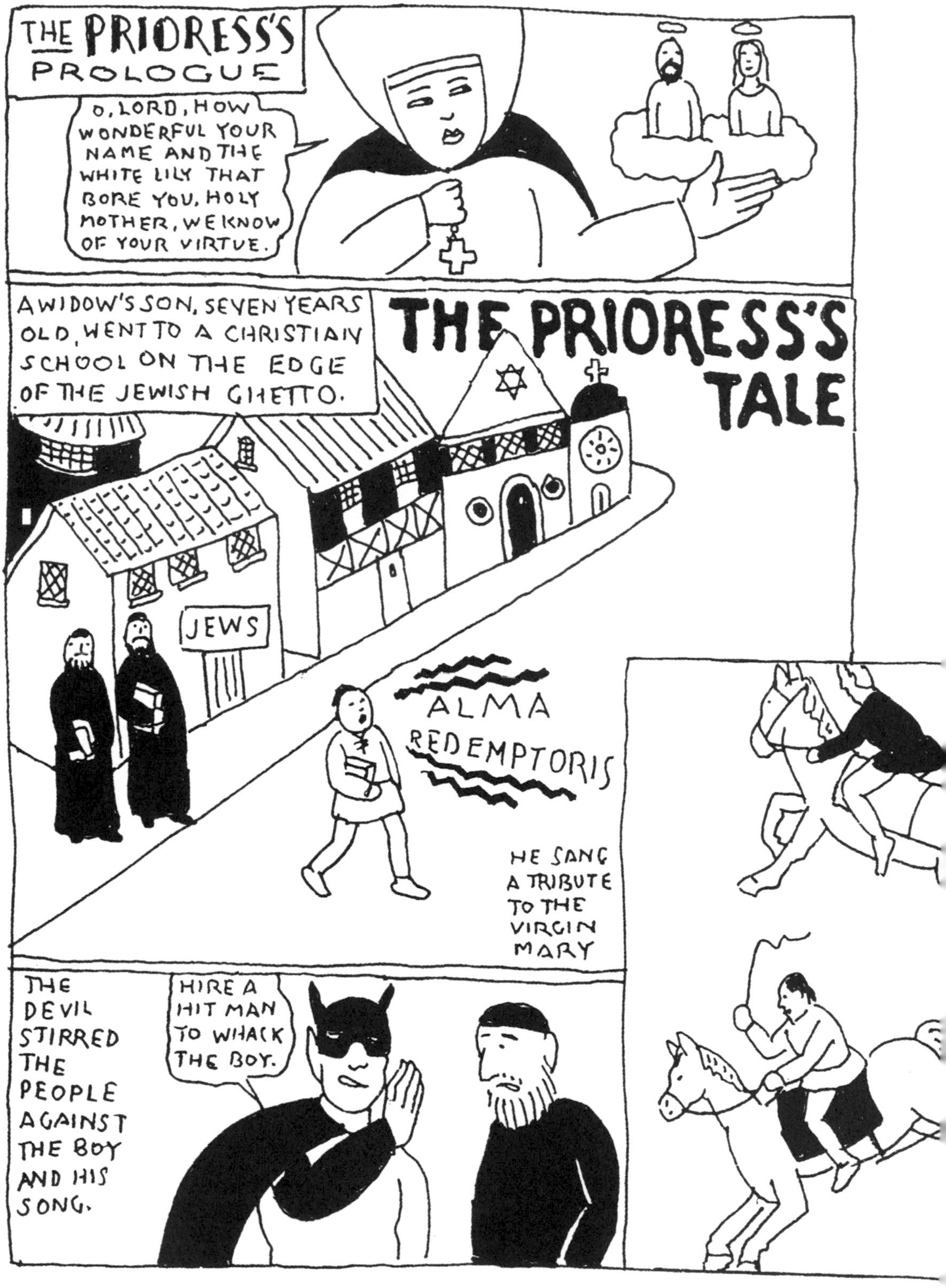
THE PRIORESS'S PROLOGUE
O, LORD, HOW WONDERFUL YOUR NAME AND THE WHITE LILY THAT BORE YOU. HOLY MOTHER, WE KNOW OF YOUR VIRTUE.
A WIDOW'S SON, SEVEN YEARS OLD, WENT TO A CHRISTIAN SCHOOL ON THE EDGE OF THE JEWISH GHETTO.
THE PRIORESS'S TALE
JEWS
ALMA REDEMPTORIS
HE SANG A TRIBUTE TO THE VIRGIN MARY
THE DEVIL STIRRED THE PEOPLE AGAINST THE BOY AND HIS SONG.
HIRE A HIT MAN TO WHACK THE BOY.

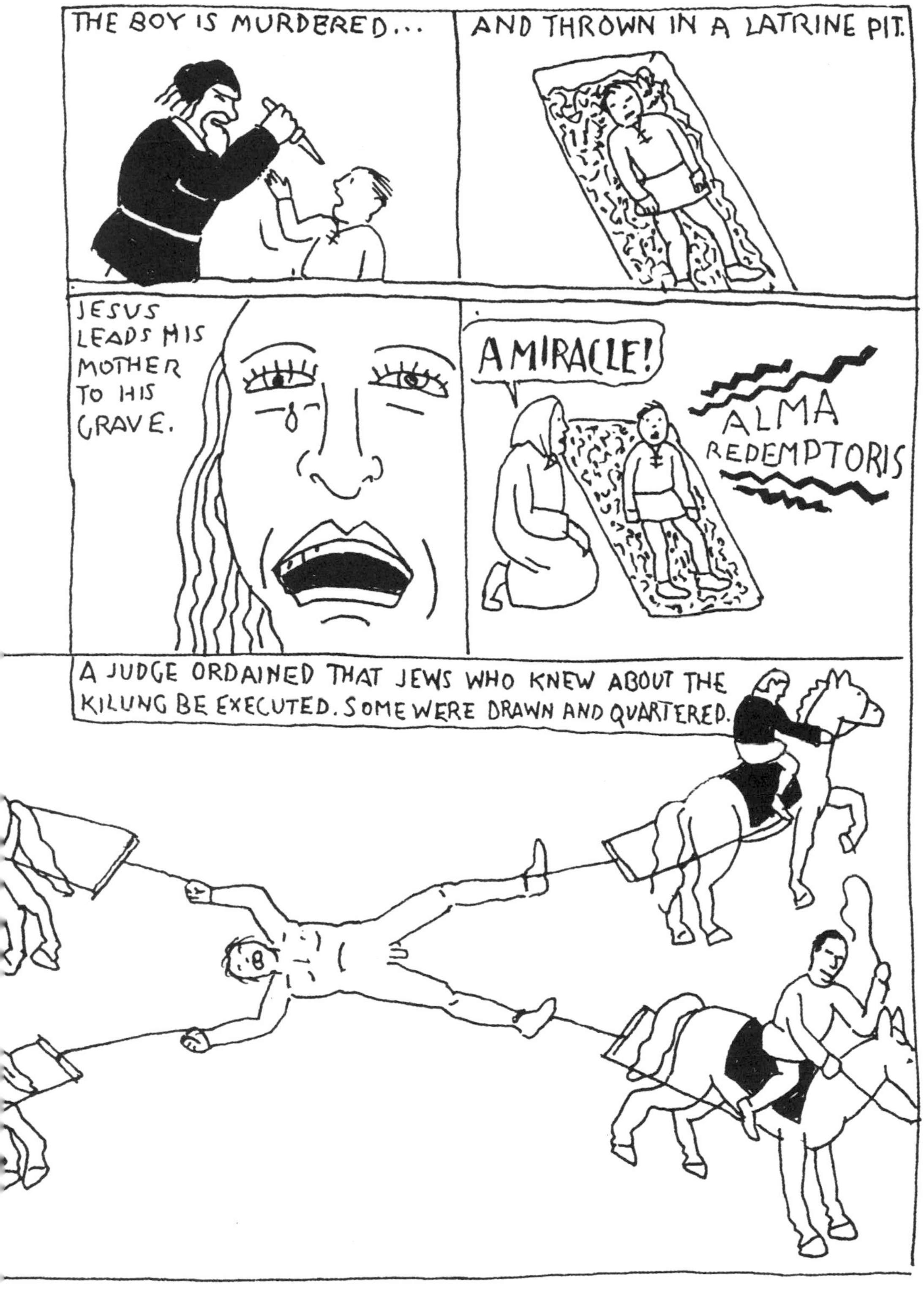
THE BOY IS MURDERED...
AND THROWN IN A LATRINE PIT.
JESUS LEADS HIS MOTHER TO HIS GRAVE.
A MIRACLE!
ALMA REDEMPTORIS
A JUDGE ORDAINED THAT JEWS WHO KNEW ABOUT THE KILLING BE EXECUTED. SOME WERE DRAWN AND QUARTERED.

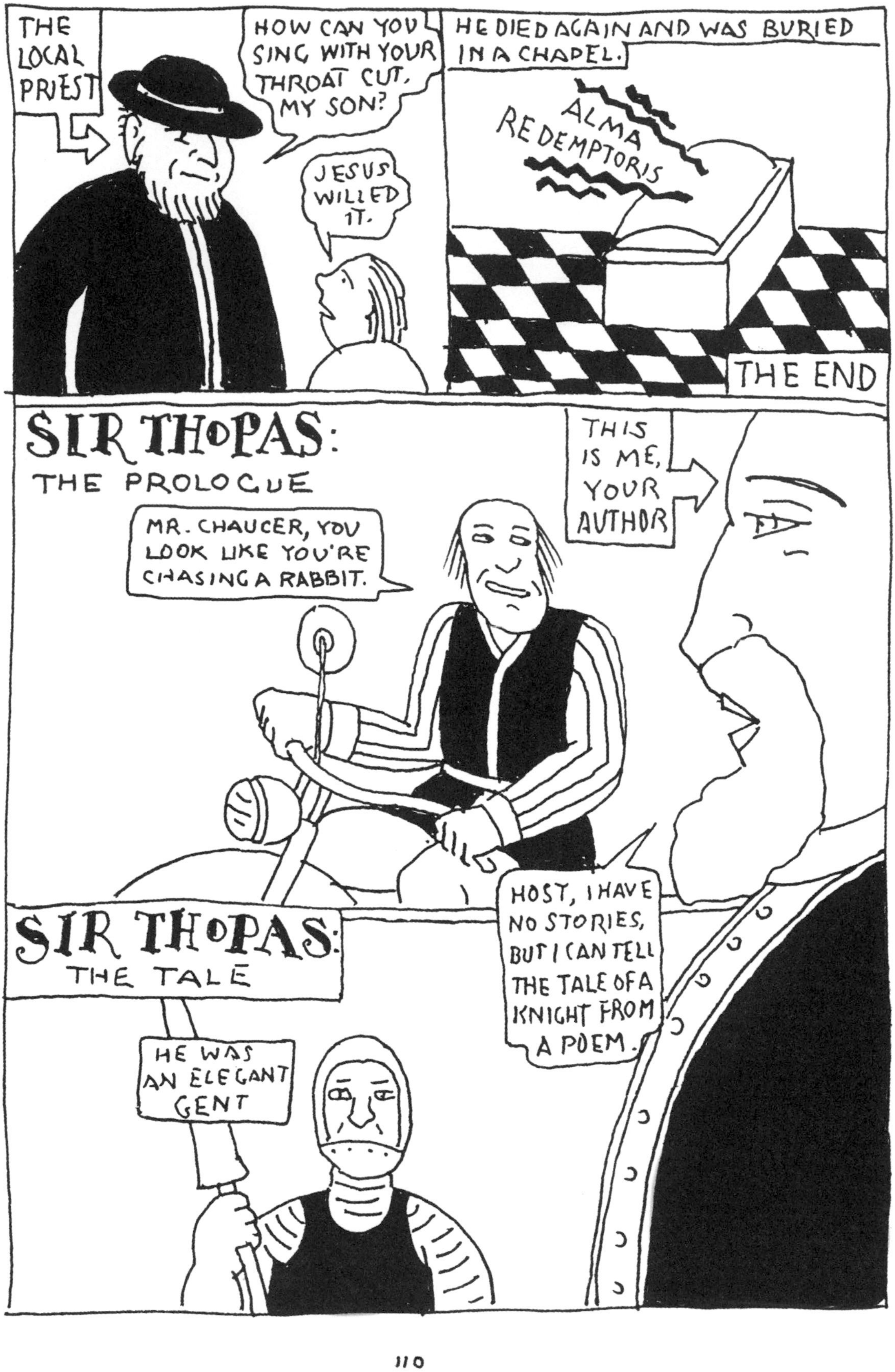
THE LOCAL PRIEST
HOW CAN YOU SING WITH YOUR THROAT CUT, MY SON?
JESUS WILLED IT.
HE DIED AGAIN AND WAS BURIED IN A CHAPEL.
ALMA REDEMPTORIS
THE END
SIR THOPAS: THE PROLOGUE
THIS IS ME, YOUR AUTHOR
MR. CHAUCER, YOU LOOK LIKE YOU'RE CHASING A RABBIT.
HOST, I HAVE NO STORIES, BUT I CAN TELL THE TALE OF A KNIGHT FROM A POEM.
SIR THOPAS: THE TALE
HE WAS AN ELEGANT GENT

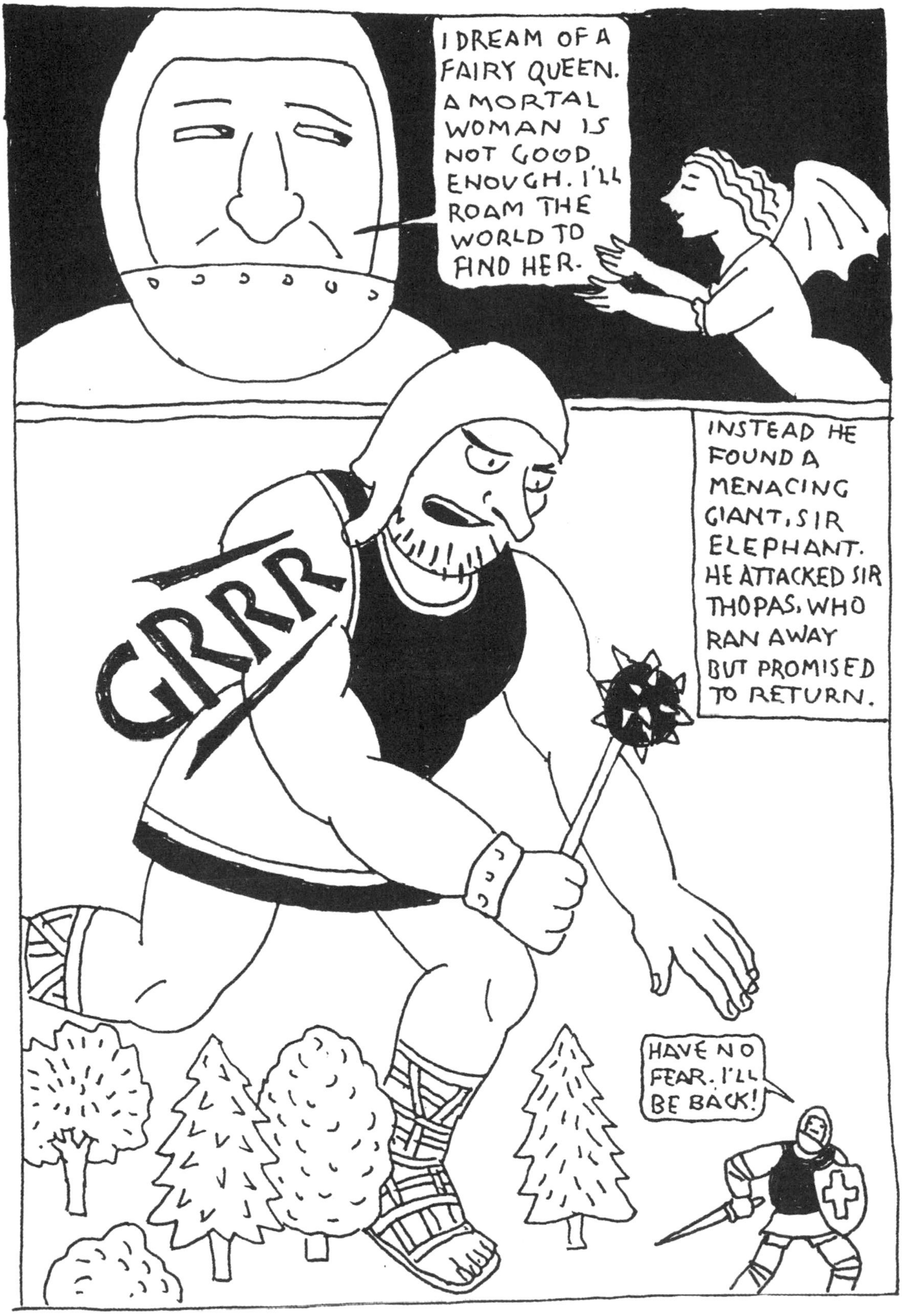
I DREAM OF A FAIRY QUEEN. A MORTAL WOMAN IS NOT GOOD ENOUGH. I'LL ROAM THE WORLD TO FIND HER.
INSTEAD HE FOUND A MENACING GIANT, SIR ELEPHANT. HE ATTACKED SIR THOPAS, WHO RAN AWAY BUT PROMISED TO RETURN.
GRRR
HAVE NO FEAR. I'LL BE BACK!

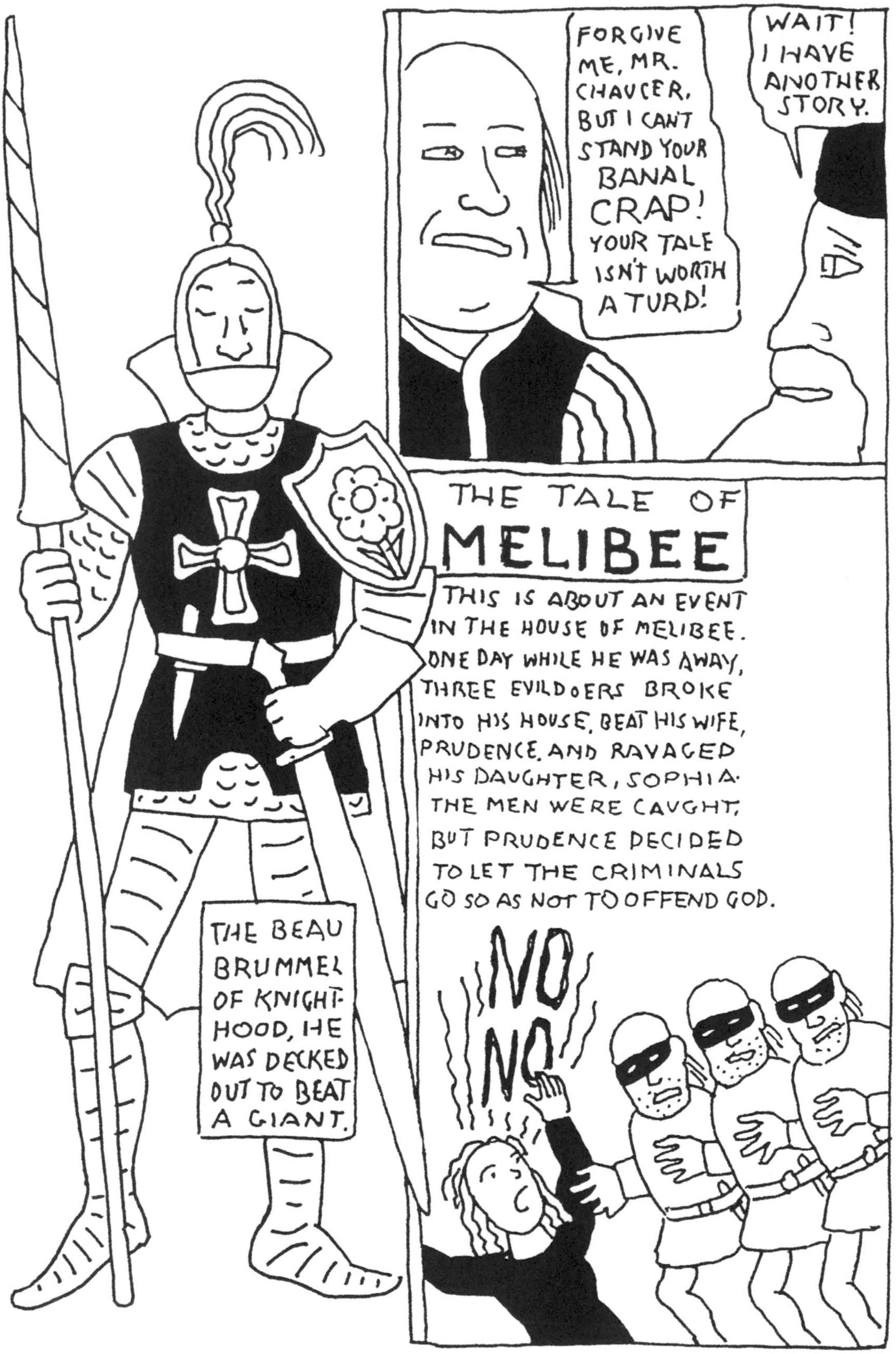

FORGIVE ME, MR. CHAUCER, BUT I CAN'T STAND YOUR BANAL CRAP! YOUR TALE ISN'T WORTH A TURD!
WAIT! I HAVE ANOTHER STORY.
THE BEAU BRUMMEL OF KNIGHT-HOOD, HE WAS DECKED OUT TO BEAT A GIANT.
THE TALE OF MELIBEE
THIS IS ABOUT AN EVENT IN THE HOUSE OF MELIBEE. ONE DAY WHILE HE WAS AWAY, THREE EVILDOERS BROKE INTO HIS HOUSE, BEAT HIS WIFE, PRUDENCE, AND RAVAGED HIS DAUGHTER, SOPHIA. THE MEN WERE CAUGHT, BUT PRUDENCE DECIDED TO LET THE CRIMINALS GO SO AS NOT TO OFFEND GOD.
NO
NO

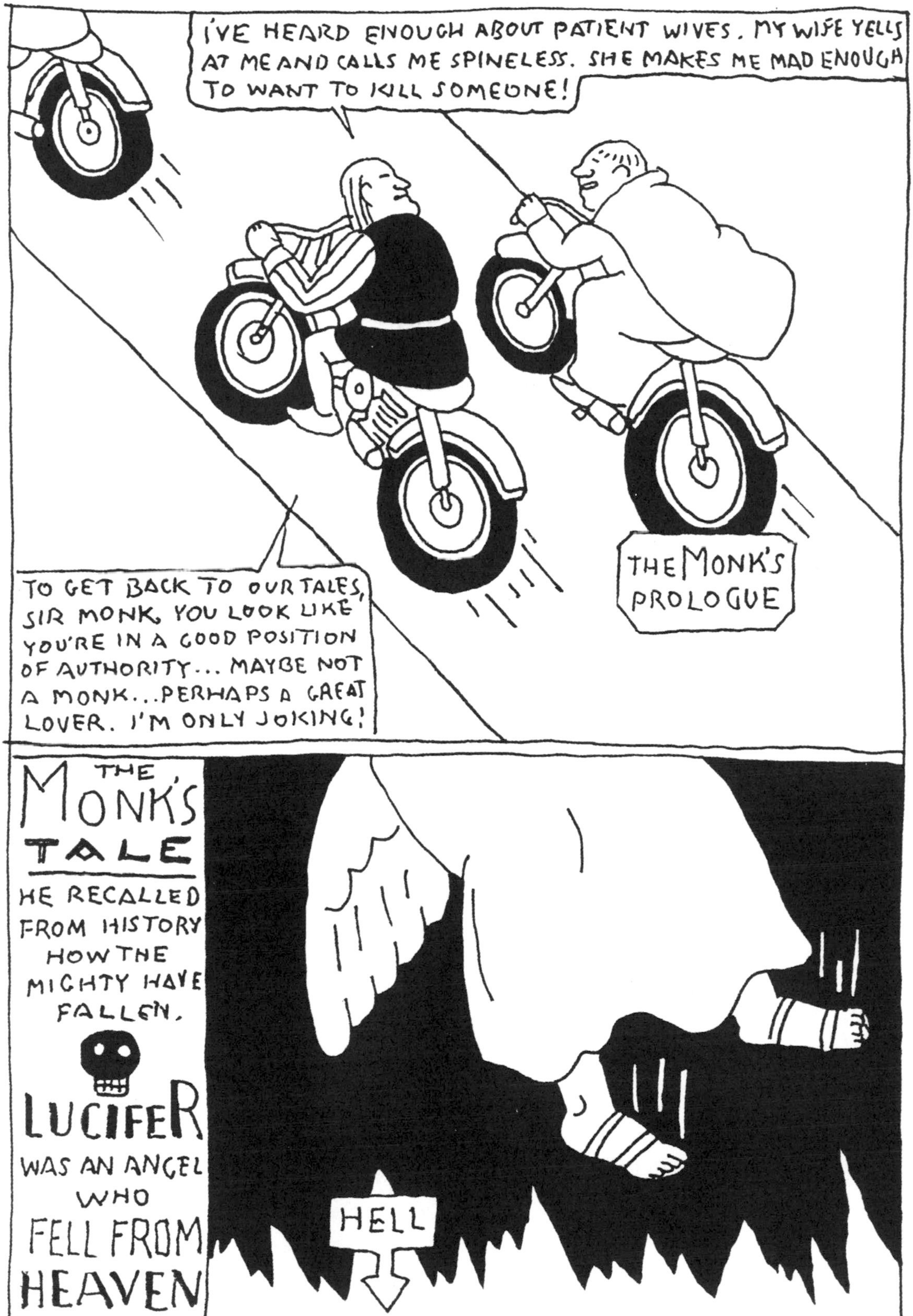
I'VE HEARD ENOUGH ABOUT PATIENT WIVES. MY WIFE YELLS AT ME AND CALLS ME SPINELESS. SHE MAKES ME MAD ENOUGH TO WANT TO KILL SOMEONE!
THE MONK'S PROLOGUE
TO GET BACK TO OUR TALES, SIR MONK, YOU LOOK LIKE YOU'RE IN A GOOD POSITION OF AUTHORITY... MAYBE NOT A MONK... PERHAPS A GREAT LOVER. I'M ONLY JOKING!
THE MONK'S TALE
HE RECALLED FROM HISTORY HOW THE MIGHTY HAVE FALLEN.
LUCIFER WAS AN ANGEL WHO FELL FROM HEAVEN
HELL

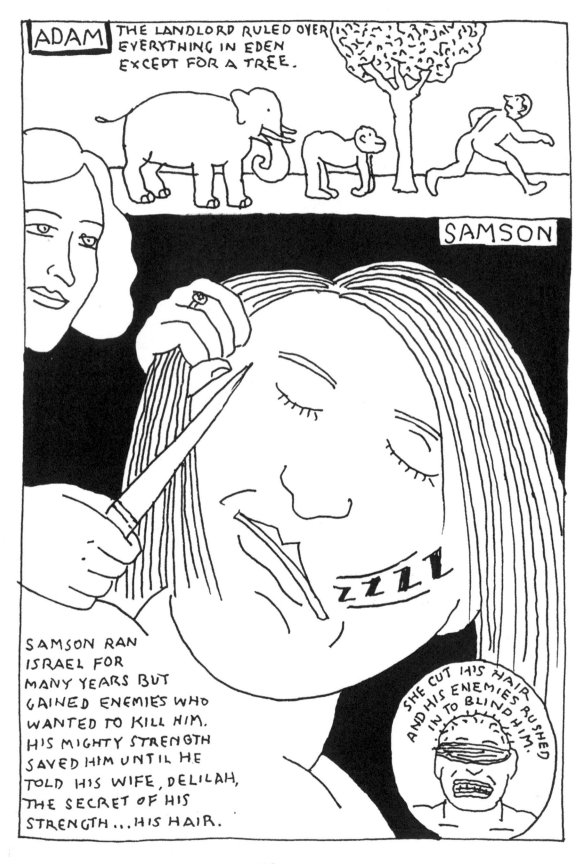

ADAM THE LANDLORD RULED OVER EVERYTHING IN EDEN EXCEPT FOR A TREE.

SAMSON

SAMSON RAN ISRAEL FOR MANY YEARS BUT GAINED ENEMIES WHO WANTED TO KILL HIM. HIS MIGHTY STRENGTH SAVED HIM UNTIL HE TOLD HIS WIFE, DELILAH, THE SECRET OF HIS STRENGTH...HIS HAIR.

SHE CUT HIS HAIR AND HIS ENEMIES RUSHED IN TO BLIND HIM.

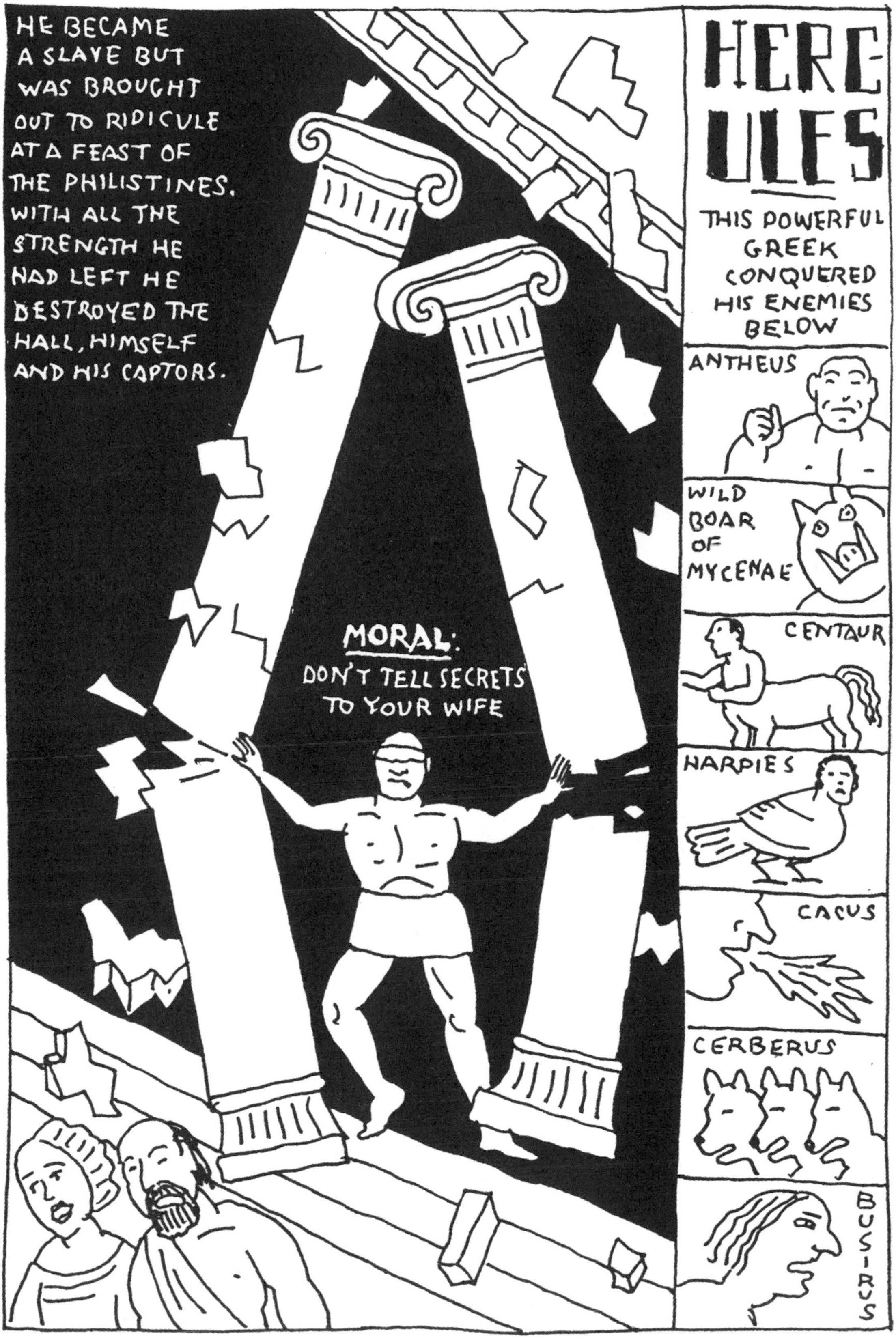

HE BECAME A SLAVE BUT WAS BROUGHT OUT TO RIDICULE AT A FEAST OF THE PHILISTINES. WITH ALL THE STRENGTH HE HAD LEFT HE DESTROYED THE HALL, HIMSELF AND HIS CAPTORS.
MORAL:
DON'T TELL SECRETS TO YOUR WIFE
HERC-ULES
THIS POWERFUL GREEK CONQUERED HIS ENEMIES BELOW
ANTHEUS
WILD BOAR OF MYCENAE
CENTAUR
HARPIES
CACUS
CERBERUS
BUSIRUS

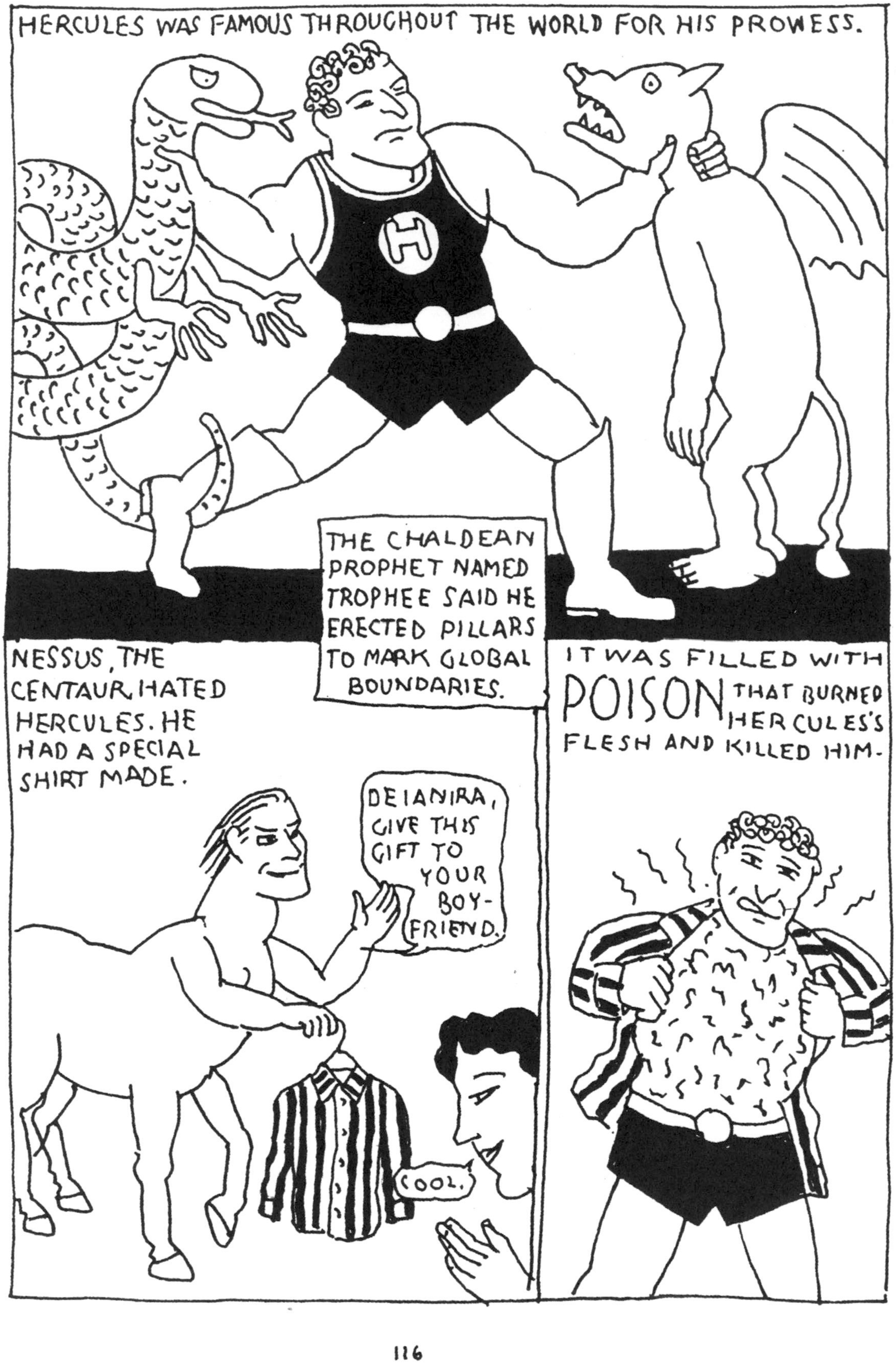
HERCULES WAS FAMOUS THROUGHOUT THE WORLD FOR HIS PROWESS.
H
THE CHALDEAN PROPHET NAMED TROPHEE SAID HE ERECTED PILLARS TO MARK GLOBAL BOUNDARIES.
NESSUS, THE CENTAUR, HATED HERCULES. HE HAD A SPECIAL SHIRT MADE.
DEIANIRA, GIVE THIS GIFT TO YOUR BOY-FRIEND.
COOL.
IT WAS FILLED WITH POISON THAT BURNED HERCULES'S FLESH AND KILLED HIM.

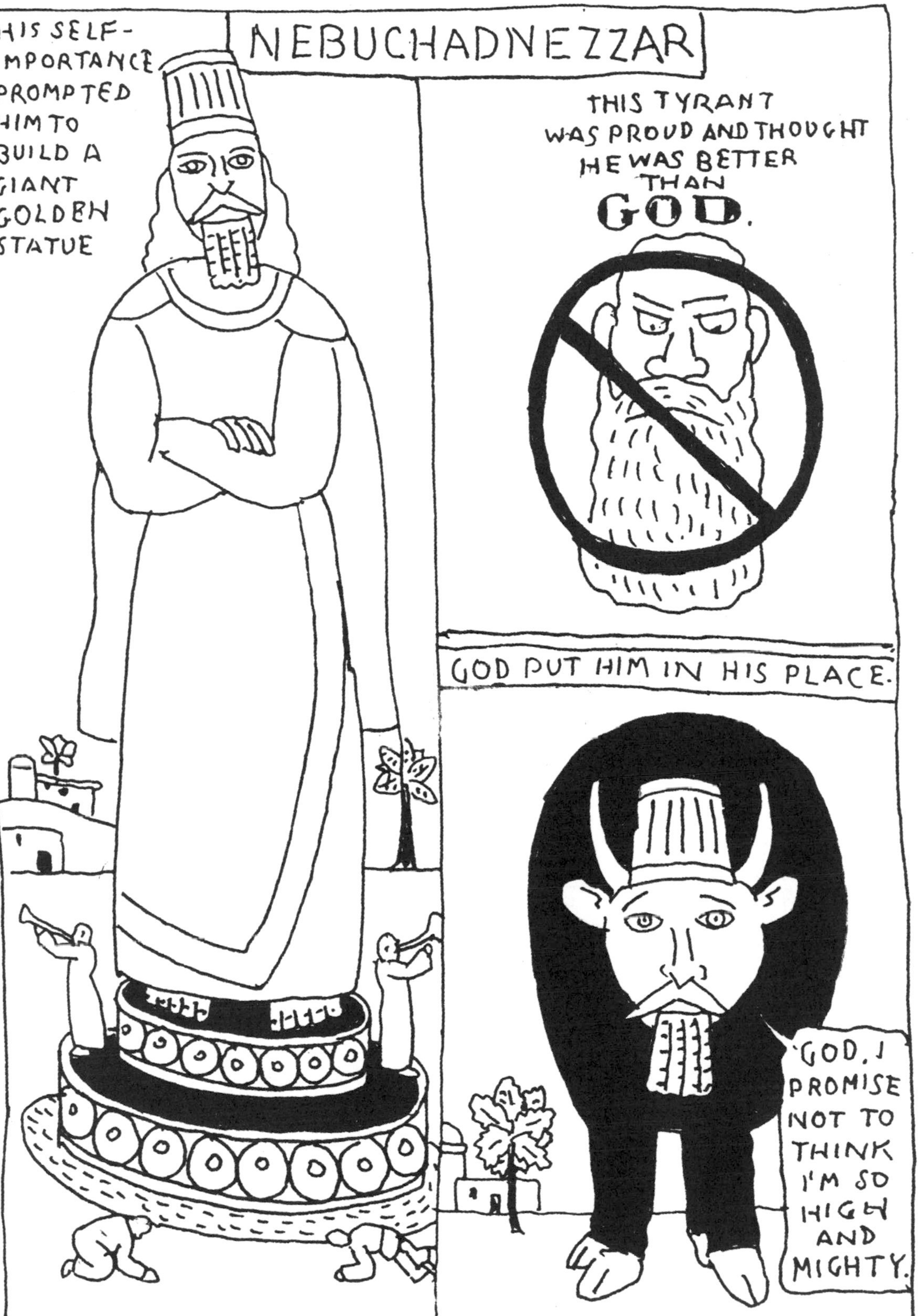
NEBUCHADNEZZAR
HIS SELF-IMPORTANCE PROMPTED HIM TO BUILD A GIANT GOLDEN STATUE
THIS TYRANT WAS PROUD AND THOUGHT HE WAS BETTER THAN GOD.
GOD PUT HIM IN HIS PLACE.
GOD, I PROMISE NOT TO THINK I'M SO HIGH AND MIGHTY.

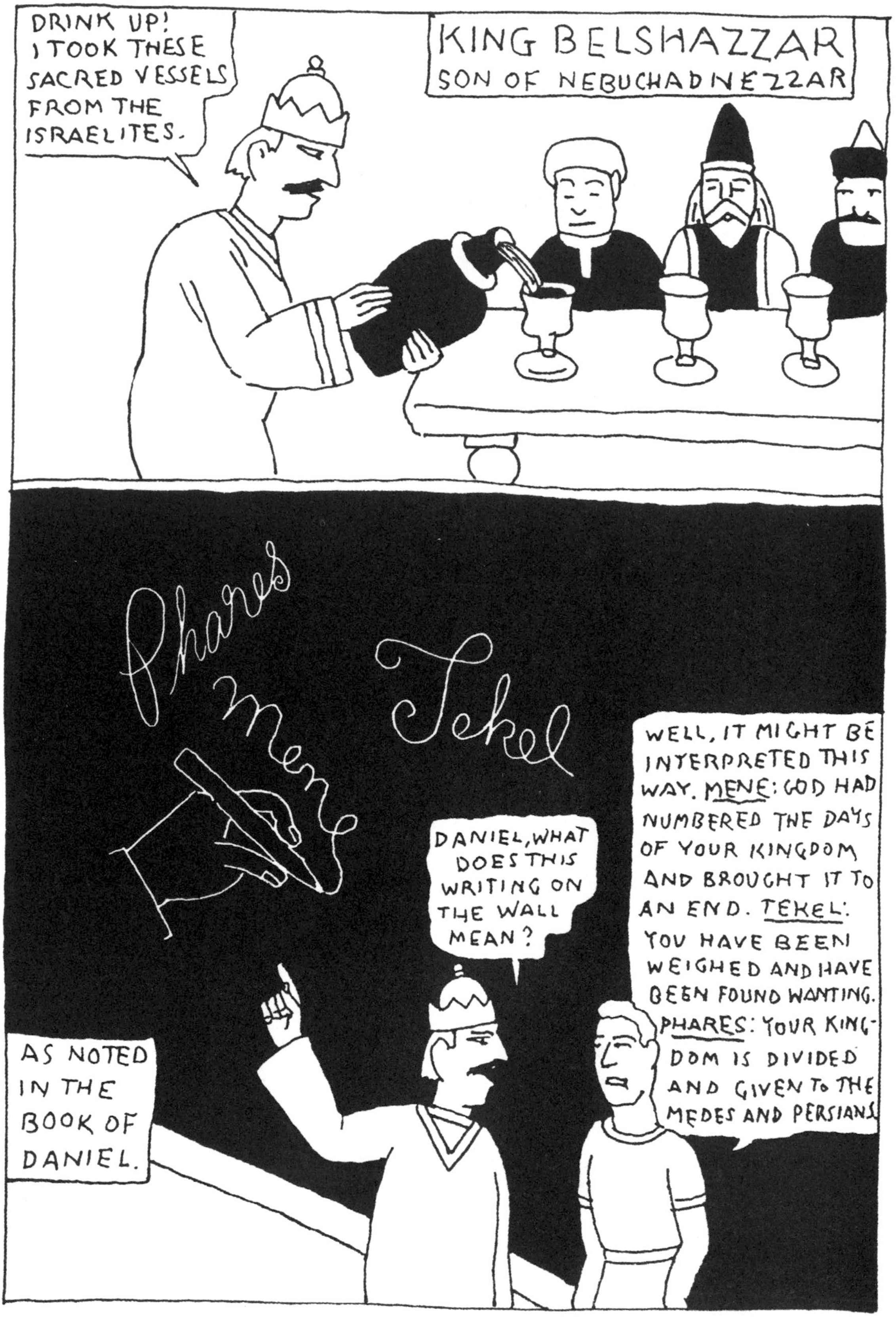
KING BELSHAZZAR SON OF NEBUCHADNEZZAR
DRINK UP! I TOOK THESE SACRED VESSELS FROM THE ISRAELITES.
Phares Mene Tekel
AS NOTED IN THE BOOK OF DANIEL.
DANIEL, WHAT DOES THIS WRITING ON THE WALL MEAN?
WELL, IT MIGHT BE INTERPRETED THIS WAY. MENE: GOD HAD NUMBERED THE DAYS OF YOUR KINGDOM AND BROUGHT IT TO AN END. TEKEL: YOU HAVE BEEN WEIGHED AND HAVE BEEN FOUND WANTING. PHARES: YOUR KINGDOM IS DIVIDED AND GIVEN TO THE MEDES AND PERSIANS.

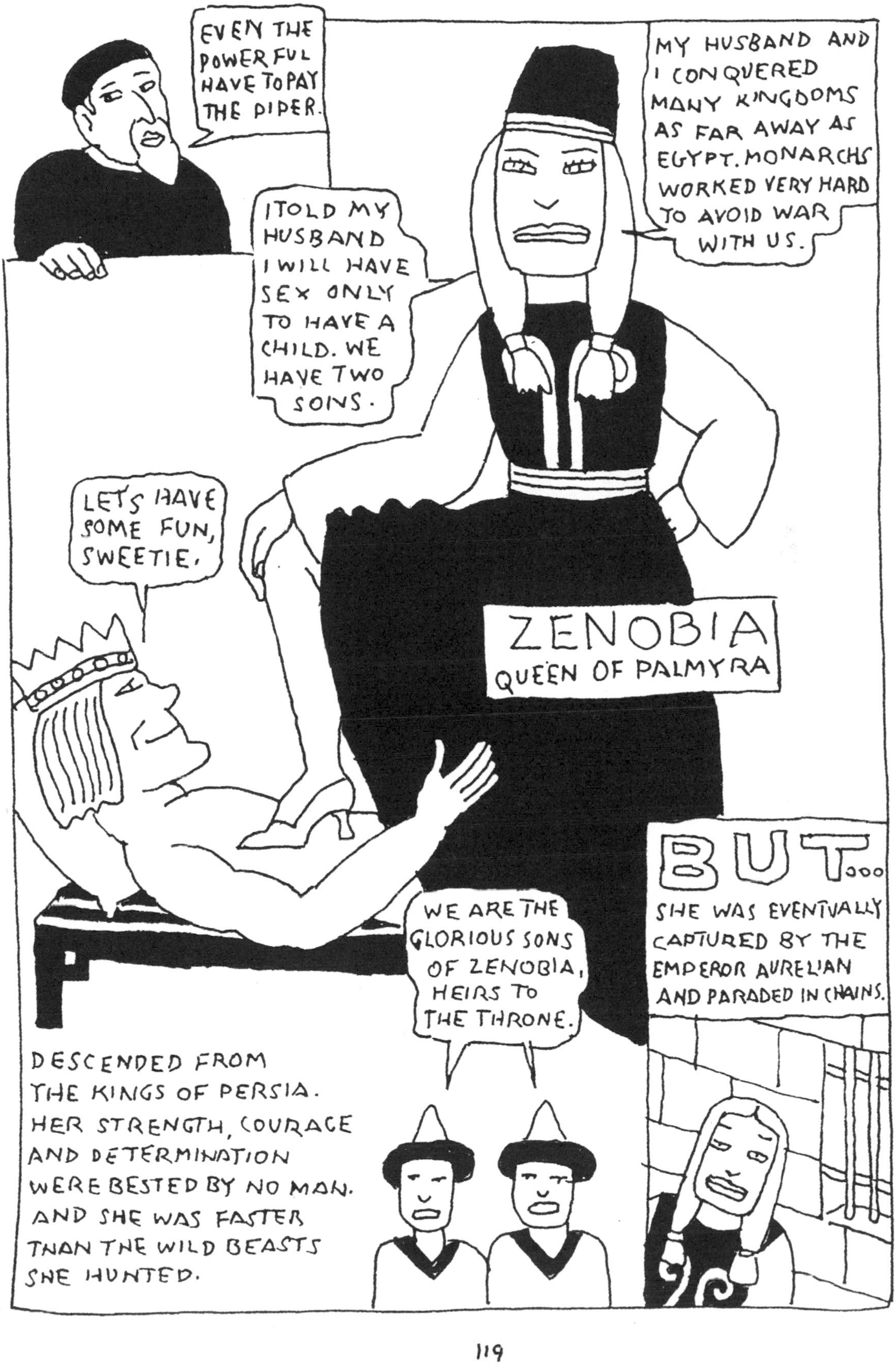
EVEN THE POWERFUL HAVE TO PAY THE PIPER.
MY HUSBAND AND I CONQUERED MANY KINGDOMS AS FAR AWAY AS EGYPT. MONARCHS WORKED VERY HARD TO AVOID WAR WITH US.
I TOLD MY HUSBAND I WILL HAVE SEX ONLY TO HAVE A CHILD. WE HAVE TWO SONS.
LET'S HAVE SOME FUN, SWEETIE.
ZENOBIA
QUEEN OF PALMYRA
BUT...
SHE WAS EVENTUALLY CAPTURED BY THE EMPEROR AURELIAN AND PARADED IN CHAINS.
WE ARE THE GLORIOUS SONS OF ZENOBIA, HEIRS TO THE THRONE.
DESCENDED FROM THE KINGS OF PERSIA. HER STRENGTH, COURAGE AND DETERMINATION WERE BESTED BY NO MAN. AND SHE WAS FASTER THAN THE WILD BEASTS SHE HUNTED.

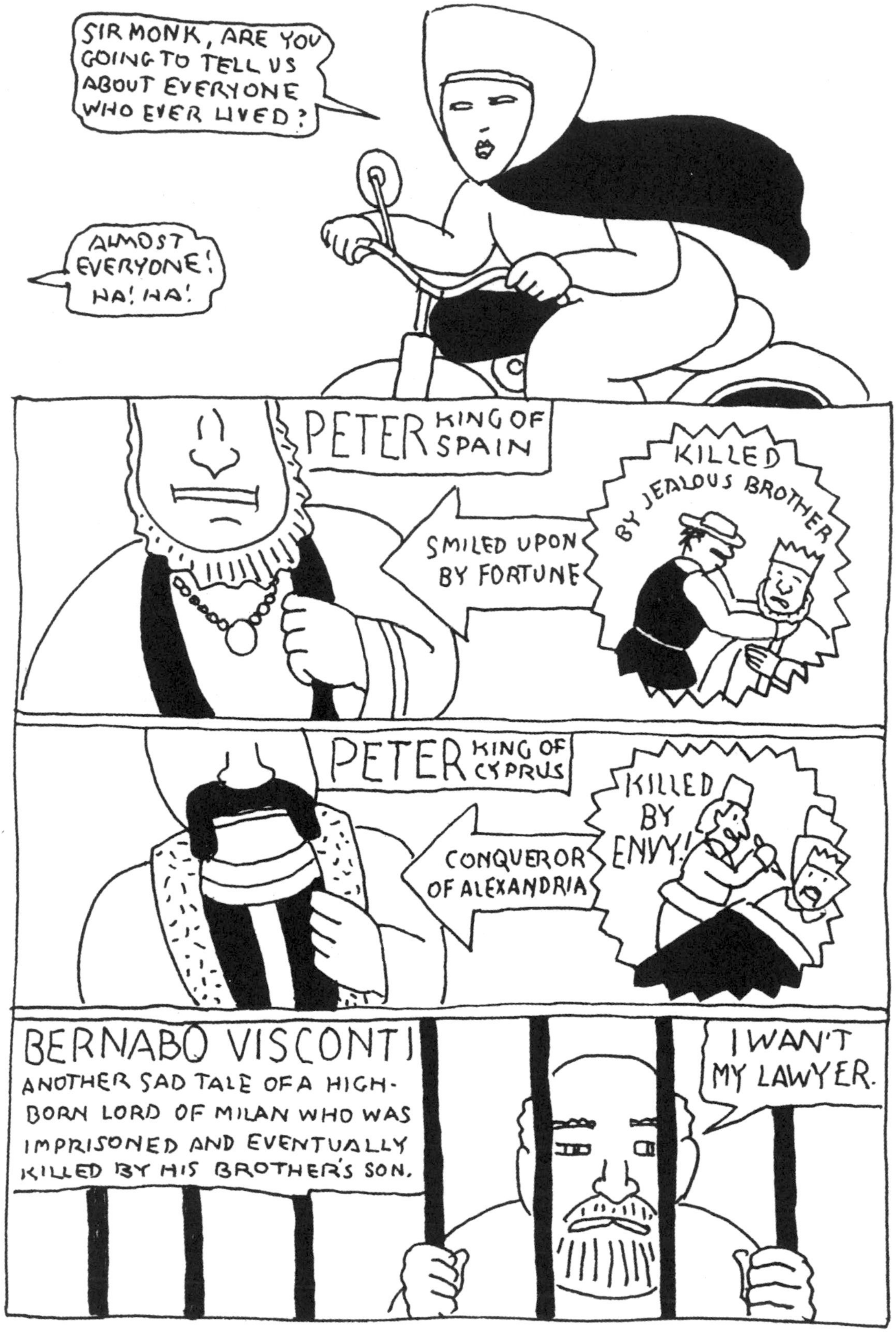

SIR MONK, ARE YOU GOING TO TELL US ABOUT EVERYONE WHO EVER LIVED?
ALMOST EVERYONE! HA! HA!
PETER KING OF SPAIN
SMILED UPON BY FORTUNE
KILLED BY JEALOUS BROTHER
PETER KING OF CYPRUS
CONQUEROR OF ALEXANDRIA
KILLED BY ENVY!
BERNABO VISCONTI
ANOTHER SAD TALE OF A HIGH-BORN LORD OF MILAN WHO WAS IMPRISONED AND EVENTUALLY KILLED BY HIS BROTHER'S SON.
I WAN'T MY LAWYER.

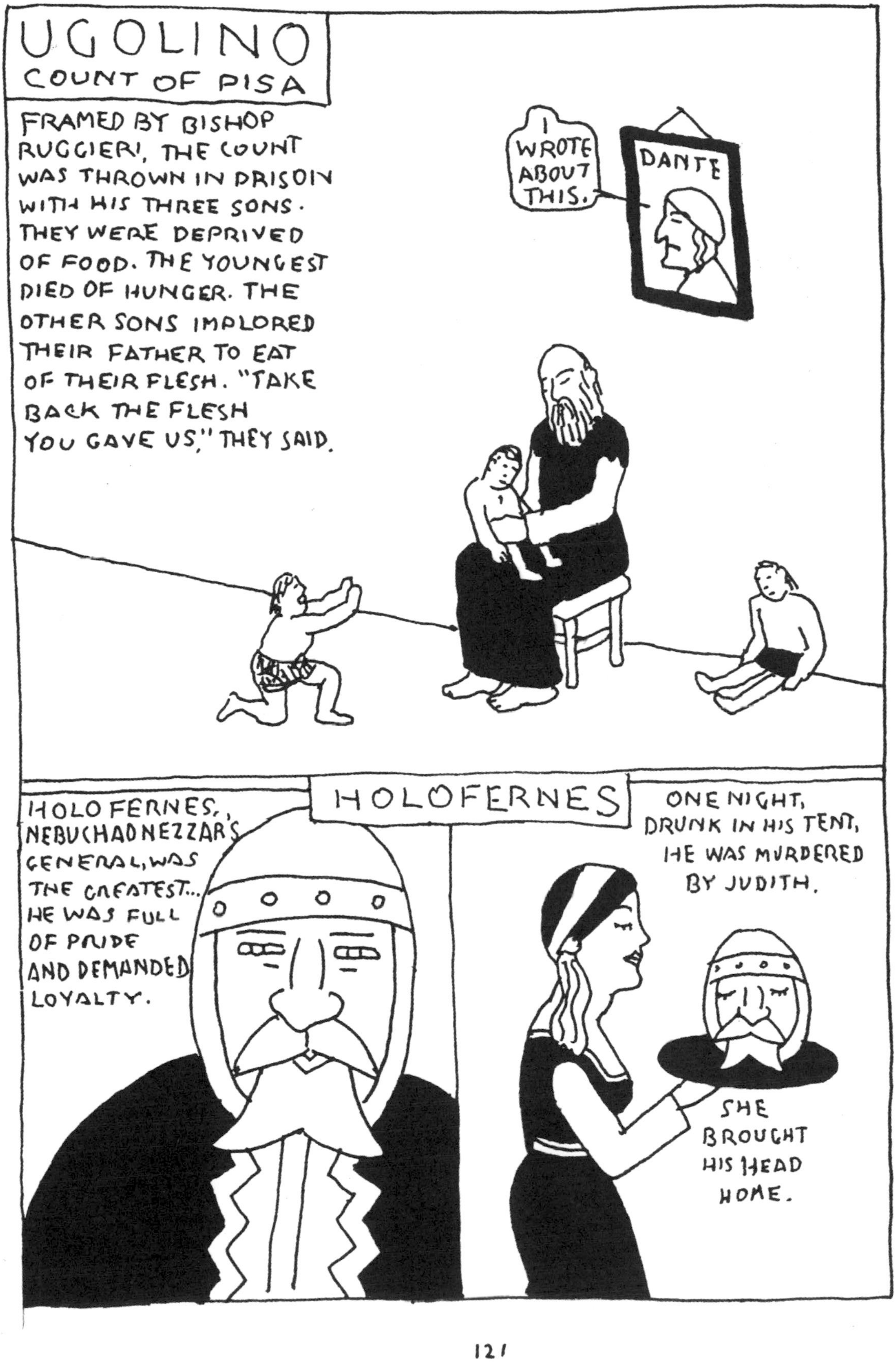
UGOLINO
COUNT OF PISA
FRAMED BY BISHOP RUGGIERI, THE COUNT WAS THROWN IN PRISON WITH HIS THREE SONS. THEY WERE DEPRIVED OF FOOD. THE YOUNGEST DIED OF HUNGER. THE OTHER SONS IMPLORED THEIR FATHER TO EAT OF THEIR FLESH. "TAKE BACK THE FLESH YOU GAVE US," THEY SAID.
DANTE
I WROTE ABOUT THIS.
HOLOFERNES
HOLOFERNES, NEBUCHADNEZZAR'S GENERAL, WAS THE GREATEST... HE WAS FULL OF PRIDE AND DEMANDED LOYALTY.
ONE NIGHT, DRUNK IN HIS TENT, HE WAS MURDERED BY JUDITH.
SHE BROUGHT HIS HEAD HOME.

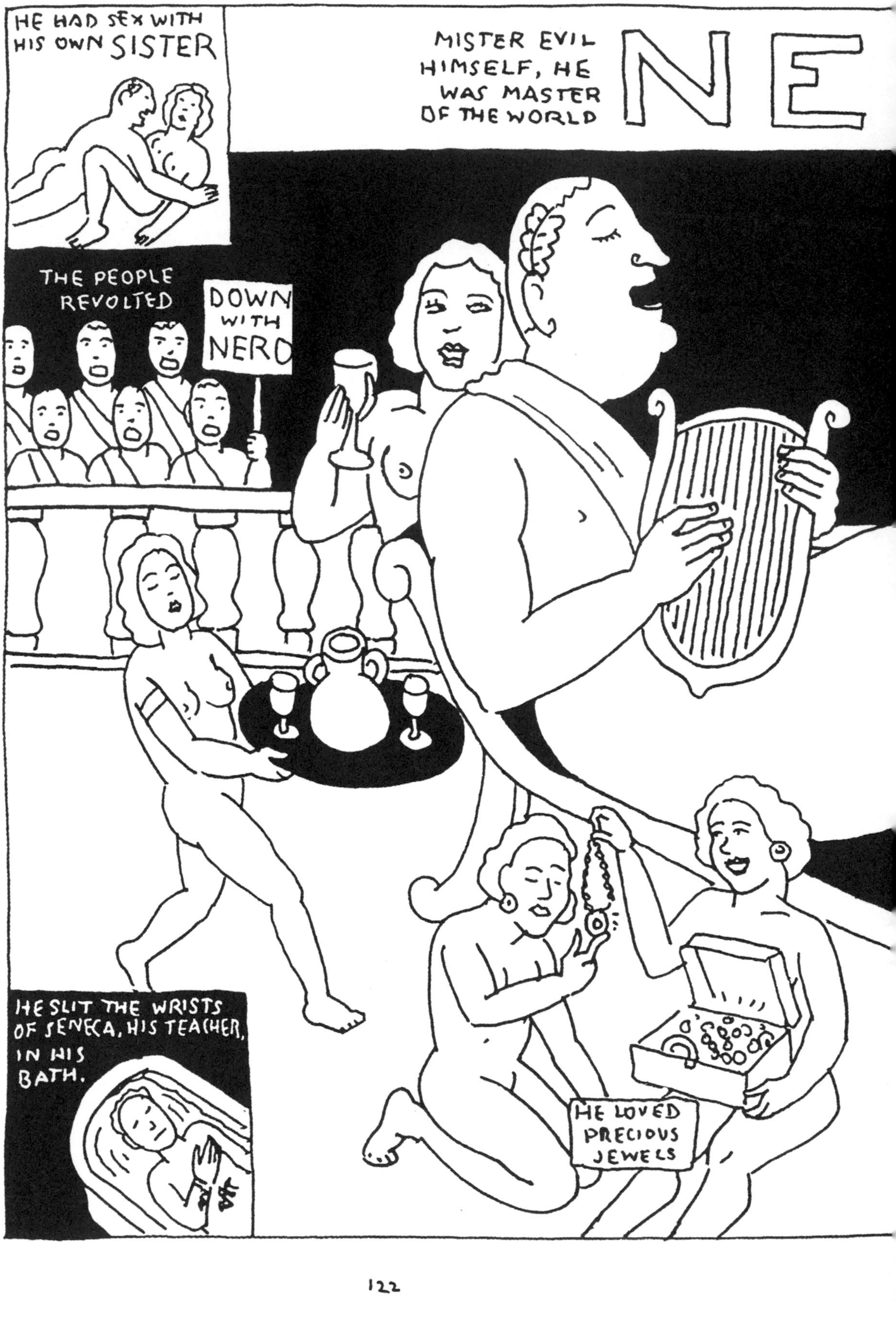
HE HAD SEX WITH HIS OWN SISTER
MISTER EVIL HIMSELF, HE WAS MASTER OF THE WORLD
NE
THE PEOPLE REVOLTED
DOWN WITH NERO
HE SLIT THE WRISTS OF SENECA, HIS TEACHER, IN HIS BATH.
HE LOVED PRECIOUS JEWELS

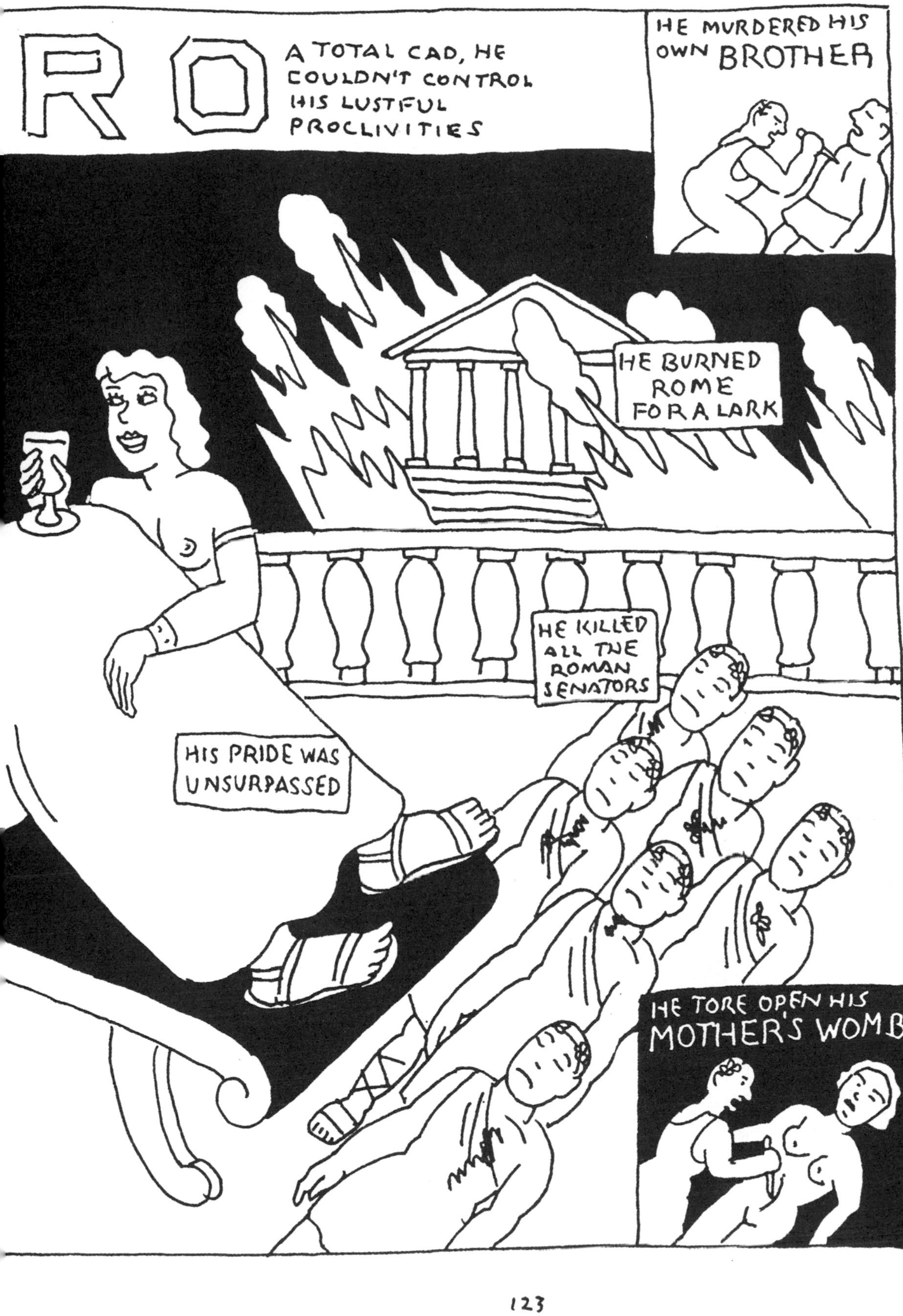
RO
A TOTAL CAD, HE COULDN'T CONTROL HIS LUSTFUL PROCLIVITIES
HE MURDERED HIS OWN BROTHER
HE BURNED ROME FOR A LARK
HE KILLED ALL THE ROMAN SENATORS
HIS PRIDE WAS UNSURPASSED
HE TORE OPEN HIS MOTHER'S WOMB

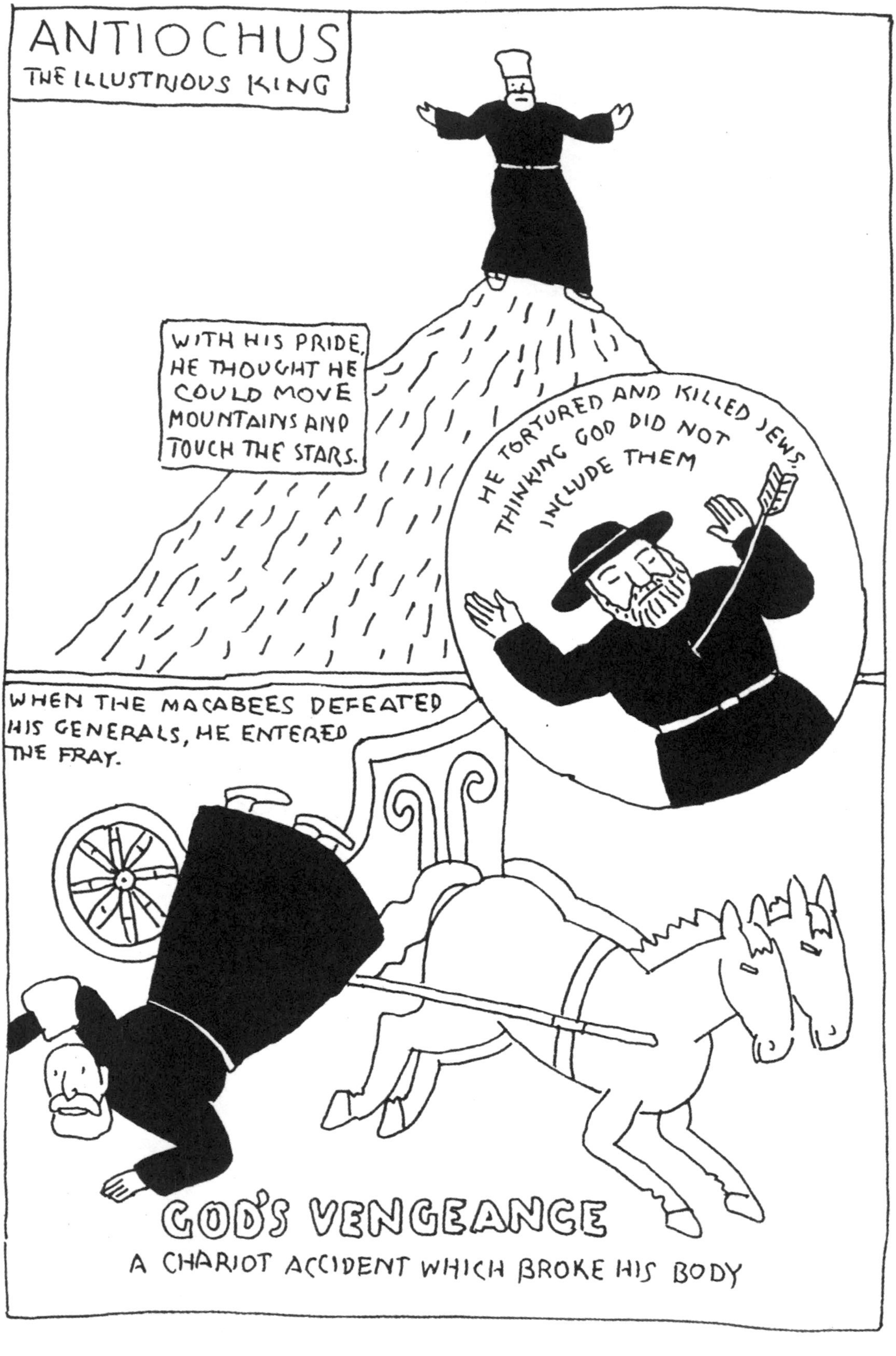
ANTIOCHUS
THE ILLUSTRIOUS KING
WITH HIS PRIDE, HE THOUGHT HE COULD MOVE MOUNTAINS AND TOUCH THE STARS.
HE TORTURED AND KILLED JEWS, THINKING GOD DID NOT INCLUDE THEM
WHEN THE MACABEES DEFEATED HIS GENERALS, HE ENTERED THE FRAY.
GOD'S VENGEANCE
A CHARIOT ACCIDENT WHICH BROKE HIS BODY

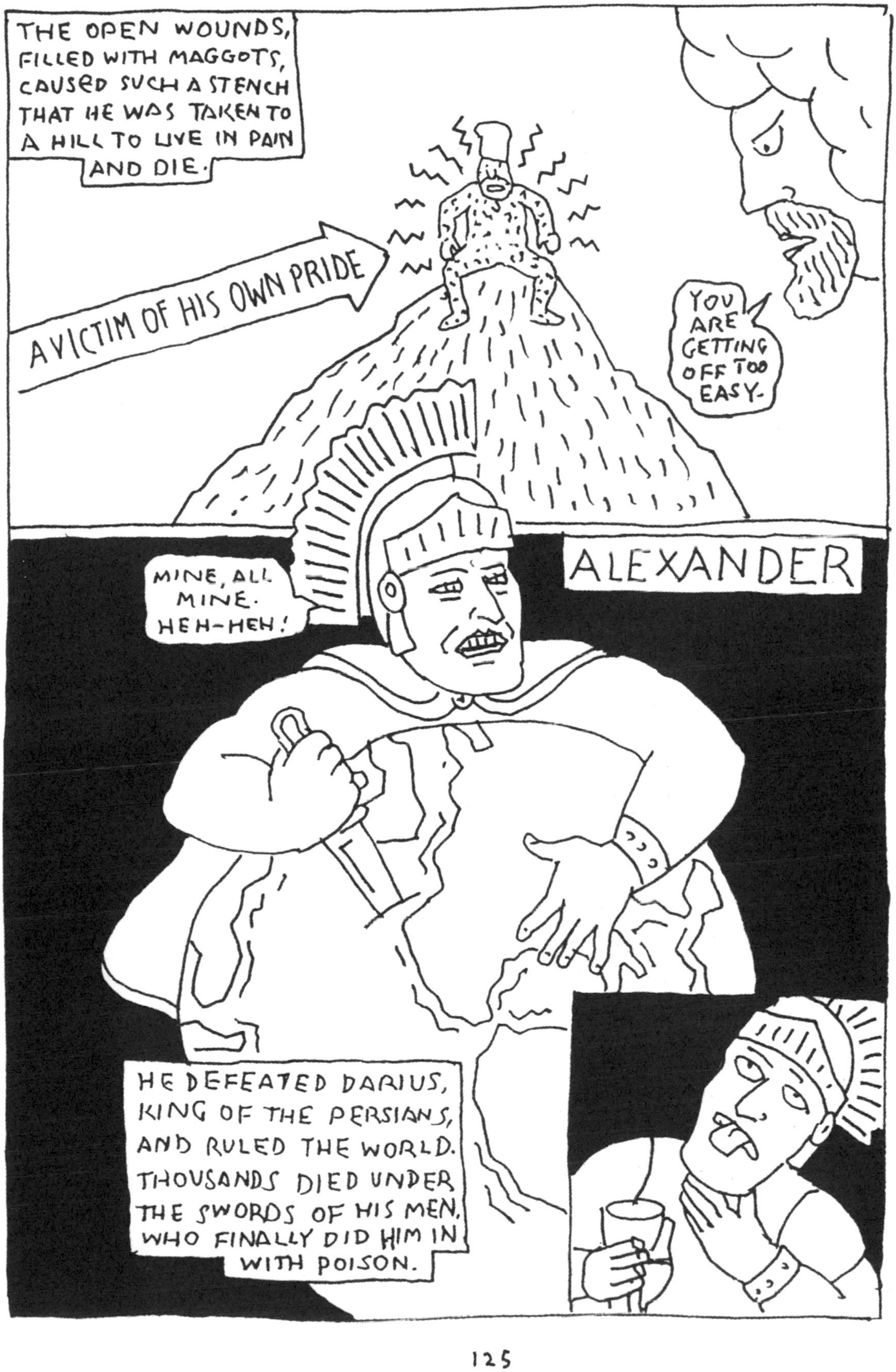
THE OPEN WOUNDS, FILLED WITH MAGGOTS, CAUSED SUCH A STENCH THAT HE WAS TAKEN TO A HILL TO LIVE IN PAIN AND DIE.
A VICTIM OF HIS OWN PRIDE
YOU ARE GETTING OFF TOO EASY.
ALEXANDER
MINE, ALL MINE. HEH-HEH!
HE DEFEATED DARIUS, KING OF THE PERSIANS, AND RULED THE WORLD. THOUSANDS DIED UNDER THE SWORDS OF HIS MEN, WHO FINALLY DID HIM IN WITH POISON.

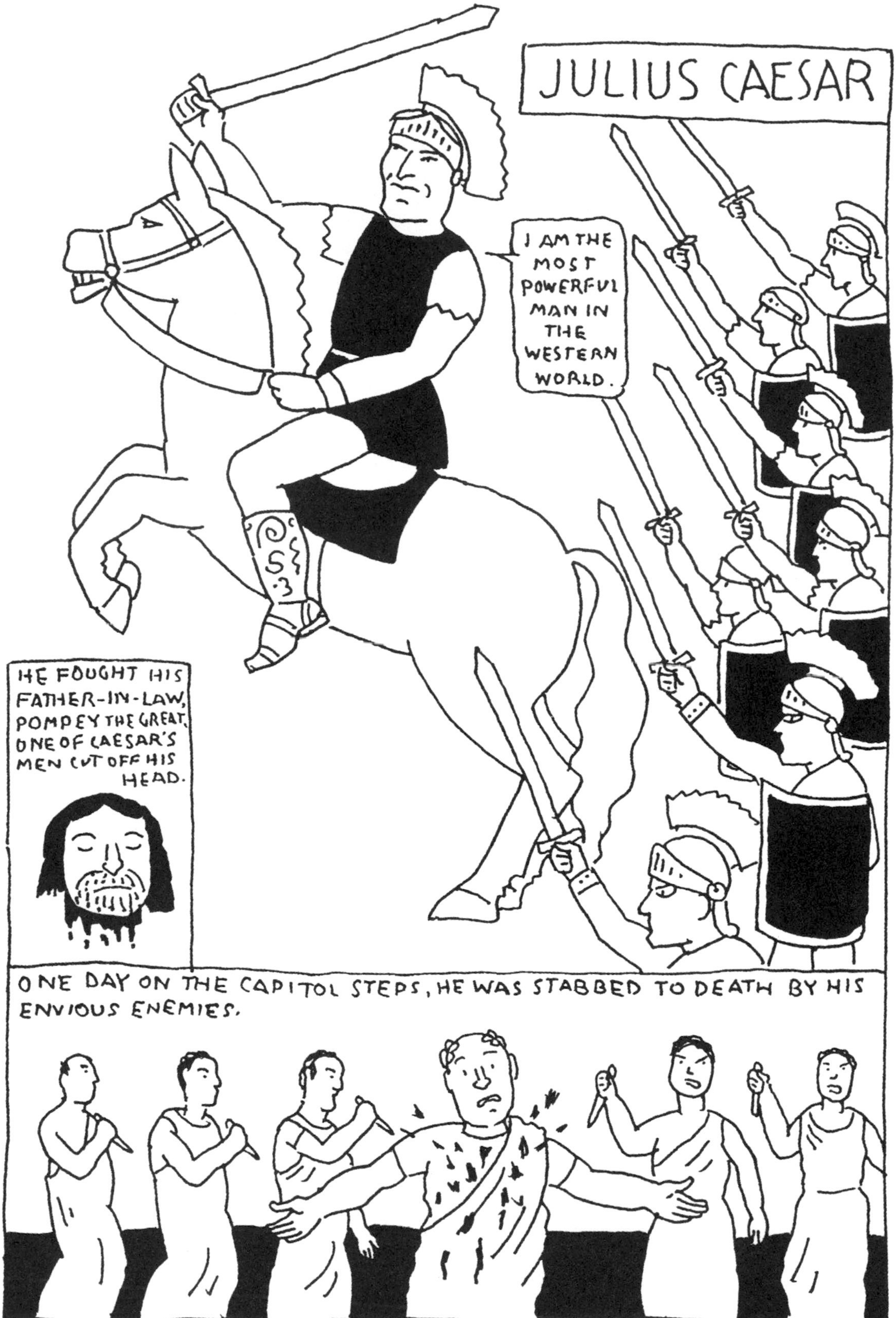
JULIUS CAESAR
I AM THE MOST POWERFUL MAN IN THE WESTERN WORLD.
HE FOUGHT HIS FATHER-IN-LAW, POMPEY THE GREAT. ONE OF CAESAR'S MEN CUT OFF HIS HEAD.
ONE DAY ON THE CAPITOL STEPS, HE WAS STABBED TO DEATH BY HIS ENVIOUS ENEMIES.

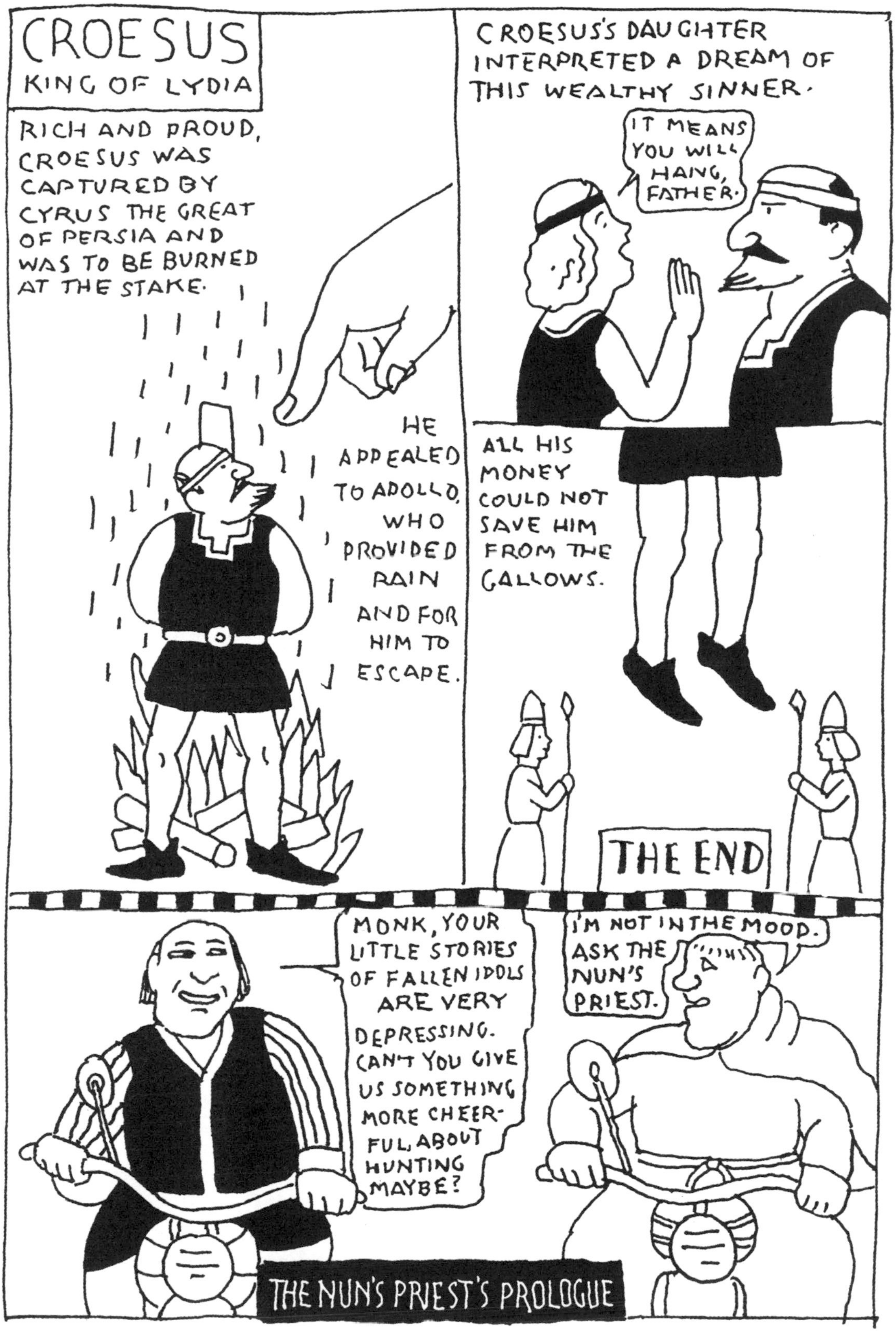
CROESUS
KING OF LYDIA
RICH AND PROUD, CROESUS WAS CAPTURED BY CYRUS THE GREAT OF PERSIA AND WAS TO BE BURNED AT THE STAKE.
HE APPEALED TO APOLLO, WHO PROVIDED RAIN AND FOR HIM TO ESCAPE.
CROESUS'S DAUGHTER INTERPRETED A DREAM OF THIS WEALTHY SINNER.
IT MEANS YOU WILL HANG, FATHER.
ALL HIS MONEY COULD NOT SAVE HIM FROM THE GALLOWS.
THE END
MONK, YOUR LITTLE STORIES OF FALLEN IDOLS ARE VERY DEPRESSING. CAN'T YOU GIVE US SOMETHING MORE CHEERFUL, ABOUT HUNTING MAYBE?
I'M NOT IN THE MOOD. ASK THE NUN'S PRIEST.
THE NUN'S PRIEST'S PROLOGUE

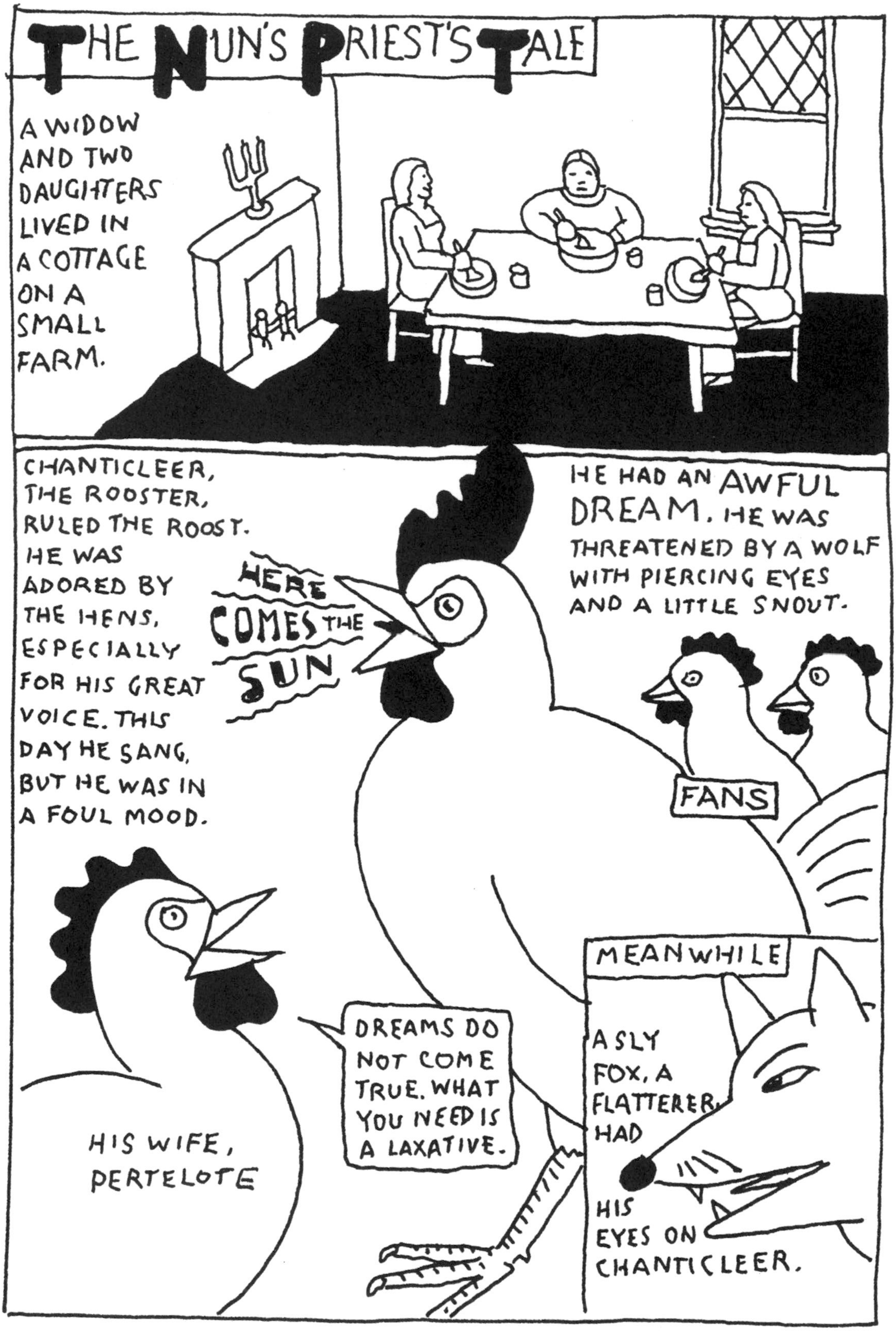
THE NUN'S PRIEST'S TALE
A WIDOW AND TWO DAUGHTERS LIVED IN A COTTAGE ON A SMALL FARM.
CHANTICLEER, THE ROOSTER, RULED THE ROOST. HE WAS ADORED BY THE HENS, ESPECIALLY FOR HIS GREAT VOICE. THIS DAY HE SANG, BUT HE WAS IN A FOUL MOOD.
HERE COMES THE SUN
HE HAD AN AWFUL DREAM. HE WAS THREATENED BY A WOLF WITH PIERCING EYES AND A LITTLE SNOUT.
FANS
HIS WIFE, PERTELOTE
DREAMS DO NOT COME TRUE. WHAT YOU NEED IS A LAXATIVE.
MEANWHILE
A SLY FOX, A FLATTERER, HAD HIS EYES ON CHANTICLEER.

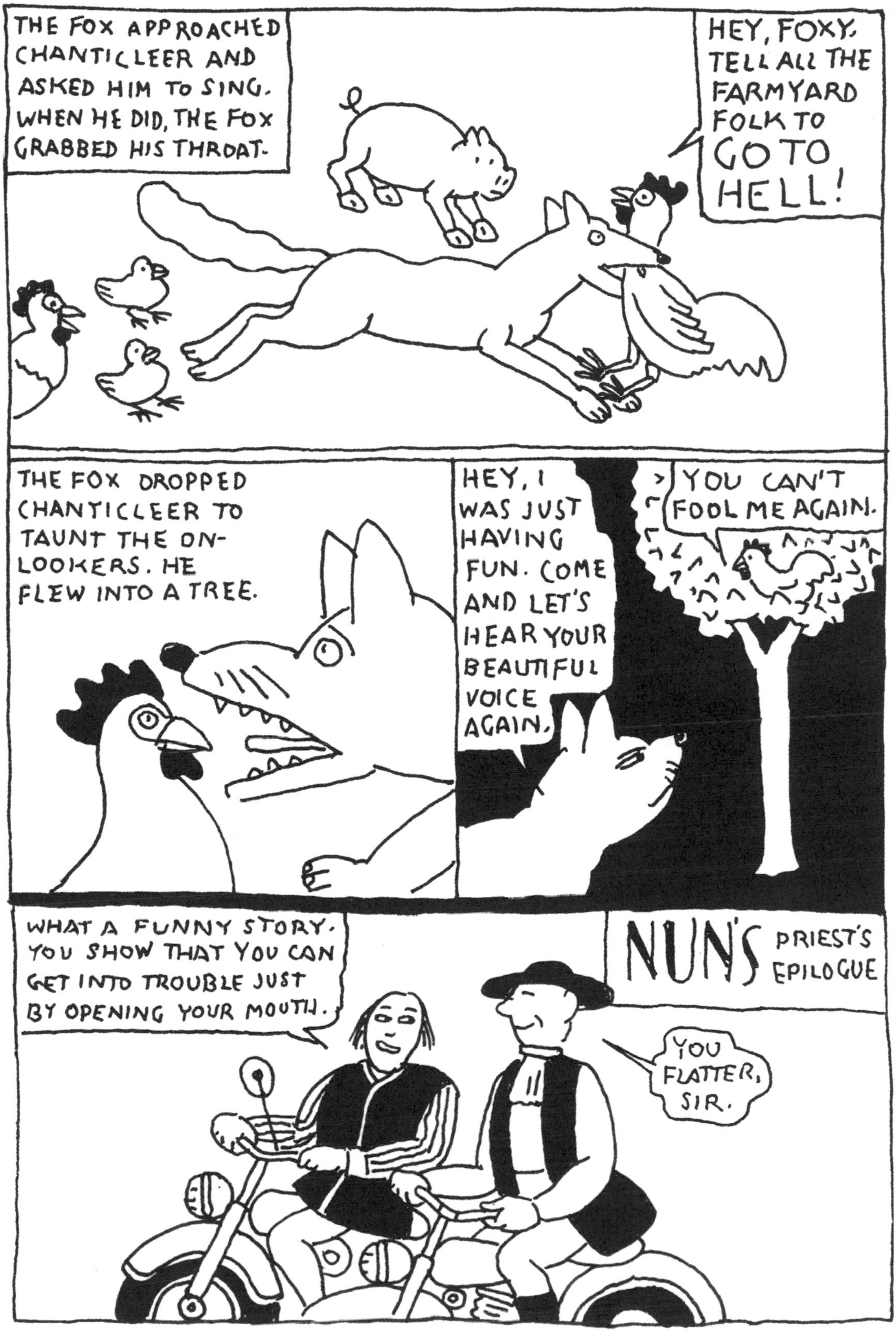

THE FOX APPROACHED CHANTICLEER AND ASKED HIM TO SING. WHEN HE DID, THE FOX GRABBED HIS THROAT.
HEY, FOXY. TELL ALL THE FARMYARD FOLK TO GO TO HELL!
THE FOX DROPPED CHANTICLEER TO TAUNT THE ON-LOOKERS. HE FLEW INTO A TREE.
HEY, I WAS JUST HAVING FUN. COME AND LET'S HEAR YOUR BEAUTIFUL VOICE AGAIN.
YOU CAN'T FOOL ME AGAIN.
WHAT A FUNNY STORY. YOU SHOW THAT YOU CAN GET INTO TROUBLE JUST BY OPENING YOUR MOUTH.
NUN'S PRIEST'S EPILOGUE
YOU FLATTER, SIR.

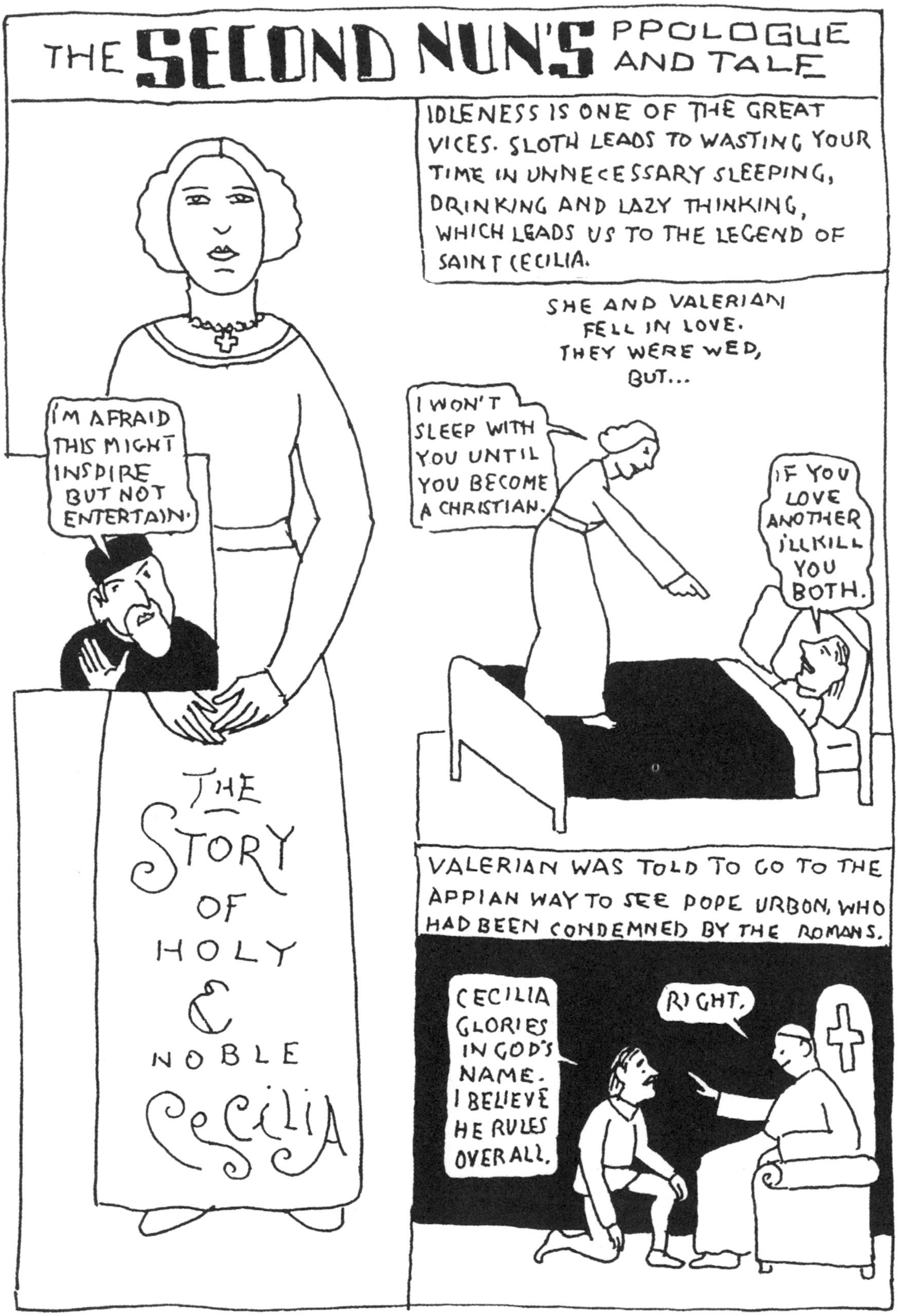
THE SECOND NUN'S PPOLOGUE AND TALE
IDLENESS IS ONE OF THE GREAT VICES. SLOTH LEADS TO WASTING YOUR TIME IN UNNECESSARY SLEEPING, DRINKING AND LAZY THINKING, WHICH LEADS US TO THE LEGEND OF SAINT CECILIA.
I'M AFRAID THIS MIGHT INSPIRE BUT NOT ENTERTAIN.
THE STORY OF HOLY & NOBLE CECILIA
SHE AND VALERIAN FELL IN LOVE. THEY WERE WED, BUT...
I WON'T SLEEP WITH YOU UNTIL YOU BECOME A CHRISTIAN.
IF YOU LOVE ANOTHER I'LL KILL YOU BOTH.
VALERIAN WAS TOLD TO GO TO THE APPIAN WAY TO SEE POPE URBON, WHO HAD BEEN CONDEMNED BY THE ROMANS.
CECILIA GLORIES IN GOD'S NAME. I BELIEVE HE RULES OVER ALL.
RIGHT.

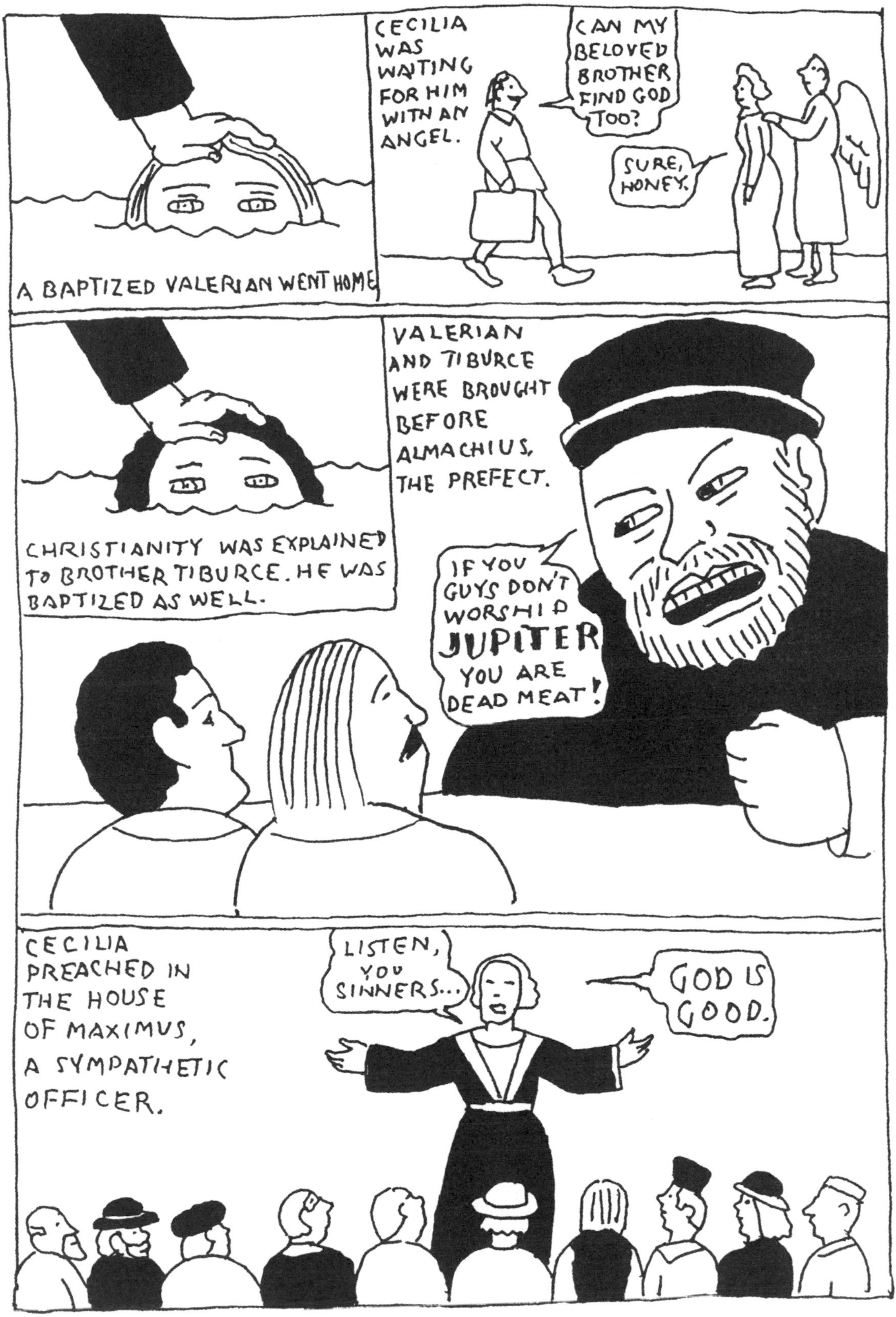
A BAPTIZED VALERIAN WENT HOME
CECILIA WAS WAITING FOR HIM WITH AN ANGEL.
CAN MY BELOVED BROTHER FIND GOD TOO?
SURE, HONEY.
CHRISTIANITY WAS EXPLAINED TO BROTHER TIBURCE. HE WAS BAPTIZED AS WELL.
VALERIAN AND TIBURCE WERE BROUGHT BEFORE ALMACHIUS, THE PREFECT.
IF YOU GUYS DON'T WORSHIP JUPITER YOU ARE DEAD MEAT!
CECILIA PREACHED IN THE HOUSE OF MAXIMUS, A SYMPATHETIC OFFICER.
LISTEN, YOU SINNERS...
GOD IS GOOD.

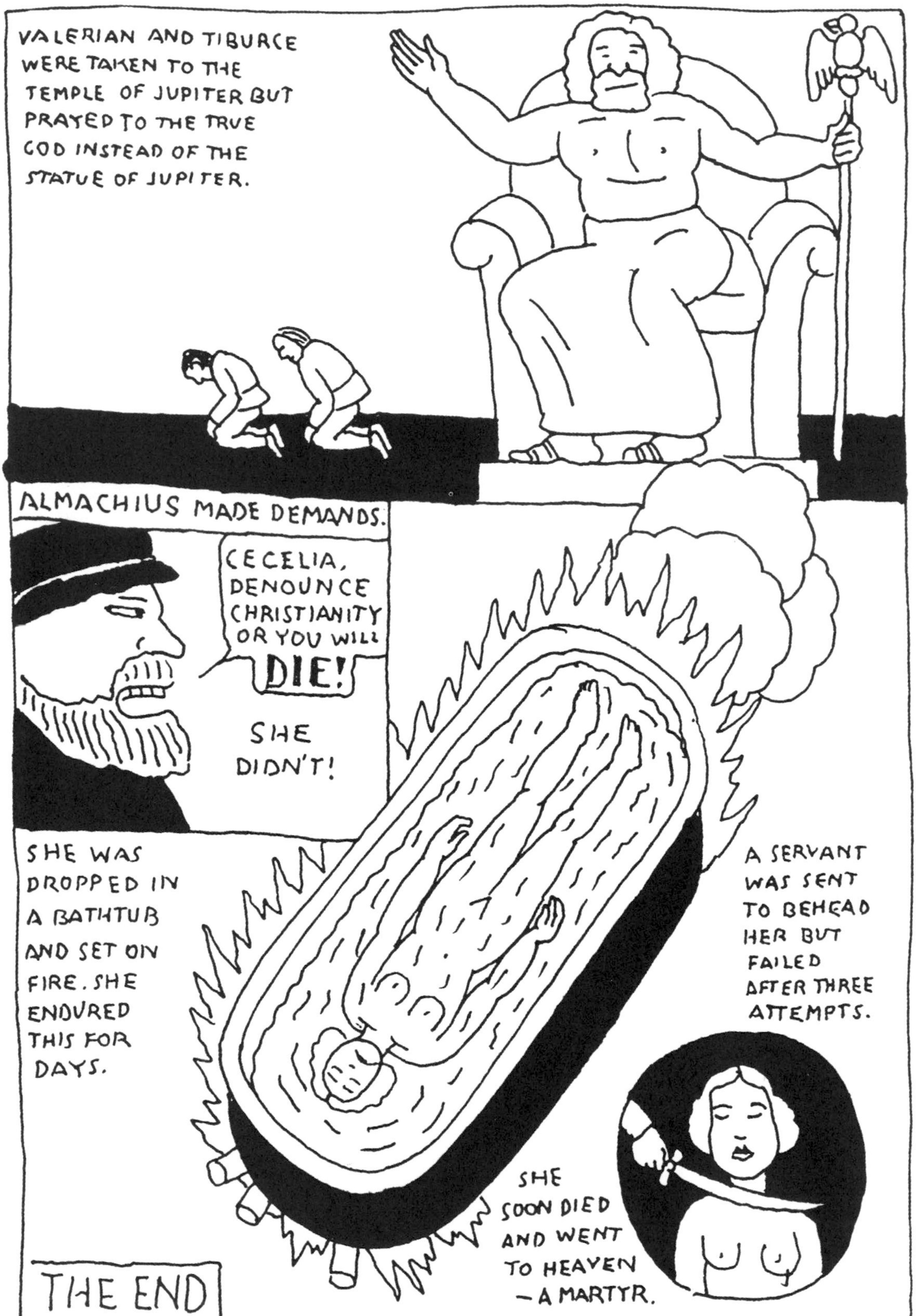
VALERIAN AND TIBURCE WERE TAKEN TO THE TEMPLE OF JUPITER BUT PRAYED TO THE TRUE GOD INSTEAD OF THE STATUE OF JUPITER.
ALMACHIUS MADE DEMANDS.
CECELIA, DENOUNCE CHRISTIANITY OR YOU WILL DIE!
SHE DIDN'T!
SHE WAS DROPPED IN A BATHTUB AND SET ON FIRE. SHE ENDURED THIS FOR DAYS.
A SERVANT WAS SENT TO BEHEAD HER BUT FAILED AFTER THREE ATTEMPTS.
SHE SOON DIED AND WENT TO HEAVEN —A MARTYR.
THE END

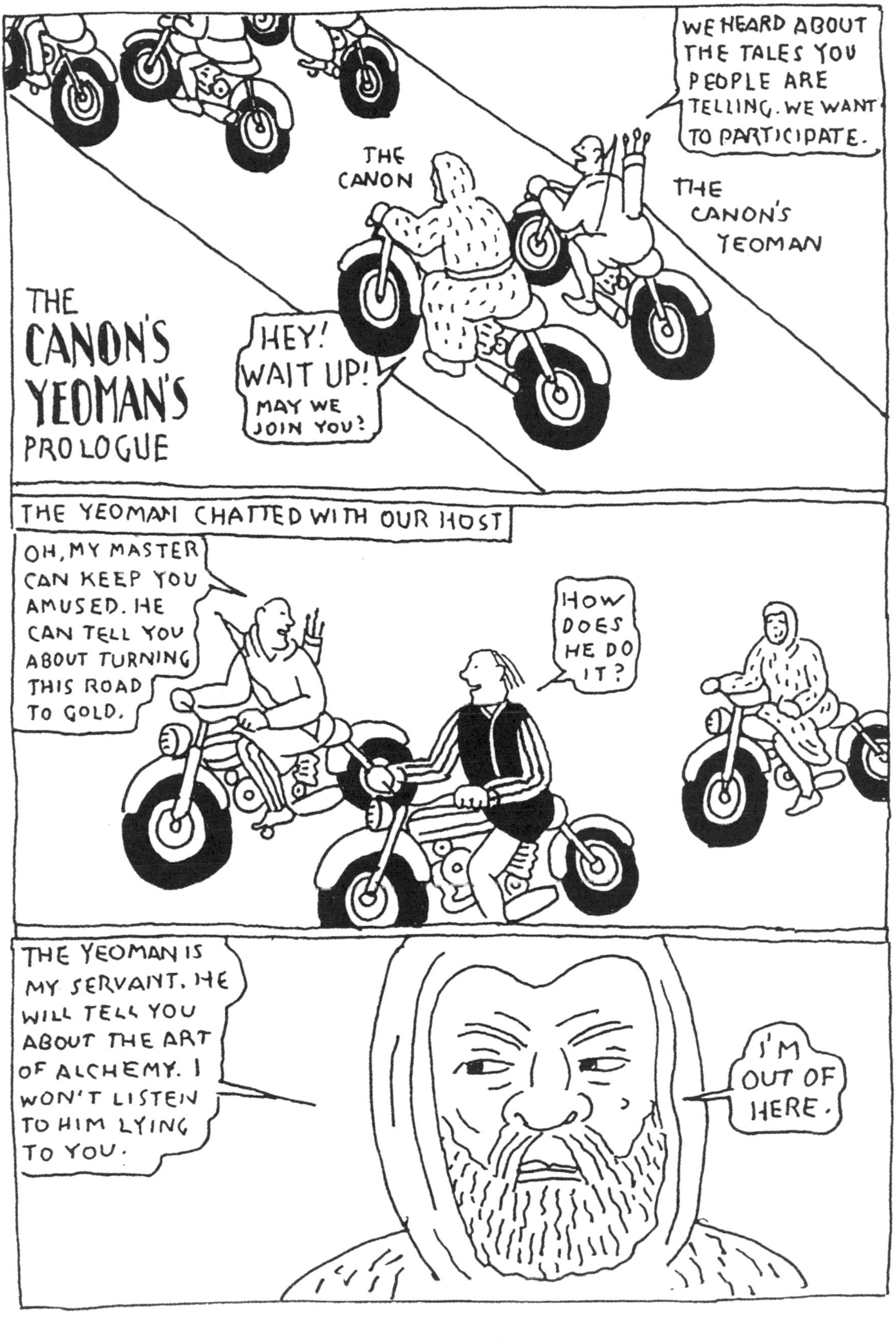
THE CANON'S YEOMAN'S PROLOGUE
WE HEARD ABOUT THE TALES YOU PEOPLE ARE TELLING. WE WANT TO PARTICIPATE.
THE CANON
THE CANON'S YEOMAN
HEY! WAIT UP! MAY WE JOIN YOU?
THE YEOMAN CHATTED WITH OUR HOST
OH, MY MASTER CAN KEEP YOU AMUSED. HE CAN TELL YOU ABOUT TURNING THIS ROAD TO GOLD.
HOW DOES HE DO IT?
THE YEOMAN IS MY SERVANT. HE WILL TELL YOU ABOUT THE ART OF ALCHEMY. I WON'T LISTEN TO HIM LYING TO YOU.
I'M OUT OF HERE.

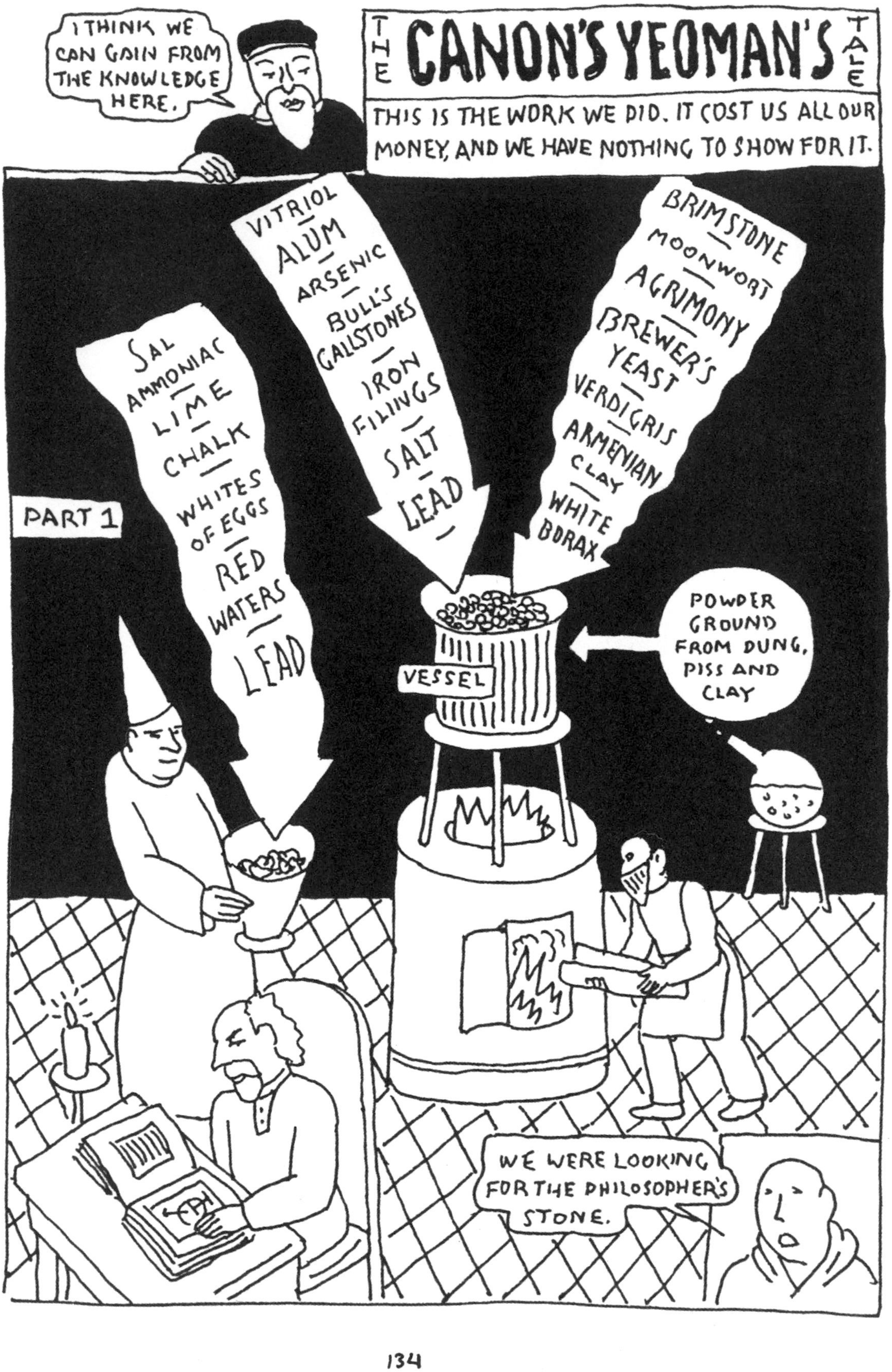

I THINK WE CAN GAIN FROM THE KNOWLEDGE HERE.
THE CANON'S YEOMAN'S TALE
THIS IS THE WORK WE DID. IT COST US ALL OUR MONEY, AND WE HAVE NOTHING TO SHOW FOR IT.
PART 1
SAL AMMONIAC
LIME
CHALK
WHITES OF EGGS
RED WATERS
LEAD
VITRIOL
ALUM
ARSENIC
BULL'S GALLSTONES
IRON FILINGS
SALT
LEAD
BRIMSTONE
MOONWORT
AGRIMONY
BREWER'S YEAST
VERDIGRIS
ARMENIAN CLAY
WHITE BORAX
VESSEL
POWDER GROUND FROM DUNG, PISS AND CLAY
WE WERE LOOKING FOR THE PHILOSOPHER'S STONE.

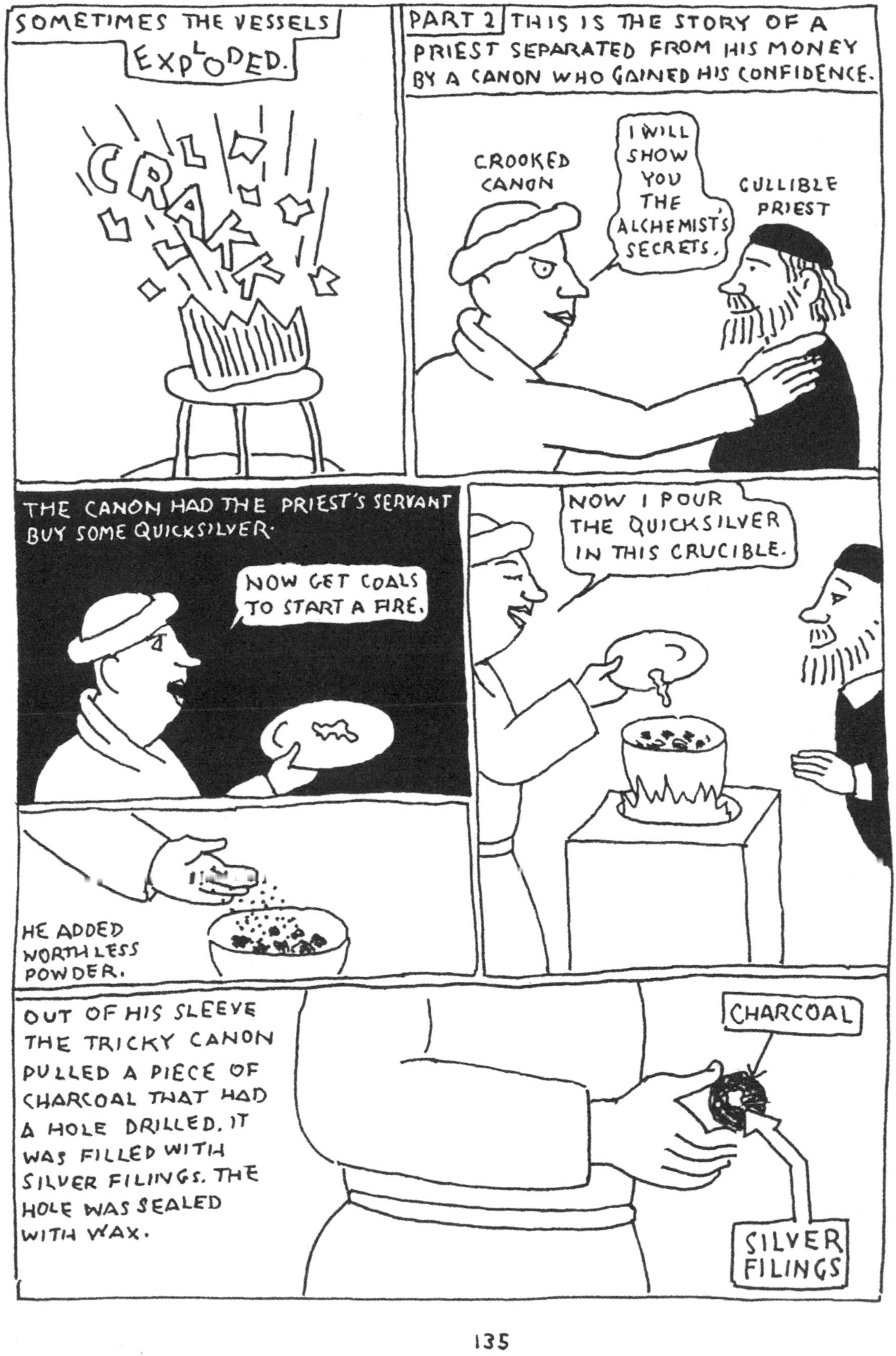

SOMETIMES THE VESSELS EXPLODED.
CRAKK
PART 2 THIS IS THE STORY OF A PRIEST SEPARATED FROM HIS MONEY BY A CANON WHO GAINED HIS CONFIDENCE.
CROOKED CANON
I WILL SHOW YOU THE ALCHEMIST'S SECRETS.
GULLIBLE PRIEST
THE CANON HAD THE PRIEST'S SERVANT BUY SOME QUICKSILVER.
NOW GET COALS TO START A FIRE.
NOW I POUR THE QUICKSILVER IN THIS CRUCIBLE.
HE ADDED WORTHLESS POWDER.
OUT OF HIS SLEEVE THE TRICKY CANON PULLED A PIECE OF CHARCOAL THAT HAD A HOLE DRILLED. IT WAS FILLED WITH SILVER FILINGS. THE HOLE WAS SEALED WITH WAX.
CHARCOAL
SILVER FILINGS

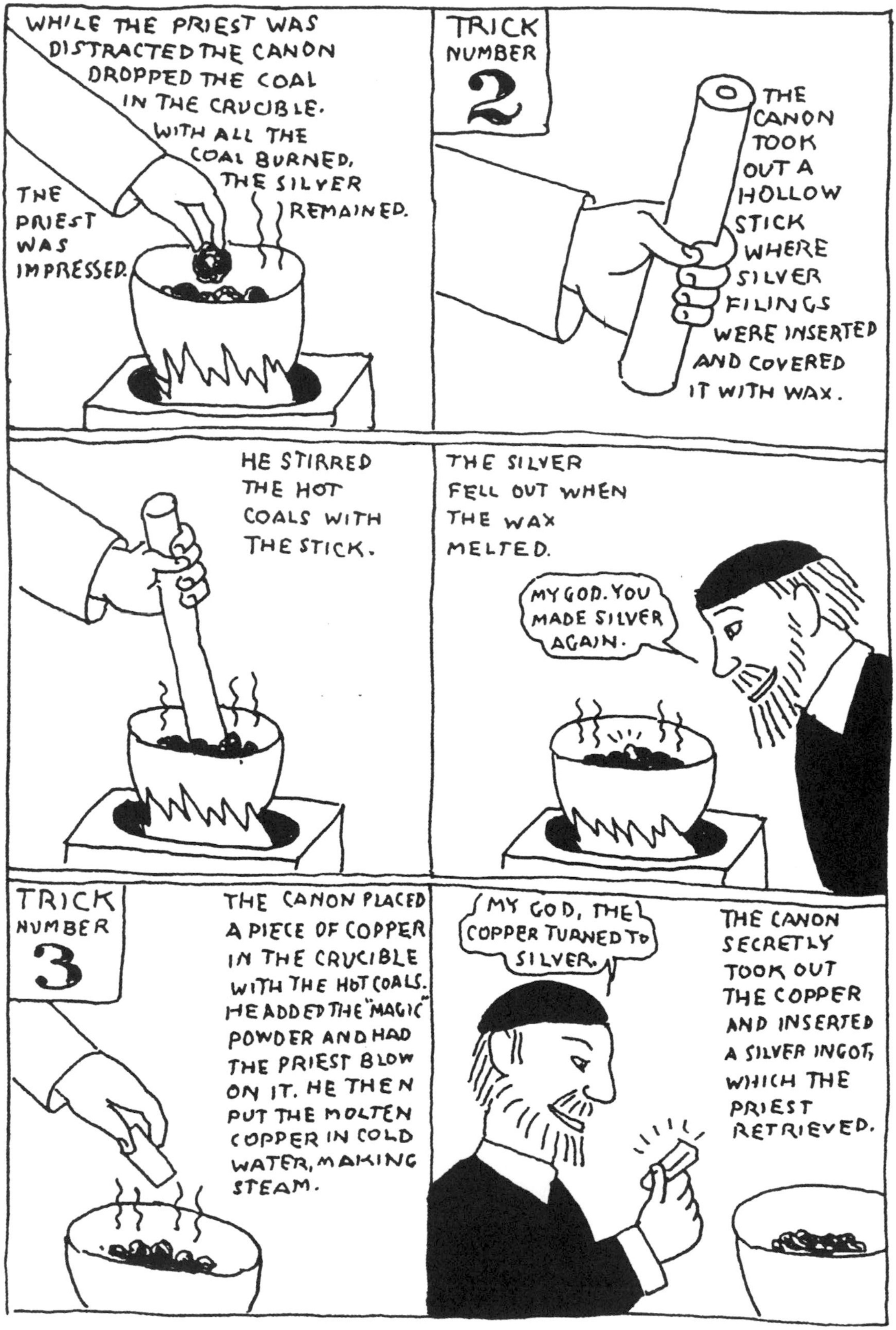
WHILE THE PRIEST WAS DISTRACTED THE CANON DROPPED THE COAL IN THE CRUCIBLE.
WITH ALL THE COAL BURNED, THE SILVER REMAINED.
THE PRIEST WAS IMPRESSED.
TRICK NUMBER 2
THE CANON TOOK OUT A HOLLOW STICK WHERE SILVER FILINGS WERE INSERTED AND COVERED IT WITH WAX.
HE STIRRED THE HOT COALS WITH THE STICK.
THE SILVER FELL OUT WHEN THE WAX MELTED.
MY GOD. YOU MADE SILVER AGAIN.
TRICK NUMBER 3
THE CANON PLACED A PIECE OF COPPER IN THE CRUCIBLE WITH THE HOT COALS. HE ADDED THE "MAGIC" POWDER AND HAD THE PRIEST BLOW ON IT. HE THEN PUT THE MOLTEN COPPER IN COLD WATER, MAKING STEAM.
MY GOD, THE COPPER TURNED TO SILVER.
THE CANON SECRETLY TOOK OUT THE COPPER AND INSERTED A SILVER INGOT, WHICH THE PRIEST RETRIEVED.

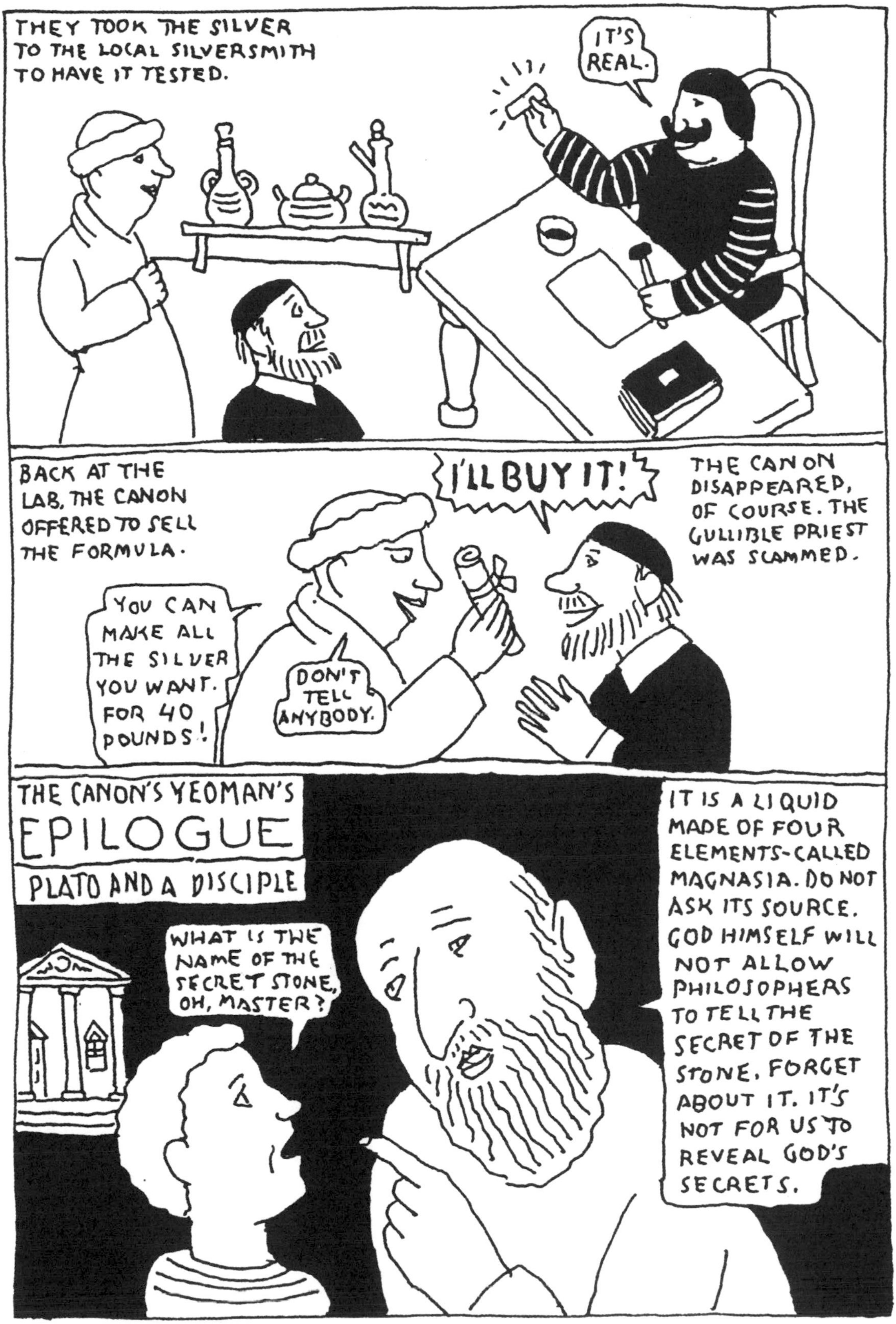
THEY TOOK THE SILVER TO THE LOCAL SILVERSMITH TO HAVE IT TESTED.
IT'S REAL.
BACK AT THE LAB, THE CANON OFFERED TO SELL THE FORMULA.
I'LL BUY IT!
THE CANON DISAPPEARED, OF COURSE. THE GULLIBLE PRIEST WAS SCAMMED.
YOU CAN MAKE ALL THE SILVER YOU WANT. FOR 40 POUNDS!
DON'T TELL ANYBODY.
THE CANON'S YEOMAN'S
EPILOGUE
PLATO AND A DISCIPLE
WHAT IS THE NAME OF THE SECRET STONE, OH, MASTER?
IT IS A LIQUID MADE OF FOUR ELEMENTS-CALLED MAGNASIA. DO NOT ASK ITS SOURCE. GOD HIMSELF WILL NOT ALLOW PHILOSOPHERS TO TELL THE SECRET OF THE STONE. FORGET ABOUT IT. IT'S NOT FOR US TO REVEAL GOD'S SECRETS.

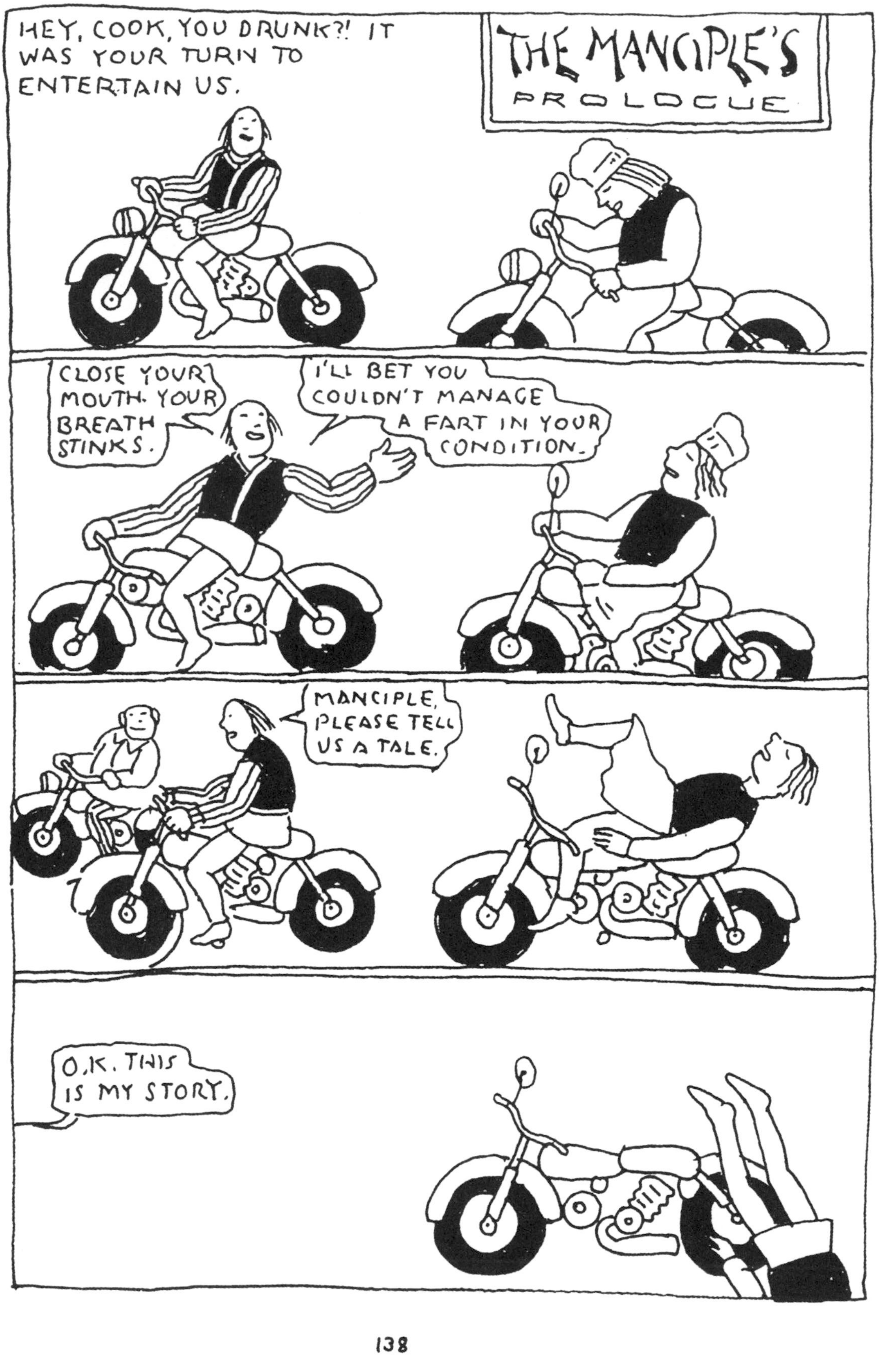
HEY, COOK, YOU DRUNK?! IT WAS YOUR TURN TO ENTERTAIN US.
THE MANCIPLE'S PROLOGUE
CLOSE YOUR MOUTH. YOUR BREATH STINKS.
I'LL BET YOU COULDN'T MANAGE A FART IN YOUR CONDITION.
MANCIPLE, PLEASE TELL US A TALE.
O.K. THIS IS MY STORY.

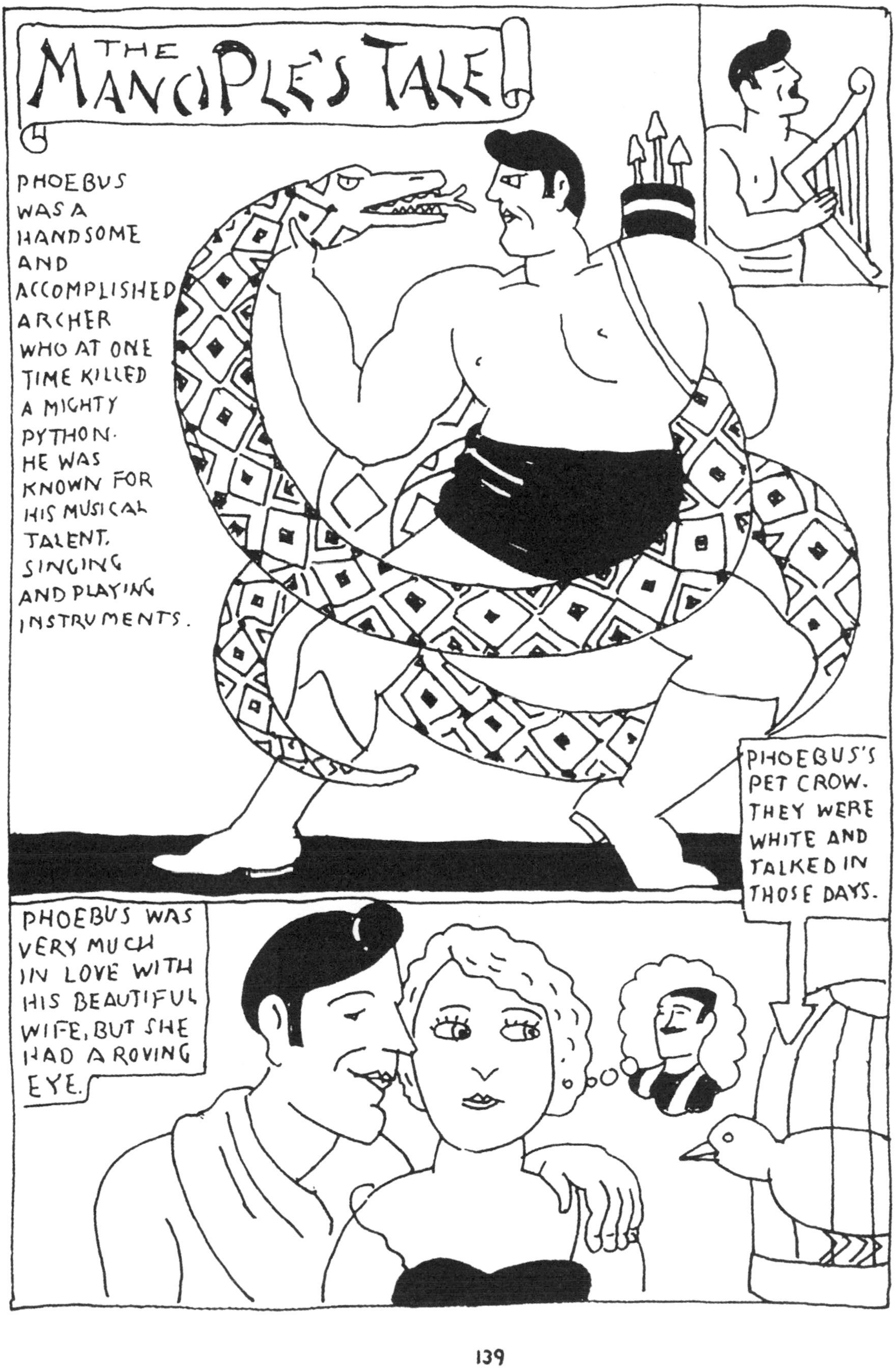
THE MANCIPLE'S TALE
PHOEBUS WAS A HANDSOME AND ACCOMPLISHED ARCHER WHO AT ONE TIME KILLED A MIGHTY PYTHON. HE WAS KNOWN FOR HIS MUSICAL TALENT, SINGING AND PLAYING INSTRUMENTS.
PHOEBUS'S PET CROW. THEY WERE WHITE AND TALKED IN THOSE DAYS.
PHOEBUS WAS VERY MUCH IN LOVE WITH HIS BEAUTIFUL WIFE, BUT SHE HAD A ROVING EYE.

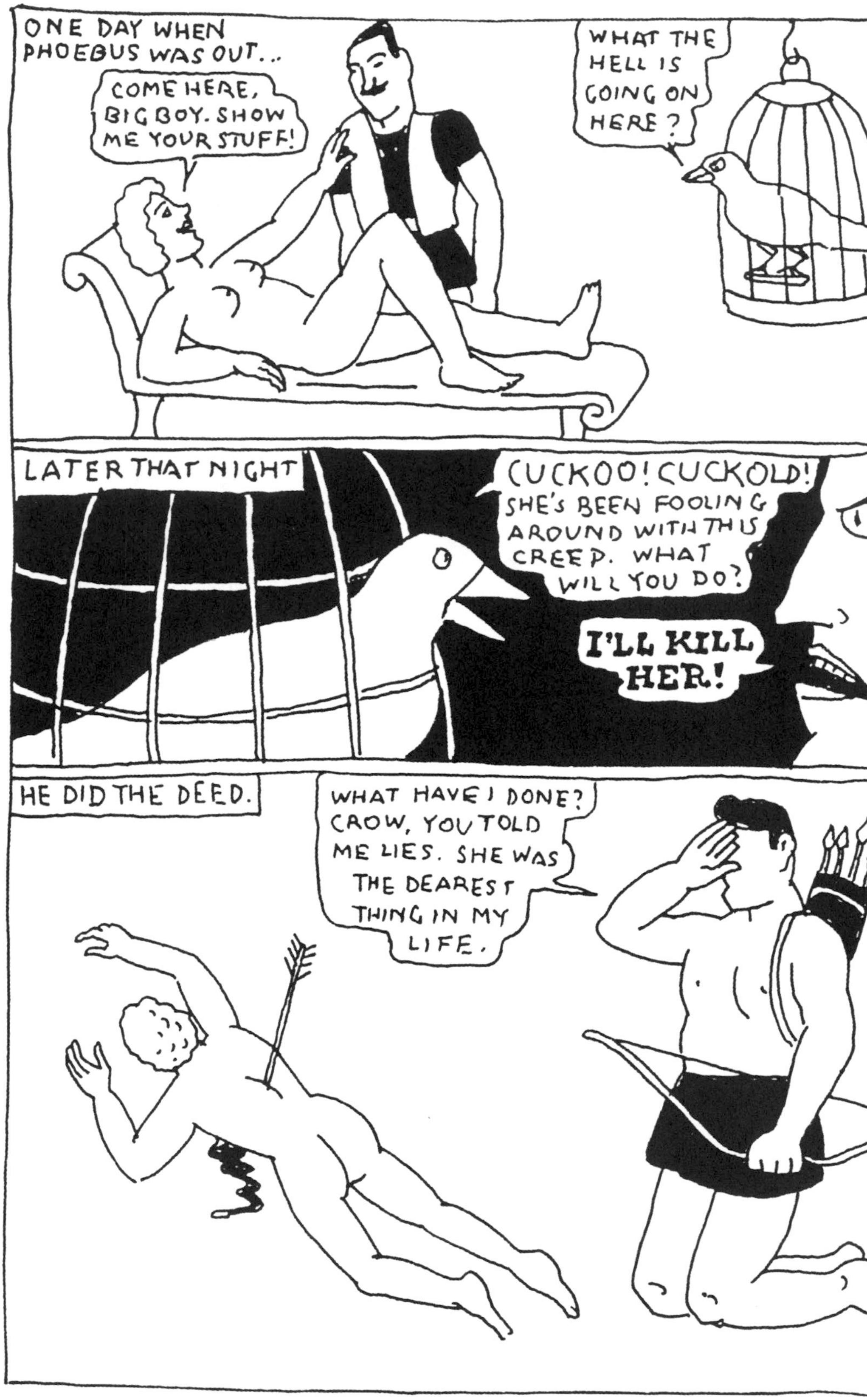
ONE DAY WHEN PHOEBUS WAS OUT...
COME HERE, BIG BOY. SHOW ME YOUR STUFF!
WHAT THE HELL IS GOING ON HERE?
LATER THAT NIGHT
CUCKOO! CUCKOLD! SHE'S BEEN FOOLING AROUND WITH THIS CREEP. WHAT WILL YOU DO?
I'LL KILL HER!
HE DID THE DEED.
WHAT HAVE I DONE? CROW, YOU TOLD ME LIES. SHE WAS THE DEAREST THING IN MY LIFE.

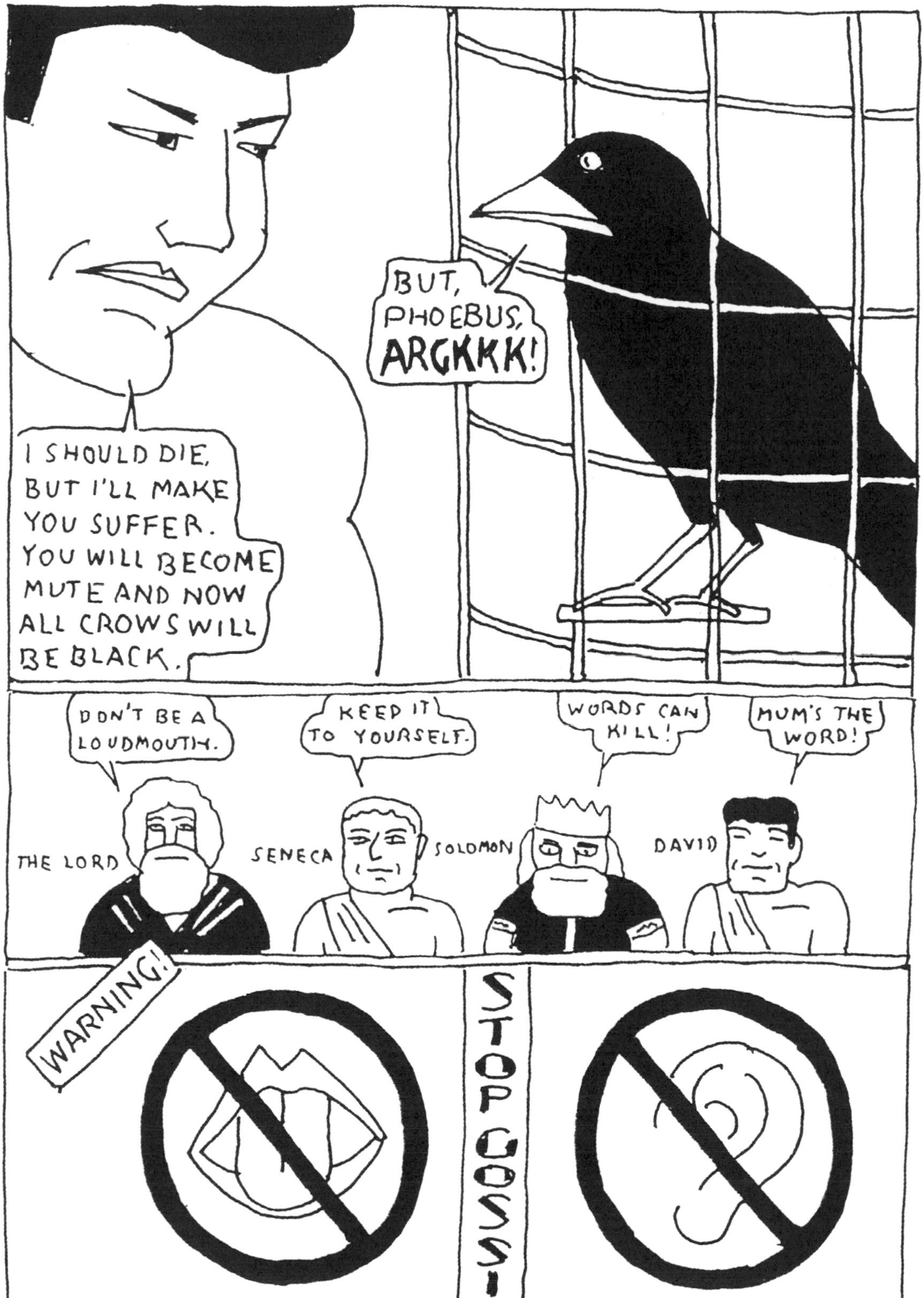

I SHOULD DIE, BUT I'LL MAKE YOU SUFFER. YOU WILL BECOME MUTE AND NOW ALL CROWS WILL BE BLACK.
BUT, PHOEBUS, ARGKKK!
DON'T BE A LOUDMOUTH.
THE LORD
KEEP IT TO YOURSELF.
SENECA
WORDS CAN KILL!
SOLOMON
MUM'S THE WORD!
DAVID
WARNING!
A LOOSE TONGUE IS DANGEROUS
STOP GOSSIP
BEWARE OF WHAT YOU HEAR

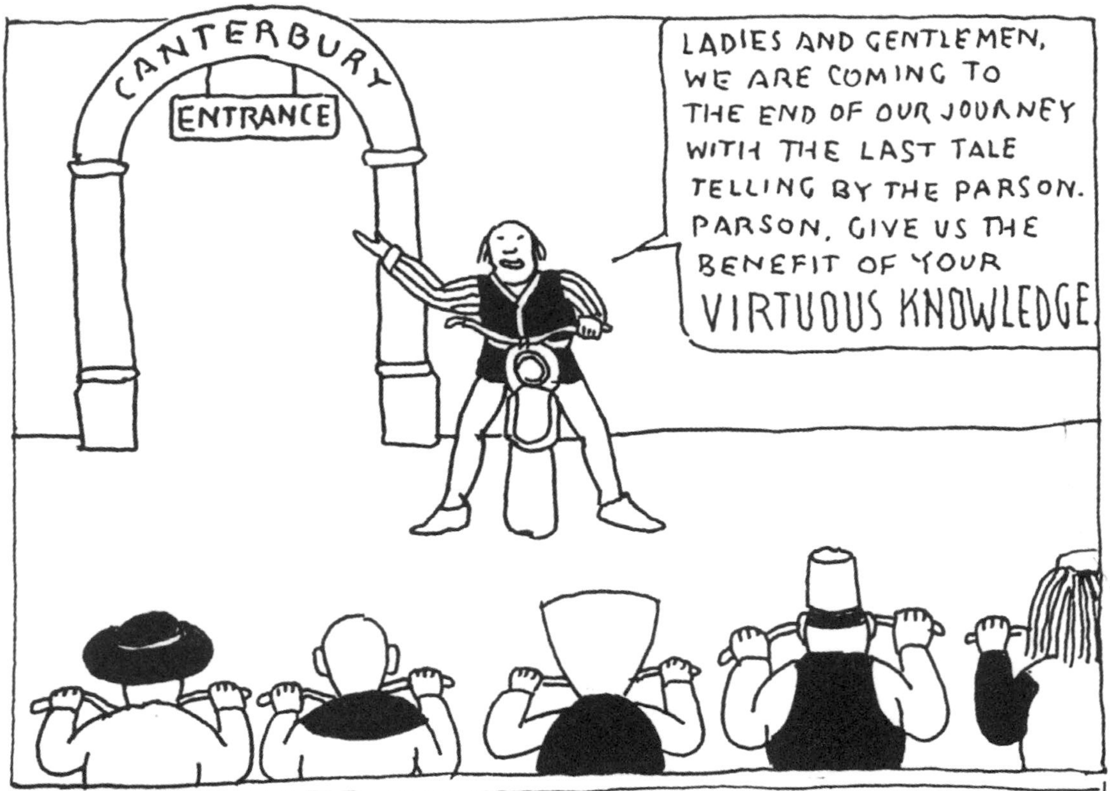
CANTERBURY
ENTRANCE
LADIES AND GENTLEMEN, WE ARE COMING TO THE END OF OUR JOURNEY WITH THE LAST TALE TELLING BY THE PARSON. PARSON, GIVE US THE BENEFIT OF YOUR VIRTUOUS KNOWLEDGE.

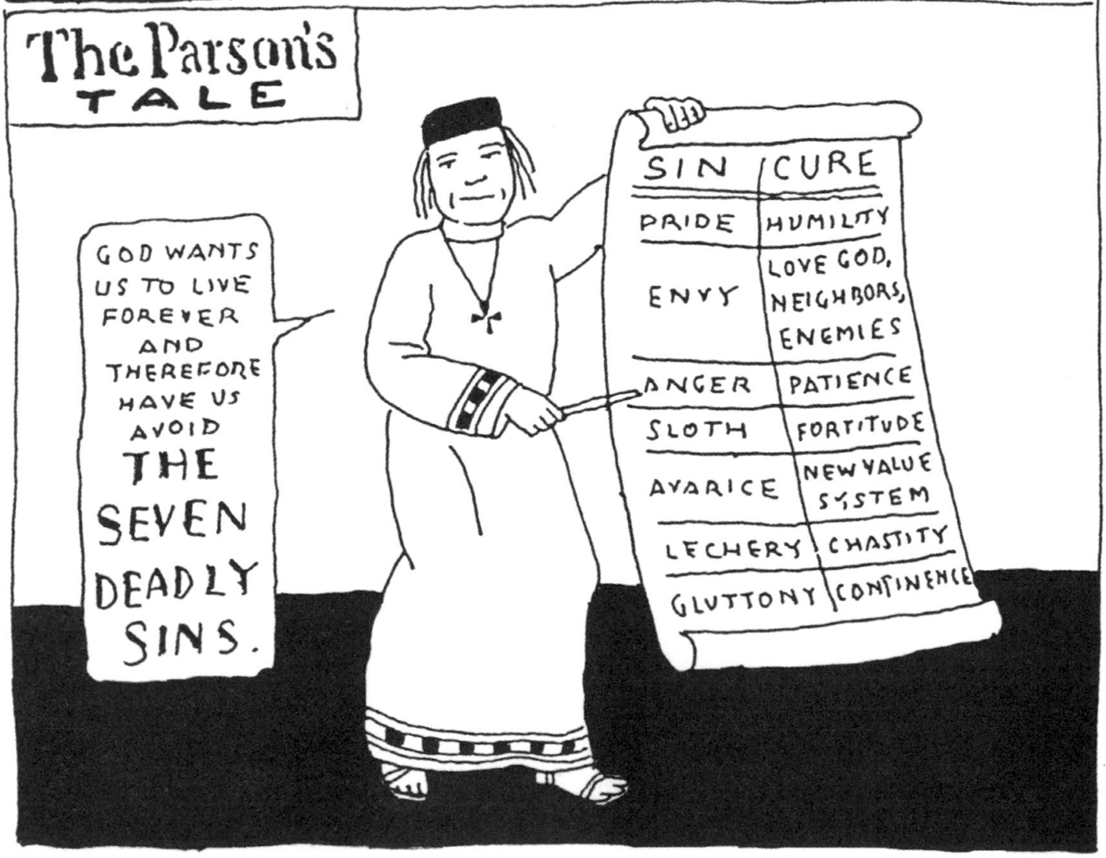
The Parson's TALE
GOD WANTS US TO LIVE FOREVER AND THEREFORE HAVE US AVOID THE SEVEN DEADLY SINS.
SIN | CURE
PRIDE | HUMILITY
ENVY | LOVE GOD, NEIGHBORS, ENEMIES
ANGER | PATIENCE
SLOTH | FORTITUDE
AVARICE | NEW VALUE SYSTEM
LECHERY | CHASTITY
GLUTTONY | CONTINENCE

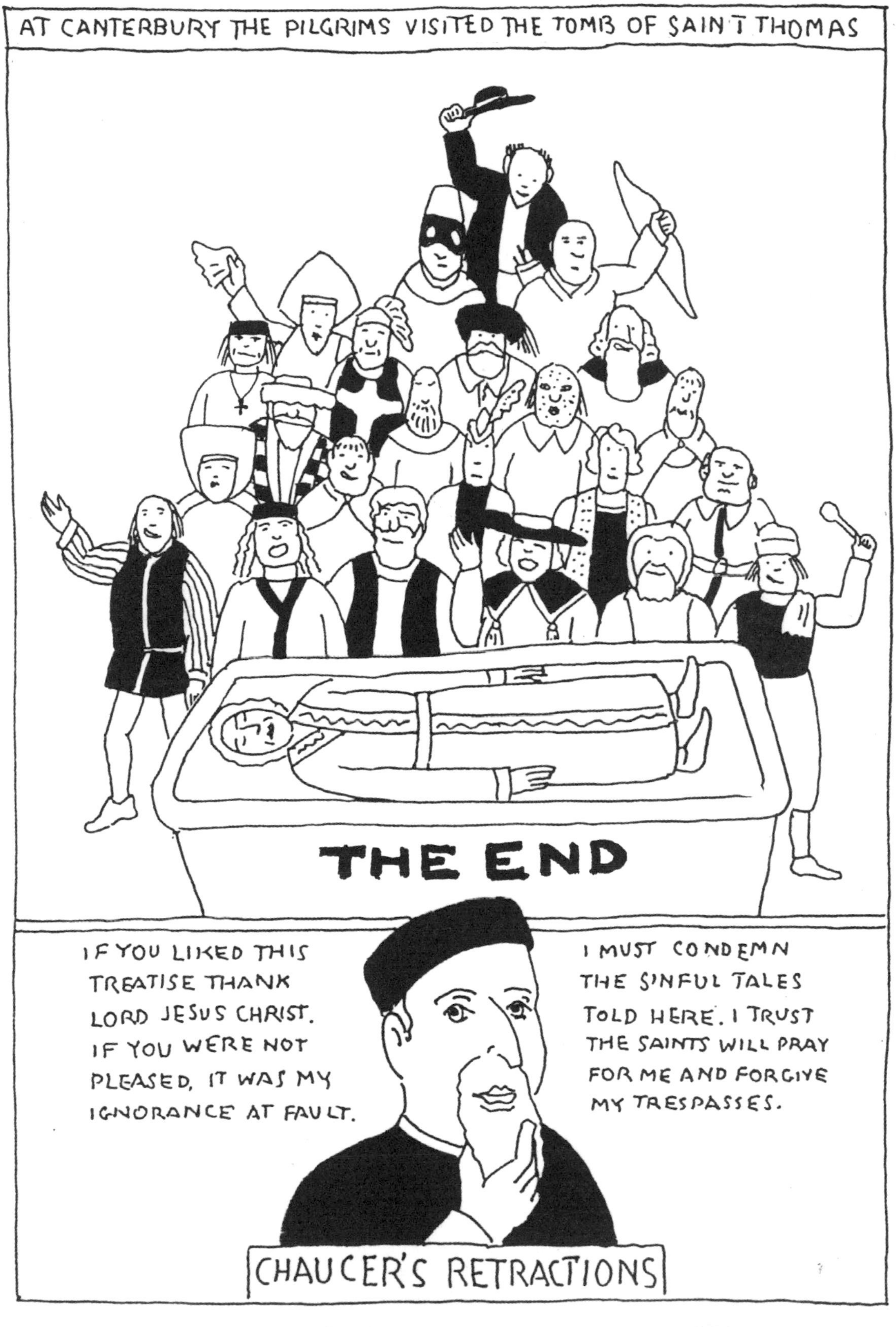
AT CANTERBURY THE PILGRIMS VISITED THE TOMB OF SAINT THOMAS
THE END
IF YOU LIKED THIS TREATISE THANK LORD JESUS CHRIST. IF YOU WERE NOT PLEASED, IT WAS MY IGNORANCE AT FAULT.
I MUST CONDEMN THE SINFUL TALES TOLD HERE. I TRUST THE SAINTS WILL PRAY FOR ME AND FORGIVE MY TRESPASSES.
CHAUCER'S RETRACTIONS

A NOTE ON THE AUTHOR

SEYMOUR CHWAST'S AWARD-WINNING WORK HAS INFLUENCED TWO GENERATIONS OF DESIGNERS AND ILLUSTRATORS.

HE CO-FOUNDED PUSH PIN STUDIOS, WHICH RAPIDLY GAINED AN INTERNATIONAL REPUTATION FOR INNOVATIVE DESIGN AND ILLUSTRATION. PUSH PIN'S VISUAL LANGUAGE (WHICH REFERENCED CULTURE AND LITERATURE) AROSE FROM ITS PASSION FOR HISTORICAL DESIGN MOVEMENTS AND HELPED REVOLUTIONIZE THE WAY PEOPLE LOOK AT DESIGN.

CHWAST IS A RECIPIENT OF THE A.I.G.A. MEDAL, WAS INDUCTED INTO THE ART DIRECTORS HALL OF FAME, AND HAS AN HONORARY PH.D. IN FINE ART FROM THE PARSONS SCHOOL OF DESIGN AND THE RHODE ISLAND SCHOOL OF DESIGN. HIS WORK IS IN THE COLLECTION OF THE MUSEUM OF MODERN ART, THE METROPOLITAN MUSEUM OF ART, AND HAS BEEN COLLECTED IN THE LEFT HANDED DESIGNER AND SEYMOUR: THE OBSESSIVE IMAGES OF SEYMOUR CHWAST. DANTE'S DIVINE COMEDY IS CHWAST'S FIRST GRAPHIC NOVEL.

HE LIVES IN NEW YORK WITH HIS WIFE, THE GRAPHIC DESIGNER PAULA SCHER.

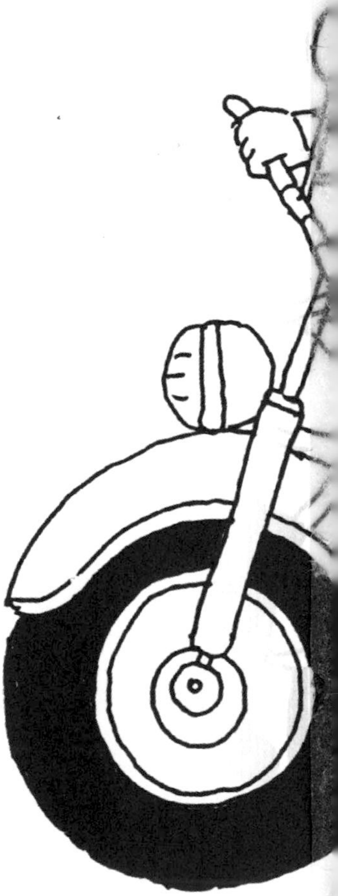

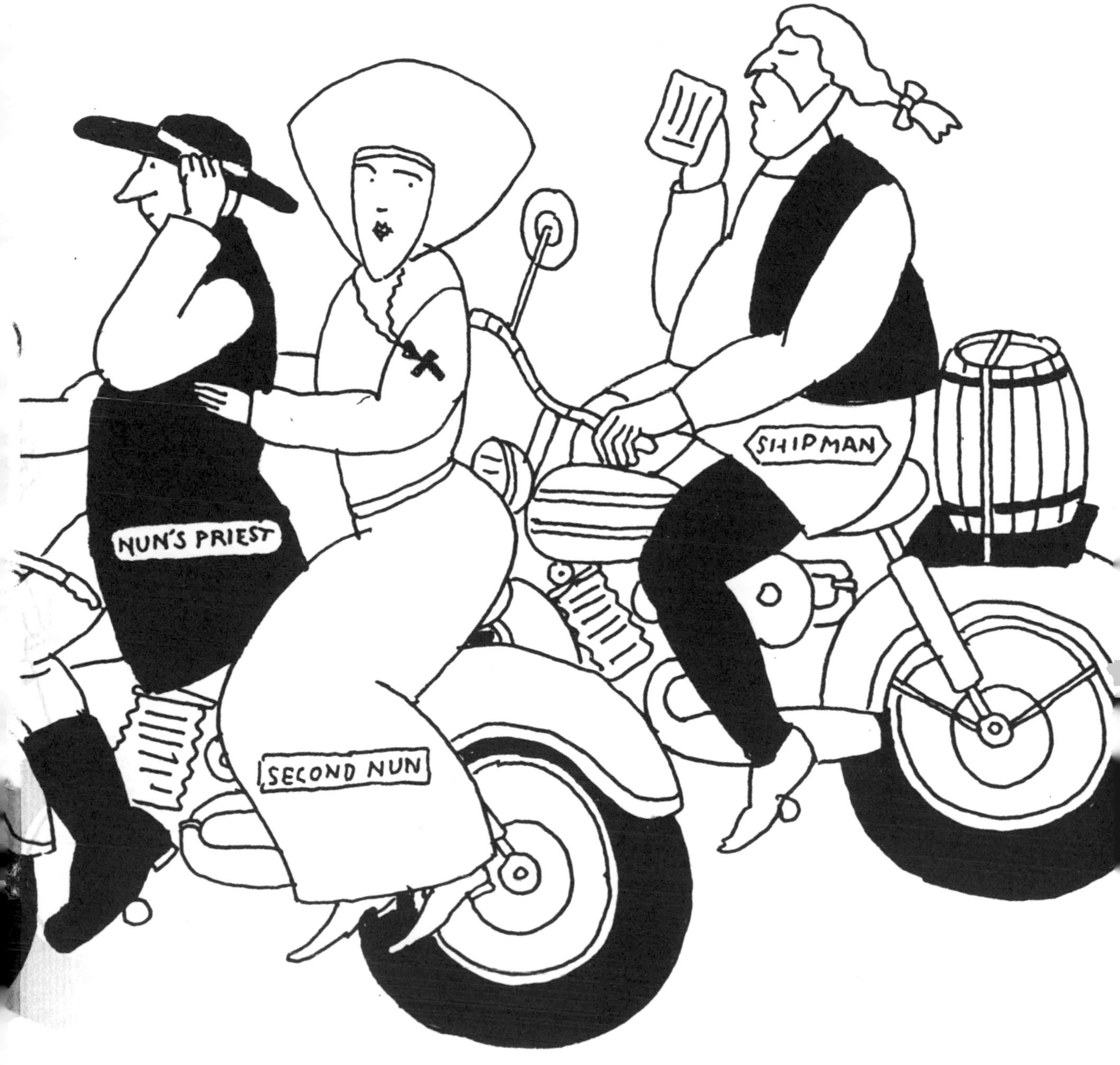
NUN'S PRIEST
SECOND NUN
SHIPMAN

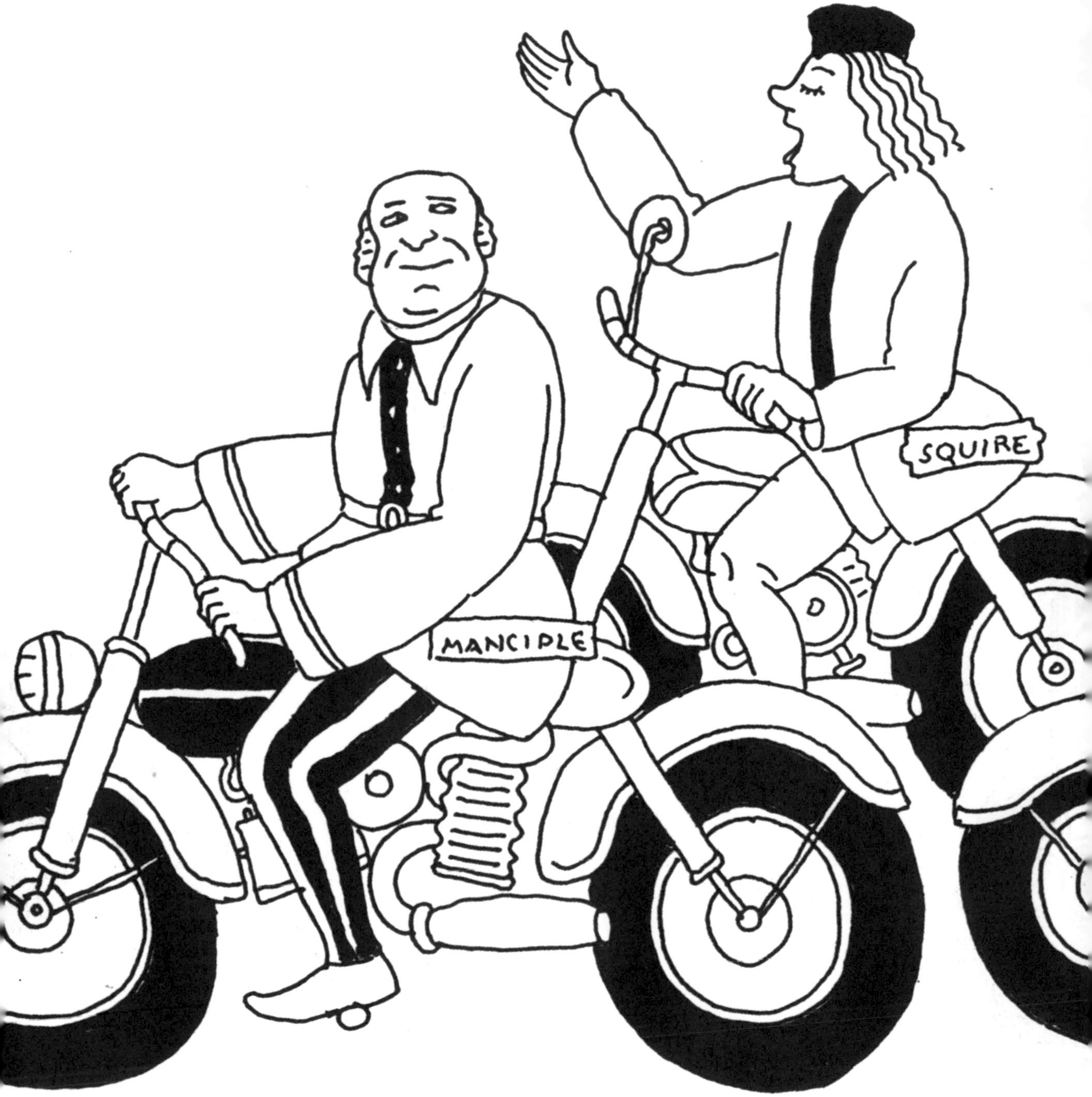
SQUIRE
MANCIPLE